Praise for A
The Book of Hip-Hop Cover Art:

"Totally absorbing" – ***FHM***

"Powerful, arresting" – ***XXL***

"Essential" – ***i-D***

"Who better to tell this story than Andrew Emery? Encyclopaedic and wickedly entertaining" – ***Time Out***

"Fantastic" – ***The Big Issue***

"The first significant study of the genre's history of design" – ***GQ***

"Provocative, witty" – ***Entertainment Weekly***

"A must for music fans and design enthusiasts" – ***OK!***

"The first to chronicle over 20 years of album covers while providing insight into the revolution that is rap music" – ***The Source***

"Brilliantly researched. What your coffee table is fiending for" – ***Jack***

"Diligent, informative. Visuals veer entertainingly between wild extremes" – ***The Guardian***

Advance praise for Wiggaz With Attitude:

"Wiggaz showcases Emery's wit and deep knowledge… and his ability to entertain the reader. It's a funny and reflective paean to hip-hop." – ***Bats Are Not Bugs***

Andrew Emery

Wiggaz With Attitude

My Life as a Failed White Rapper

Fat Lace Publishing

Wiggaz With Attitude: My Life as a Failed White Rapper

Published by Fat Lace Publishing 2017

Wiggazwithattitude.com
Contact: drewhuge@gmail.com

ISBN: 978-1-9997607-0-0

Cover design: Richard Firth/upperechelon.co.uk

For

Justin Quirk, for inspiration, editing and the whole idea.

Greenpeace & Countdown, for being the P.A. Posse.

Andy Cowan, for helping me find my way.

Richard Firth, for your generosity and for being Toot Hill fam.

My family, now and always.

Tam, for unwavering love and support. "This world is cold; you make me warm."

A quick note on footnotes:

You'll notice, as you read the book, that there are lots of footnotes dotted throughout. Whether you read them as you go, or at the end in one chunk, is entirely up to you. However, I just wanted to point out that they're not those dry but essential reference footnotes like you might get in a history book, pointing you to sources and further reading. These footnotes are packed full of further information, they're riffs on various people, artists and aspects of hip-hop, and they explain some of the more obscure references for a) people who don't know everything about hip-hop, b) people who aren't from the UK and c) people who didn't live through the 80's. And, let's be honest, they're chances for me to go off on one whenever the mood strikes me without completely derailing the narrative.

Again, it's up to you, but I think some of the best stuff in the book is stuffed away in the footnotes. At least you haven't got to put up with those hovering numbers and pop-ups like the e-book people. Trust me, you've got off lightly.

To My Own Aspiring Rap Star –
Love You Gus!
Merry Christmas 2017 –
– Mom

Prologue
The Show

Summer 1995, an illegal warehouse party, somewhere in York. An historic town better known for its Viking Heritage and milking of same for tourism than for its commitment to cutting edge musical events, but here we are. It's happening over three floors of an abandoned building that presumably violates every building code ever thought of, and we're in the basement. Sweat drips down the chipped walls, and my best friend Daniel Goldberg and I await the moment we take the next step in our careers as Leeds' future finest rap group of all time.

The act before us – memory says it was Shed Seven but memory is fickle[1] – finish their set to shrugs of indifference from a pissed-up, pilled-up audience who stand with arms folded throughout. Tough crowd. But we can do this, and the adrenaline kicks in as our backing tape starts up.

We've only got time to perform two tracks, but then again we only know the lyrics to about four out of the dozens of songs we've written in our lustre-less career anyway. We'd debated long and hard

---

[1] History hasn't been kind to these plodding indie dirge-merchants, but they did have quite a few Top 40 hits. Then again, the Nazis were once ballot box gold, so draw your own conclusions. They were definitely there that night, but probably not on our floor, truth be told.

over the merits of “Pretty Boys Don't Survive Up North” versus “Grab The Mic And Drop Bombs”. In the end, we choose “Three Nipples Of Scaramanga” to open with, only the other two 'nipples' who rap on the track are missing, so it'll be a truncated version.

For some reason – a misplaced sense of 'wackiness', perhaps, maybe a forlorn attempt to stand out from the sullen hip-hop crowd – we're wearing record sleeves on our heads. But we're so nervous that looking cool doesn't matter, and we're not trying to be an overly serious hip-hop group anyway. Hip-hop in 1995 was still trying to rebuild its reputation and self-belief a mere four years after MC Hammer and Vanilla Ice simultaneously set the charts alight and the art form back creatively by ten years. This meant hardcore, independent music that didn't care much for airplay, and lots of po-faced talk about 'keeping it real' – more on this later, but suffice to say we 'kept it real' insofar as we often liked to wear record sleeves on our heads even when we weren't performing.

We explode into action, dousing the microphones with spittle, holding them like we've seen our heroes do on MTV and on stage, the momentum ensuring we don't forget our lyrics. And it's working. The crowd are moving. Most are just nodding their heads, but that's par for the course at rap concerts. That's approval. We're golden. A couple of kids with the kind of tie-dye apparel and monged-out expressions that suggest they're on the wrong floor of this party launch into some freaky dancing. We finish “Scaramanga” to a few whoops, both say something like “What up, York?” to muted cheers, then launch into our closer “Street Pilgrims”. The crowd stay with us, despite the complete lack of hook, chorus or memorable lyrics. We can do no wrong. In the brief career of Progressive Agenda – Scam (myself) and DJ Greenpeace (Dan) – this is thus far the undoubted highpoint. We came to rock the place, and all of the 12 people we played to were left looking distinctly rocked.

Maybe one day each of those 12 people, older and wiser, will sit in an armchair, their children and grandchildren perched nearby, a Werther's Original clacking against a denture, and tell for the umpteenth time, with a moist twinkle in their eyes, of how they were there when the P.A. Posse played their breakthrough gig. How they were there to see us before the fame, before the record deals, the classic 12"s and albums, before the groupies, the platinum plaques, the endorsement deals and the invitations to 10 Downing Street to rub shoulders with the cultural mavens du jour and uncomfortable-looking politicians. Before the high-profile guest appearances on records by the cream of the world's rap stars. Before the 'interesting' solo albums, the quadruple coloured vinyl concept album, the dalliances with abstract painting and self-funded gallery exhibitions, the awkward drunken chat-show appearances, the marriages, glamorous lovers and divorces. Before we invited *Hello!* Magazine into the homes we bought and built with our rap-made millions. Before the split-up, the recriminations, the bankruptcy and the triumphant reunion tour that was obviously to pay for crippling alimony bills. Before we woke up.

One
Children's Story

It was a boy called Richard Kirk who saved me from a life more ordinary. It was 1984 and I'd just started at Toot Hill Comprehensive School in Bingham, Notts. My days consisted of dreaming of what ZX Spectrum game I'd load up when I got home, running scared of the 2nd year boys who were threatening to kill me just for being a) a 1st year and b) tall for my age, and what fresh humiliation would be visited upon me when I turned up to PE without the kit that I'd lost and was forced into the ill-fitting tatty spares the PE teacher kept as a sartorial punishment for such occasions. In other words, my days were the days of most 11-year-olds in market towns the nation over.

My ambitions were small: getting to see Manchester United play at Old Trafford again, buying more ZX Spectrum games, and making life hell for my 15-year-old sister, Susan. My latest trick in that ongoing campaign was to trap her and her best friend Fiona in Susan's bedroom, and scrape a butter knife down the door, while they cowered inside. Perhaps I also have Richard Kirk to thank for me not turning into Nottinghamshire's Ed Gein.

Kirky was just another boy at school, one who wasn't faring very well in the few classes we shared but who – crucially – didn't care about it (most schoolboys pretend not to care, but really do; he genuinely didn't). I'd vaguely known him since primary school, a lanky graceless lad and one of those boys who seemed eerily adult because he boasted a wispy bumfluff moustache at the age of 11. He was so preternaturally hairy, I imagine him looking like Brian Blessed by the age of 15. Combine that with his effortless truancy – a potent combination, I'm sure you'll agree – and he reeked of cool (as well as Brut aftershave[2]). We weren't close mates, but he knew me well enough to invite me back to his house one day after school to play on his Spectrum.[3]

Yet it wasn't Kirky's Spectrum or the games he had that stuck with me that day. It was the cassette of music he had on in the

---

[2] Brut by Faberge is a cologne that was ubiquitous in the 1970's, due to its masculine advertising – sporting idols such as David Hemery, Barry Sheene and Kevin Keegan endorsed it. Its famous 'splash it all over' tagline is synonymous with boxer Henry Cooper, and you couldn't escape its 'unique' musk in the playground or at school discos, as it only cost a couple of quid. It is irredeemably naff, but survives on into a new millennium like the cockroach of the fragrance aisle. And you can't say that about Hai Karate.

[3] I realise I've mentioned the mighty ZX Spectrum three times in this first chapter already, and I'll be careful to ration such references from now on. I'm aware that, like most sane people, you may well have no interest in gaming computers from the past that had less processing power than the old Nokia mobile phone your mum texts you in all caps on. But in 1984, you were either a Spectrum or a Commodore fan when it came to home computing, and friendships hinged on which camp you fell into. The Spectrum was a truly English thing – low-powered and with a weird rubbery keyboard, it was the brainchild of Sir Clive Sinclair, who spunked the profits on developing the mobile death-trap he called the C5 (well done, Clive) and married a lapdancer. The Commodore 64, meanwhile, was an American interloper that cost more than twice as much and looked like an actual computer should. The plucky Brit Spectrum was all about games, whereas Commo-bores banged on about how they could do homework and accounting on their machines, as well as play more powerful games, if the mood took them. Yes, there was a class issue here, with us Speccy loyalists dissing the innate snobbery of the Commodore crew and they in turn laughing at our quaint machines with their 48k of memory and tinny sound. They'd win eventually, of course. We didn't know it but we Spectrum lovers were like the cavalry advancing at a stately pace to be chewed up by tanks. Of course, some lucky people had both computers, and they were just dead posh.

background while we played. I had, quite literally, never heard anything like it before. I thought of myself as one of Bingham's leading musical connoisseurs, because my Dad not only had stacks of records but also owned a mobile disco. He rarely operated it himself, and I'm not even sure why he came to have it, or what its benefits were. I can only assume that, because my dad always loved to dance (footage is available upon request), he wanted to have the means of dancing within his grasp at all times.

If there was a new pop single to be had, we had it. My sister taped the top 40 from the radio every Sunday and I'd nick those cassettes too. I had my finger on the pulse of pop, but the stuff Kirky was playing wasn't in the top 40 – it wasn't the Flying Pickets, Hazell Dean or Lionel Richie's weird clay head.[4] It wasn't in my Dad's extensive singles collection. It wasn't even something which fitted in with what I thought conventional music was allowed to sound like. I asked what the hell it was, this mixture of bleeps, squelches, robotic yelps and percussion sounds that no drum kit on earth could have given birth to. He nonchalantly popped the cassette out and said, "You can borrow it if you like." I scorn the suspiciously total recall of most memoirists but, from what I can remember, Kirky had just scrawled "Electro Megamix" on the cassette. Those two words – and that one tape – were the point at which my life changed.

I say it was Richard Kirk that saved me, but perhaps it's really Neil Falconbridge I should be thanking. After all, Kirky and I fell out shortly after the "Electro Megamix" handover, because I'd had a

[4] The Flying Pickets hit on the kind of wheeze that is usually doomed to failure: Attempting to make pop records that were entirely a cappella. It worked, with their debut single, a cover of Yazoo's "Only You", spending five weeks at number one in 1983. And, true to their name, they did lots of picketing during the miner's strike, so fair play to them.

playground scrap with a mate of his who I'd called a 'Joey'.[5] Neil 'Falco' Falconbridge was the first new mate I'd made at Toot Hill, one of my few classmates that hadn't been at my primary school. He was from a place called Cropwell Bishop and he had a swagger that I wanted to be near in case some rubbed off, largely attributable to him being the only person I knew with a highly desirable Campri skiing jacket.[6] He also smoked and had bumfluff – 11-year-old dynamite. I got my wish when, at break time, we were discussing music and I mentioned the tape of Kirky's that had made such an impression on me. Falco was clearly more clued in than me, as he knowingly imparted the information that what I probably had on tape was *Electro 2*.[7] He had it on vinyl, as well as its companion, *Electro 1*. Did I want to borrow them?

---

[5] *Blue Peter* did a laudable thing when they featured Joseph 'Joey' Deacon as an example of someone who'd overcome their disability (in his case severe Cerebral Palsy) to live a rich life. The unfortunate side effect was that playgrounds were immediately populated by cruel kids mocking his voice and appearance. Joey was up there with 'flid' – short for Thalidomide – as a pejorative playground name in the early 80's, conclusive evidence that it's not really worthwhile trying to educate most young boys about disability. They will merely turn it into playground nastiness until they reach 6th form at which point they will be become po-faced and pretend they always had an enlightened and progressive view on such issues.

[6] Campri ski jackets first came out in the 70's, but in the 80's they ruled the playground due to their combination of eye-wateringly fluorescent colours and bulkiness, added to the picture of a mountain on the front with lettering down the arms. Many had bright pink lining. Subtle they weren't, and it goes without saying they weren't actually the kind of things worn in real life aprés-ski. Their reign was cut short by the arrival of Cabrini jackets from around 1987.

[7] The *Electro* series was put out by Morgan Khan's London-based StreetSounds label. He licensed the tracks from the labels and artists involved and then had them turned into megamixes by various DJ's, most notably Herbie the Mastermind. They were the best way for fans not plugged into the scene or the latest vinyl releases to stay up to date. As the music evolved, the series eventually morphed into *Hip-Hop Electro* and then by number 17 the word *Electro* was dropped altogether. The series ran to 22 instalments, in addition to a few spin-offs, before the label went bankrupt in the late 80's.

Let's be clear. If I'd answered no, I don't know who or what I'd be today. I don't know who my friends would be, I don't know where I'd be living. I would not be with my beloved wife, that's for certain. Nearly everything I'd have done would be different from the things I have done. That's what saying 'yes' meant to me. Saying 'yes' took me down the rabbit hole. It was the blue pill – the red pill would have meant a different life entirely, of this I'm convinced. I took *Electro 1* and *2* home and, from then on, I was into hip-hop.

Although hip-hop is well chronicled in books, its origins and impact analysed and assessed, its inventors and innovators quizzed at length, its legends and myths finely polished, I've long harboured the dream of writing the definitive book on what rap music meant to white teenagers living nowhere in the 80's and 90's – about how it politicised them, how it stirred them from their apathy and got them interested in the impact of racism, poverty and social disenfranchisement. That was the aim – but, of course, all people will remember is the big trainers and that time you performed Public Enemy's "Rebel Without a Pause" at the school talent show while your nerdy mates wore fake gold medallions and backwards baseball caps.

Maybe a book can combine both. Maybe it can capture the innate ridiculousness of a culture where rappers are called things like Aggressively Intense Fierce MC and Shamar Da Boonkie (not to mention Shorty Shitstain and the deeply regrettable Peedo) but also the serious socio-political side of rap that changed lives and kicked a moribund pop generation up the arse. But you just want more of the funny names, right? There's plenty of those coming, and many of them were mine.

This story is all about the impact hip-hop can have, and the specific impact it had on a normal 11-year-old from Bingham, a market town 12 miles outside Nottingham. It's about the dream it gave him of being an international hip-hop star and of how that dream flickered and foundered. It tells of the absurd hopes of a useless white rapper and his equally useless white rapper mates.

I've always been contemptuous of memoirs written by people who haven't done anything. Books by the non-famous or by non-achievers. Well, I'm not famous and I haven't achieved anything. But I'm taking a leaf from hip-hop's braggadocio ethos where every MC, from the bedroom to the studio to the stage, raps about being the best rapper who ever lived. Well, if that's the case, then this bedroom writer can be the hottest memoirist since Samuel Pepys.

Two
Step in the Arena

Let's pause, before we get into my own tale, and very briefly tell that of hip-hop. Many of you will know what it is, where it came from and what it sounds like. Many of you will have grown up with it, or had your life changed by it. Some of you will just like that one where they shout "Jump Around" a lot and pretend to be Irish. It's always fascinated me that a revolutionary musical culture like hip-hop (and stop me if you've heard this one before, but there's supposedly a big difference between hip-hop and rap. People have gone blue in the face and written essays about this, but no-one has ever come up with a pithier description of the difference than legendary rapper KRS-One who, I paraphrase, said that rap is something that you do, while hip-hop is something that you live.[8] I'm not sure that it's actually true, but it's on enough T-shirts to have become an article of faith[9]), born in such a particular environment

---

[8] And if you wonder why I'm paraphrasing rather than quoting directly, I refer you to the very tricky laws on copyright and quoting lyrics in books, even for the purposes of criticism or parody. Laws that I wish I'd Googled before I wrote a 1000 word section for this book about 'lyrics you always got wrong' that I had to shred after doing so.

[9] I'm using the lower case for hip-hop here, as I do for all musical genres. Were KRS-One to ever read this, he'd probably be apoplectic because he has very, erm, particular views on how you use the phrase hip-hop. Fair enough, he's

(the South Bronx, New York in the mid 70's), could translate so universally.

The social and economic factors that gave birth to hip-hop – poverty, gun crime, crack use, unemployment, boredom with disco music – were in no way prevalent in the town I lived in in 1984 (well, apart from unemployment. Cheers, Thatcher) but the kids I hung out with threw themselves wholeheartedly into hip-hop culture anyway. Simply, it was the coolest music around (it still is), which meant it could spread like a virus, acknowledging few boundaries. It helped that it came with the tang of parental distaste, the single fastest and most reliable guarantor of teenagers latching onto something.

A snapshot of the birth place of hip-hop in the early 80's: Block parties, DJ's scratching and mixing the best parts of funk and disco records (the 'breaks') while young kids in turtlenecks rap over them and the party people dance, all this in clubs with shonky music systems, overcrowded beyond all fire regulations. The first breakout stars are in the studios cutting seminal 12" records bankrolled by fly-by-night labels often set up with drug money or backed by pimps. Street gangs that were born out of the struggle for civil rights and morphed into crews that defended their territory with threats and violence. The sense – one you no longer get in contemporary New York – of something about to kick off, a switch about to be thrown.

---

dedicated his life to it, but his *The Gospel of Hip-Hop* (Powerhouse, 2009) book is nothing if not tedious and preachy about the issue. Apparently there are three spellings, all with different meaning, including Hiphop, hip-hop and Hip Hop. He goes on to say, "It's extremely important to spell Hip Hop at least with a capital H but also to know the difference between what means what." Thankfully he also acknowledges that, "the average person doesn't need to know this." I'd argue that nobody does. And while I love many of KRS' records and he's a legend, if I tell you that he's the kind of person who spells 'culture' with a 'k', you can draw your own conclusions about whether or not he wears a tinfoil hat.

A cauldron where something interesting – either delicious or hard-to-swallow, who knew which? – was being cooked up.

My home town of Bingham, Nottinghamshire, by contrast: Darts nights at The Crown pub. Dave Pinder's mobile disco playing chart hits out at the RAF base. The opening of the town's first video rental shop (*Porkys*, *Who Dares Wins* and *Sudden Impact*, among the cineaste treats on offer). Bejam or the VG supermarket for all your frozen food needs, Barrett's for chocolate and toy soldiers, the sweet shop in the arcade for pick 'n' mix. The music scene was strictly confined to covers bands playing the pubs and clubs. A TV crew turning up to film some of *Auf Wiedersehen Pet* in our market square, with Bomber (Pat Roach) spending time in Go Sing, our Chinese takeaway. The late wrestler-cum-actor was also generous enough to tell my teenage sister that she ought to be a model – and as her little brother, with the concomitant and onerous teasing duties that are part of the job description, I'm reluctantly duty bound to inform you that career choice would have described a similar arc to the rapping one I'm about to regale you with.

In the Bronx, they used to set up parties in the park, powering the sound system by running cables into hacked street lights. At our park, we tried to smoke, played British Bulldog and lied about which of us had fingered girls.[10]

---

[10] For those unfamiliar with this playground staple (of Britain and many of its former colonies), British Bulldog is a game where a couple of kids – the 'bulldogs' – stand in the middle of the playground, while a much larger mass of kids attempt to get from one side of them to the other. Anybody tagged by the bulldogs as they try to pass becomes a bulldog as well. The winner is the last free person. It sounds innocent, but the reason it has been banned from many playgrounds is that the 'bulldogs' were often not content with just tagging you to pull you over to their side. Often they resorted to kicking, punching or tripping you onto the concrete and sitting on you – this variation was known in our school as 'Bring Down Bulldog'. When you were one of the last free people, you'd often be hunted by a group of bulldogs who would basically kick the shit out of you.

Of course, the people at the clubs and block parties in New York weren't gangly 11-year-olds with nascent pubes, and by the time that hip-hop had filtered through to the UK, it had already evolved in the US. We were playing catch up from the start. Maybe if we'd been in London we'd have had a chance of not being hopelessly out of the loop. We didn't even have a record shop in Bingham (unless you count the charity shop selling old *Top of the Pops* albums for 50p, the chief delights of which, with their cheeky covers featuring barely clad 70's models, were masturbatorial) – we had to travel on the bus to Nottingham for that. Hip-hop was mutating in New York – and LA, Boston, Philadelphia, New Jersey, Miami and many more places, taking on different regional flavours – but in Bingham we were passing round cassettes of stuff from two years ago. We thought we were too cool for school, but in fact we were as cutting edge as an episode of *Highway*. Word to Harry Secombe.

I was also held back in my young hip-hop days by something else other than living in a dull town: Heavy metal. Despite the vast number of records that combine heavy metal and rap – most famously Run DMC's "Walk This Way" – there used to be a time when hip-hop and heavy metal fans defined themselves in opposition to each other.[11] Metallers sneered at B-Boys, B-Boys

---

The only reason you'd play – other than coercion – is that you'd occasionally get to do this yourself.

[11] While "Walk This Way" may be the most famous – and arguably the most musically successful – of all rock/rap crossovers, it's far, far from being the only one. Hip-hop has always gone through phases where the artist throws in a track as a sop to current tastes. When house music was first popping up, rap artists would throw in an always dreadful house remix or hip-house track. LL Cool J's "I Need Love" spawned endless rap ballads. As for rap and rock, this marriage has usually fared better when it's just a matter of a sample rather than an actual collaboration and notable triumphs include Boogie Down Productions use of AC/DC's "Back in Black" for "Dope Beat" and Deep Purple's "Smoke on the Water" for "Ya Slippin". I personally can't stand Public Enemy's remix of their own classic "Bring the Noise" with Anthrax, and Jay-Z's link-up with Linkin Park was commercially

sneered at metallers with their poodle hair and wack trainers. They said we didn't use real instruments, we said they had poodle hair and wack trainers. Personally I never went in for this pathetic rivalry, but that's because I used to be a metaller myself.

So much of my life has been indelibly linked with hip-hop – my listening, my friendships, my career, my dress sense, the stuff I collect, my economic fortunes, even the holidays I took – that it's strange to think I could have lived a life defined by heavy metal instead. For many kids, your dad is your hero, and my dad was a heavy metal fan. He wasn't a casual music listener – he'd grown up on 50's and 60's rock 'n' roll and now he came home from Saxon concerts with his ears bleeding. He owned the previously mentioned mobile disco set-up, and his friend Dave Pinder took it out on the road. I was pretty popular at school discos because we had everything, so I'd take along a bunch of records to get the party started. So that they didn't get lost or stolen, I put 'This belongs to Andy' stickers over many of them, which didn't go down a treat when I returned them to my dad.

But my dad's personal collection was something else entirely. That was where the AC/DC records resided, the live album *If You Want Blood... You've Got It*, with a thrilling gatefold sleeve that showed Angus Young being impaled on a guitar. There was Saxon, Motorhead, Deep Purple, Led Zeppelin, KISS, Rainbow and Whitesnake. This was my musical education before hip-hop washed ashore. Like kids all around the world, I'd wait until my parents were

---

successful but artistically negligent. As for the Beastie Boys and "Sabotage"? They started out as a punk group and segued into being rappers, and their combination of both genres was often wonderful and effortless, rather than the mash-up confections that seem to be the brainwaves of record labels or self-indulgent artists trying to explore their rock/rap side (that means you Lil' Wayne – and we'd really rather never hear another crushingly awful guitar solo from Outkast's Andre 3000, thanks).

out, cue up "Whole Lotta Rosie" or "Since You've Been Gone" and rock out. I did a bit of air guitar but my heart wasn't in it.[12] I graduated to air drums, which again wasn't my niche and, eventually, settled on air keyboards, usually by standing behind the sofa and pretending to play that. It was neither here nor there whether the song I was playing along to actually had any keyboards on it. Despite my passion for records, I didn't actually know the first thing about music per se. Then again, by this point I was pretty much an air keyboard prodigy and that was entirely self-taught.

In terms of live music, I can't boast of having spent this period of my life seeing all the major bands that would form the future of metal, concerts that would allow me to tell stories about the time I saw so-and-so guitar legend shredding for two hours. No, instead I could boast a grand total of two gigs at this point. A family outing to see Tina Turner, at the behest of my dad, and the same to see Def Leppard. I don't think my dad even liked Def Leppard, who were then in their first flush of fame, and played Nottingham's Royal Concert Hall in December of 1983. But the drummer Rick's dad was my dad's accountant, so we got free backstage passes, which to a 10-year-old metaller was a BIG FUCKING DEAL!

---

[12] Quite simply the act of playing the guitar while not actually having or holding one. At a basic level, an air guitarist should at least give the appearance of holding an invisible guitar in roughly the correct way, although you can get away with just thrashing away at it, rather than picking out the correct chords and doing all the fingering. At an advanced level – and there are actually championships for this kind of thing (the existence and popularity of which will make you feel either that the world is a wonderfully colourful place full of rich diversity and endless human ingenuity or that we're all going to air hell in an air handcart) – you need to be a lot more convincing in your playing of the instrument you're not holding. Good air guitar, along with vigorous air drumming, is a staple at weddings and parties where lots has been drunk and vintage hair metal is being played. It is incredibly cathartic and joyous.

After the concert, of which I remember precisely nothing, we went backstage where I acted like the bored, petulant boy I was, and my sister acted like the pubescent 14-year-old she was, picking up beer cans the group had drunk out of and the like. Lead singer Joe Elliott asked my dad what he thought of the concert, and he tactfully replied, "It was okay, but no AC/DC." Accurate, but hardly likely to cement his place in Mr Elliott's affections. I don't believe Rick's dad is still my dad's accountant, which is one way of ending this particular anecdote.

My hair in the early 80's was an unholy mess of curls, an absolute bastard to try and get a brush through, but I wasn't allowed to grow it long like a proper metal fan, or like my other metal god, my cousin David. He was several years older, had a wardrobe that consisted 100% of denim items covered in band-related patches, knew all the bands and the members and the albums, who played what kind of guitar and he also had long hair. We went to visit his family in Sheffield a couple of times, and he was lumbered with me for the day, so he took me, wide-eyed, into the record shops in town, where he talked chummily to record shop assistants in a way that filled me with awe. The last time we visited I pestered my mum all the way home about her stitching some stuff onto my denim jacket when we got back.

My ruthless haranguing of my poor mother worked, and she agreed that I could have AC/DC's logo stitched into the back of my treasured jacket. The year before, my dad had taken me to London for the very first time, as he'd got a couple of tickets for the FA Trophy at Wembley from a mate who was supposed to be playing in it but didn't even make the substitutes bench. We went to Madame Tussaud's and the London Planetarium and I went on the London Underground for the very first time. At one point we got off at a stop and realised on the platform that I'd left my denim jacket on the tube. My dad, knowing how much I loved it, rushed back on to get it for me, squeezing back off through the closing doors as I panicked on the platform.

I painstakingly traced the AC/DC logo onto the back of my beloved jacket for my mum to sew, asking her to get some red thread so it stood out. She promised she would. Red – because if you want blood, stitch it into your denim. I couldn't wear the jacket in the meantime, as it had a slightly unconvincing biro'd logo on the back. But when it was finished, I was basically going to rule the primary school playground.

No matter how cool your mum, no matter how much she likes to tap her foot to music herself, she will never understand the explosive passion a young boy has for music. It's all-consuming. That's my somewhat weak justification for the tantrum I threw when she finished stitching my jacket. Tears? Yes. But there was also shouting, accusations and recriminations. There was wrenching, scrunching and throwing of the garment in question. There was a boy sent to bed early with no tea, even though it was a bright summer day outside.

I said in the previous chapter that it was a tape from my school-friend Richard Kirk that was the catalyst for my hip-hop life but, thinking back, maybe I was already on my way. Perhaps the thing that kick-started my life-long love affair with hip-hop was the day my mum brought the curtain down on heavy metal Andrew by stitching the AC/DC logo onto his denim jacket in shocking, girly pink.

Three
Back to the Old School

My flirtation with every other form of music in the world over with by age 11, I embraced hip-hop, and Neil 'Falco' Falconbridge was now my official hip-hop mate. It may seem like a weird thing to say in the 2000's, where it's a dominant culture and everyone knows about it, but it was so niche in 1984 that we huddled together in tiny groups, all of us true believers, keepers of the flame. We played tapes together, we went record shopping together and, at playtimes at school, we tried to do breakdancing together.

My state comprehensive, Toot Hill, was divided up into different houses, with each of them known for a particular attribute, which usually reflected the predilections of the Heads of House, who seemed to select their pupils from local primary schools based on that sole prejudice. So Windsor House was known for sporting ability and would always triumph on school sports day. Rutland, my house, was known for being brainy, and for coming dead last at sports day. Every year since the school was founded.

Being placed in Rutland, someone must have thought I was reasonably intelligent (or too awful at sports to contemplate), and I had been one of the bigger bookworms at primary school, a wannabe poet at the age of eight. As my old friend Kevin Strachan puts it, "I remember you writing fantasy novels in class that you could club a whale to death with." Teachers like the wonderful Mr Sparrow had fostered my love of reading by lending me books from his own collection. He gave me Anita Desai's *The Village by the Sea* when I was nine, hoping to pique my interest. Such faith in me was badly misplaced, as my first year at comprehensive saw me trade my passion for books for listening to music by the likes of The Great Peso, Afrika Bambaataa and Pumpkin, the King of The Beat. The only things at school that remotely interested me were girls and the breakdancing sessions that kicked off in Thoroton House at breaks and lunch. I can't remember what aspect of the curriculum Thoroton House was known for – perhaps it was bodypopping.

Falco and I would rock up (a modern phrase that sounds like we were very casual about the whole thing, whereas we were actually clenching our buttocks very tightly in order to avoid actually shitting in our shoes), nervous of most of the other older kids, and watch them do their thing. They seemed to have the same music as us, the same *Electro* tapes, but in all other ways were leagues ahead. They had cool trainers, they had the bodywarmers we knew US breakdancers wore to cushion their backs, and they could do the moves. There is, of course, a chasm between being 11 and being 13 at school. At some point on that continuum I always assumed someone would take me in hand and tell me about the downy hair on my body, how to breakdance, how to speak confidently and chat girls up properly.[13] That someone never appeared.

---

[13] Breakdance, or 'breaking' as we actually called it 'in the streets', was another of the seemingly unique aspects of hip-hop that appealed to me in my search for a cultural identity that wasn't the norm in Bingham. Before discovering it, I used to headbang at school discos, as that was linked with heavy metal. Once I was into hip-hop, I did robotics to pretty much any song played, no matter how ill-fitting (Kenny Loggins' "Footloose" or Fun Boy Three's "The Lunatics are Taking over the Asylum", for example). Breakdance eventually took up a life separate from hip-

I'd practised backspins on the kitchen floor at home, with results that can best be described as mixed, although the floor came up a treat. Headspins were way out of my league – the sporting ability that got me put into nerdy Rutland House meant that at age 11 I'd

---

hop, and disappeared from hip-hop concerts and jams as the 80's progressed. It didn't fit with the music as it evolved, and as wonderful as breakdancing can be, it did have its time. Not that it died. Some die-hards kept it going, it experienced a revival at retro events in the late 90's, and still has annual awards and battles with crews from all over the world competing at a very high level. It also begat 'street dance', which is now a staple of 'let's do the show right here' teenage films and TV shows like *Britain's Got Talent.* Street dance is really an amalgam of breakdancing – simply put the stuff you do on the floor that involves spinning and strenuous activity – and popping, which is a series of jerky movements usually performed while stood erect. There's also locking as well, but by now we're really getting specialised.

I can't help but feel that there's something regrettable about men in their 40's still wanting to see breaking at shows, as if hip-hop should be preserved in amber or in a time loop where only the first few 'pure' years of it are allowed to be celebrated and repeated. Middle-aged men and women should be allowed to reminisce about how they used to breakdance when they were kids, and to perhaps jokingly throw a few moves when drunk at a wedding party or school reunion. They shouldn't make a habit of trying to reintroduce breakdance to a world that has moved on. After breakdance had died out in New York clubs, other dances were created to fill the void, not that any of them caught the public imagination in the same way. The Wop did reasonably well, the Pee-Wee Herman, Running Man, Robocop, Tootsee Roll, Kickstep and the Bankhead Bounce all had their moments too. Usually they were promoted by a song or two which was either a cash in on a currently popular dance or a slightly desperate attempt to crowbar a new one in. Even seemingly no-nonsense Ice Cube played his part, ghostwriting a 1987 song for Dr Dre's World Class Wreckin' Kru called "The Cabbage Patch". The Gucci Crew II and RP Cola also released songs about that particular craze, while Digital Underground's "The Humpty Dance" is a phenomenal song but probably only Humpty Hump himself could carry off the moves.

All this light-hearted fun disappeared in the more serious early 90's, when headnodding ruled the roost, apart from the stiff, jerky and limited moves that everyone did – called colloquially 'The 93 Dance' by people who remember that time of hardly dancing at all – to dark songs from the likes of Onyx and Rumpeltilskinz. The 93 Dance is basically stomping on the spot, raising your knees to about your waist, combined with repetitive arm moves. It was so pervasive and so ugly that it's no surprise that people drifted away from NY hip-hop back then to other regions in the US where they still liked to have fun and dance properly.

still never done a proper forward roll as I was scared of breaking my neck. Attempts to climb the rope in the school gym led to mild chafing and me reaching the heady, vertigo-inducing heights of five inches from the floor. I'd done robotics at school discos along with Peter Crouch and everyone else you've ever heard speak on *I Vaguely Remember The 80's* on TV, but that's not real dancing.

Also, it's not like you could hide in a crowd if you actually wanted to breakdance or bodypop. You don't all dance at once like at a club – you take it in turns to get on the floor, briefly become the centre of attention and bust your best moves, and hope people approve with a nod of the head, before sliding away and watching who was up next. It means it's hard to disappear if your moves aren't up to snuff, but it's also quite meritocratic. You get your chance and have to seize it. Of course, another reason for you being given so much space is that you need it. If you're performing windmills, at least five metres of space is recommended, or you'll kick someone in the head.

So if Falco and I were going to make our mark, we had to step up in front of the big boys. Falco was nerveless, sticking to his trademark bodypopping that he practised at home in front of the mirror. It was low key, but he got some sweet moves off and resisted the temptation to go beyond what he could do – he didn't dabble in breakdance itself. Heads were nodded, if grudgingly (13-year-olds can't be seen to publicly approve of 11-year-olds) as he made his way back to the side. My rectum clenching, I knew I couldn't just stand there – I had to do my thing as well.

I suppose it would be funnier if I had fucked up royally. If I embarrassed myself in some physical way, or split my trousers and set off some farcical Harold Lloyd chain of events, or got booed off or fell over or something shameful and inadequate, but none of those things happened. Nor was it a triumph, a series of technical spins and boogaloos that drew impressed 'oohs' and 'aahs' from the onlookers, and cemented my arrival in the hip-hop world and had the big boys making me an honorary 3rd year. People weren't going to be taking the piss out of how awful I was as I skulked back to Rutland like a scolded dog, and neither were they going to be telling their mates that 'Emmo', as I was known at school, was an amazing breaker and popper. Instead, I shuffled into the middle and spent about 30 seconds delivering some routine bodypopping moves that were the dancefloor equivalent of beige. I was exactly, precisely average. A shrug. Not the worst there, thank god, but no-one would be inviting me to join their breakdance crew in a hurry. Spoiler alert: As in all things with hip-hop and me, this was very much a taste of things to come.

As Falco lived in Cropwell Bishop (shout out the Stilton massive) and I in Bingham (no notable cheeses, unfortunately), I was often left to my own devices at evenings and some weekends. We were only a few miles apart, but neither of us had the pocket money to spend on bus fare, and to BMX there meant taking a chance on some tricky unlit country lanes in the dark. Instead, I'd see my non hip-hop mates, bullying them relentlessly into listening to the three or four records I now owned. Their reactions veered from the nonplussed to the physically violent.

Often I'd go to my friend Adam's house for a warmer welcome. Adam was a big, cheerful lad who didn't have many friends and, consequently, was happy to be gently pushed along into doing whatever you wanted to do. Luckily for both of us, what I wanted to do didn't involve pre-ASBO pranks, but instead getting three tape recorders lined up. We'd have tapes of music in two of them and a blank cassette in the third. We'd play the two with music in simultaneously, adjusting the volume constantly, moving them nearer and then further away from the deck that was recording. This was what we thought 'mixing' was, in our naivety. We'd then listen back to the discordant mess and point out what we thought the good bits were. As most of the tapes we played were megamixes anyway, we were remixing mixes in the most cack-handed fashion possible, so that there were often four separate records playing at once.

Over the last 27 years I've lost dozens of prized cassettes that I wish I could track down, one-off recordings, sought after live shows from classic artists and the like. I get a nostalgic pang when I think of them and I curse myself for my clumsiness in letting this gold slip through my fingers. But thank fuck the tapes that Adam Slater and I made over a long school holiday are consigned to the dustbins of history. What a dreadful racket they were. What were we thinking of?

As time went on, it became apparent to Falco and I that we needed to form a crew. You might be familiar with artists like

Tupac[14], MC Hammer[15] and Biggie Smalls.[16] They only appear to be solo artists. In fact, they have behind them a posse of producers,

[14] Tupac Shakur is an incredibly divisive hip-hop legend. He began as a dancer and back-up rapper for colourful Funkadelic-inspired West Coast rap crew Digital Underground (which, for me, is definitely his career high point). He went on to have a hugely successful and controversial solo career that resulted in his becoming perhaps the biggest rapper in the world, wildly notorious and a protagonist in an East/West coast feud that fuelled hip-hop for a couple of years and ended with his premature death after he was killed in a drive-by shooting in Las Vegas in 1996. This death was both incredibly predictable – he was Icarus-like for much of his career – and sadly messy. Also predictable, in the light of the killings of other famous rappers, was the police mishandling of the case. As we move beyond the 20th anniversary of his death, Tupac continues to release records from beyond the grave, most of them studio footnotes of little interest, and no-one has ever been charged or arrested with his murder. He also did time for sexual assault and spent much of his fame being a total dick, though, so don't mistake me for one of those people who see him as a fallen hero. It's a real bugbear of mine but, like several other rappers and sportsmen (Mike Tyson, for example) who've physically abused women, Tupac seems to be afforded a pass by a certain breed of hip-hop fan who seem to think that the women either asked for it or entrapped a rich star and then cried rape for publicity. Whatever the individual merits of each case, for some reason you'll never hear a hip-hop fan round on a hero of theirs for being a rapist – only for making a record that isn't as good as their last. We're similarly blind to the 'lovable' pimps of rap music, without really stopping to contemplate what it is a pimp does for a living.

[15] MC Hammer was an Oakland, California rapper who, for a brief period, was the biggest rapper in the world (before Tupac) even if you couldn't find any hip-hop fans who actually liked him. His biggest hit was 1990's "U Can't Touch This", which sampled Rick James' "Super Freak" and, all cynicism aside, is a pretty fine pop-rap record, largely because it's pretty hard to fuck up a song like "Super Freak". Hammer was also known as a dancer, a choreographer, for wearing huge 'Hammer' pants that could fit three people or one 80's darts player in, for lavish spending leading to bankruptcy, for being the subject of numerous diss records by the likes of LL Cool J and 3rd Bass (and by me, in some of my lyrics, although I don't think he knows about those unless he was a secret fan of the Leeds bedroom rap scene) and for becoming a minister in the church. I don't own any MC Hammer records, but I do think the world would be a less interesting place without him, not least because hip-hop was always more fun when there was a bit of conflict going on.

[16] Biggie Smalls aka The Notorious B.I.G (known as Christopher Wallace to his family) was the other main protagonist in the East/West Coast hip-hop war of the 1990's and, like Tupac, would end up the victim of an unsolved murder after

DJ's, dancers, mates and hangers-on – the excellent phrase 'weed carriers' has been coined for the latter, the star needing a mate to not only carry his marijuana in case of police interest, but to roll his spliffs for him. This posse is a hangover from the late 70's birth of hip-hop where pretty much any rapper worth the time of day was in a crew. The names, to me, are incredibly evocative and an example of how fresh hip-hop was when it came into my life. Chart artists in 1984 had names like Nik Kershaw and Blancmange. By contrast, hip-hop crews were called Grandmaster Flash and the Furious Five, Knights of the Turntables, Afrika Bambaataa & The Soulsonic Force, Freddy B & The Mighty Mic Masters, The Crash Crew, The Fearless Four, The Fantastic Romantic Five, The Cold Crush Brothers, Awesome Foursome and The Treacherous Three. They sounded innovative, space age and incredibly tough to my naïve ears. Gangs of like-minded rappers and DJ's at the forefront of the world's most cutting-edge music, banding together to rid the world of stodgy middle-aged guff and vacuous pop mediocrity. I still feel that way about them now, nearly thirty years later, even though time and experience has given me a different perspective on the names.

When I was 11 and desperate to be a rapper, I only saw their adopted aliases in terms of how cool they were. Furious, Mighty, Awesome, Treacherous – all superlatives any kid can get excited about. This applies outside of music. The Morphin Power Rangers? A bunch of lightweight milksops that anyone could chin. The Mighty

---

a drive-by shooting in Los Angeles in 1997. He'd been implicated – with little evidence – both in an earlier robbery of Tupac and his eventual death. Biggie's recorded legacy – two proper albums called, prophetically, "Ready to Die" and "Life After Death" (which was released a fortnight after his shooting) is somewhat more consistent than Tupac's, largely due to the executive production influence of the unfairly maligned Sean 'Puff Daddy/P-Diddy' Combs. Combs corralled some excellent beat-makers to produce some of their best work for Wallace who, on his day, had legitimate claims to be the best rapper alive.

Morphin Power Rangers? Whoa! Those dudes are hardcore! Now I see those names in different ways – yes, still with elements of cool, but I can perceive now that a lot of rapper's names weren't just based on supposed attributes (let's take it as read that 'Soulsonic' is an actual thing you can be), but also on where they lived, on slang terms and argot, witty bits of wordplay, or ones based on trends and even other people's names.

We'll talk more about battle records later, when I get onto cross-Leeds inter-hip-hop warfare (with all the thrills that implies – no skipping ahead now), but for now let's touch on the 'Roxanne Wars'. In 1984, a group called UTFO (the Untouchable Force Organization, obviously) released a song called "Roxanne, Roxanne", a typical tale of a hard-to-get woman who rebuffed the advances of the group. The story would have ended there, except UTFO pissed off influential New York radio DJ and promoter Mr Magic and his producer friend Marley Marl by cancelling an appearance at one of their events in New York. A young female rapper they knew called Lolita Shante Gooden offered to make a song hitting out at UTFO, and did it in the form of an answer record called "Roxanne's Revenge". She released it under her adopted rap alias of Roxanne Shante. And after this, it gets crazy. UTFO bite back, hiring women called Elease Jack and later Adelaida Martinez to perform as 'The Real Roxanne'. This phony war then spins out of control, with at least 30 (and some say more) records making up the Roxanne craze. I personally own records by and about The Parents of Roxanne, Roxanne's Doctor, Rocksann, Little Roxanne, Roxanne's Brothers, Roxanne's a Man, Roxanne's Sister, Roxanne's Real Fat and, with an air of finality, the East Coast Crew's "The Final Word – No More Roxanne (Please)".

What's most striking to me is that none of the participants in the Roxanne Wars were actually called Roxanne. To an 11-year-old discovering a new musical genre, an 11-year-old with an easily blown mind, this was mind-blowing. It also shows how thinking of a name for yourself as a rapper or crew isn't just as simple as adding Amazing to Andrew. Although there are plenty of people who do just that.[17] For the record, I would be prepared to wage an entirely new kind of 'Roxanne War' that would be solely about never having to listen to Sting sing "Roxanne" again.

Falco and I sat in the bedroom of his house with pen and paper going through lists of names. We came up with and crossed out dozens. Despite the fact that I couldn't rap, and hadn't tried, and he couldn't DJ, and hadn't tried (and his mum's Alba midi system didn't look too promising as a stand-in for any real crew's 'wheels of steel'), we decided that I was the rapper, and he was the DJ. I can't remember what names he rejected on the way, but before long he was newly minted as DJ Touché. I found it harder to decide, but then hit upon what I thought was a perfect combination of alliteration, hip-hop's penchant for deliberate bad spelling, and the first letter of my surname.[18] And thus Kold Kid E was born.

Or stillborn, more like. As I BMX'ed home that very night I thought better of it, and Kold Kid E was consigned to history. I was

---

[17] For example: Fresh Gordon, Messy Marv, Prince Paul, DJ Mike Smooth, Kool Kyle, Master Rob, Disco Dave, Krazy Eddie (emphasising just how crazy by using a 'K'), Rockmaster Scott, Jazzy Jeff (x 2), Jazzy Joyce and Def Jef.

[18] To truly chronicle this would take about another 100 pages. But here's a few that capture the peculiarly tortuous manner in which rappers would go out of their way to take perfectly nice words and mangle them on purpose: Kukoo Da Baga Bonez, Invisibl Skratch Piklz, Jeru the Damaja, Outkast (and one half of Outkast, Big Boi), Fabolous, Da Lench Mob. There are very few hip-hop groups that don't turn 'The' into 'Tha' or 'Da' or transform 'Clique' into 'Klick'. Consequently, rappers tend not to be very good at *Countdown* or *The Times* crossword. To this day I'll get messages on Facebook or from people buying records from me on eBay where about one word in ten is spelled correctly, and the rest are in hip-hopese, which I always think must take them a lot longer to write.

reborn as MC Melody Ski. I've never skied in my life, but it sounded cool (still does, if you ask me). DJ Touché and MC Melody Ski – yep, we were ready to go places. If only there'd been any places for us to actually go...

Four
I Can't Live Without My Radio

Bingham, as I've hinted, wasn't exactly the world centre of hip-hop, and it's telling that I had to look to the far-flung reaches of Cropwell Bishop to even find myself a DJ. The closest thing to a fan I knew in my own town was my sister, Susan. I have three sisters, but Tracy and Beverley had left home before I was born – I can only assume they'd had some premonition of what a malicious little shit I'd be as I grew up. So Susan had to bear the brunt of my behaviour, and while I'm very close to her now, and I'm sure she's forgiven me my many trespasses, it's fair to say my actions at the time could be classified as those of an obnoxious twat.

Yet even when we were generally at loggerheads we could still bond over music. Before I started to eschew everything else when hip-hop came into my life, we liked a lot of the same pop, and still share a deep love for Adam Ant now. And Susan, although she was into Billy Idol amongst other hormone-induced crazes and crushes, really liked some of the same hip-hop I did. Grandmaster Melle Mel & The Furious Five's "Step Off" hit the UK charts in 1984, and to this day she and I can often be persuaded by the charms of a couple of bottles of red wine to perform an unwanted duet of this classic rap song.

In 1984, however, I didn't want to hang out and rap with my sister[19]. I wanted to hang out and rap with mates. Playground discussions had thrown up the fact that there was another big hip-hop fan in the school (imagine that now – a mere handful of hip-hop fans in a school. Impossible, unless in some horrible apocalyptic future scenario where UKIP or the BNP are allowed to run free schools), but he was a few years older than me. Older years didn't talk to first years, even if they were related to you, so it took quite a bit of pluck for me to go up to Pete Littlefair in the school playground, surrounded as he was by his burly peers, and tremulously say, "I hear you like hip-hop, I do too, who do you like?" Unfortunately, I got told to bog off before I got chinned, by one of his friends, and I retreated to my side of the playground, suitably chastened.

Fair play to Pete, he sought me out himself later, away from the disapproving looks of his mates. I still know Pete a little bit today – he turned into an excellent DJ and producer under the name of DJ Ivory (seek out the works of The P Brothers), so perhaps he'll forgive me if I don't paint him in an entirely flattering light here. Suffice to say, he was a teenage male, a boastful breed. He suffered my little conversation with him semi-stoically, but when I told him I only owned two records, he sneered at me. 'Two records? Ha! I spend £50 a week on records!' And so that was that. I'd been put in my place. I didn't believe him either – what 14-year-old had that much disposable income in 1984? – but as I've developed my own

[19] Susan would, for many years, put a little rap she'd written in all of my birthday cards. I have a Public Enemy postcard she gave me for my 18th which reads: "Yo! Andy you are now eighteen / You can live it up in the pub and club scene/ You can dance about with a girl called Jean / Or if on that idea you are not keen / You could stand by the bar and on it lean / By the way your sister's a beauty queen." Her talents were wasted.

extremely expensive vinyl addiction over the years, I'm prepared to give him the benefit of the doubt. But my brush with the older, cool kids had reinforced one thing – as far as the hip-hop scene for 11-year-olds in Bingham was concerned, I was on my own.

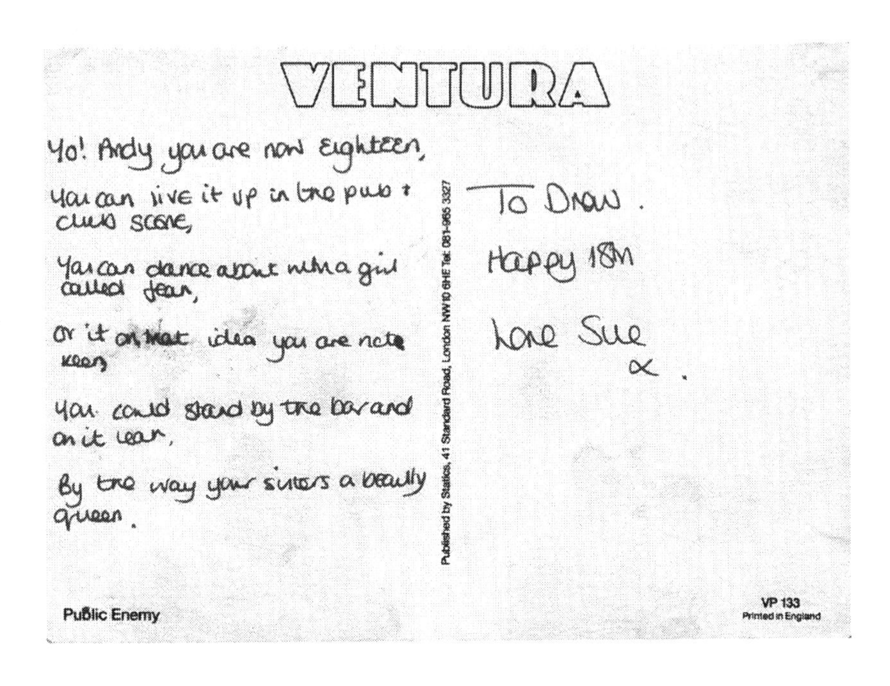

I'd learned from the telly (by which I mean extremely patronising bits of evening news about the 'hip new craze called breakdancing', which the more I think about it seems like the Trojan horse that got rap music into the UK) that fans of hip-hop enjoyed their music in a particular way – pumped out of a massive stereo carried on the shoulder, about two inches from the ear. I find it hard to reconcile my opinion of people who drive around, windows down, blasting music from their cars – 'pricks' – with my romantic notion of people who carried their boomboxes on their shoulders blasting out Electro – 'heroes and cultural pioneers'. All I can say is that I formed my attachment to the latter during my impressionable years. And while

I couldn't drive (still can't), I could certainly carry a stereo around on my shoulder.

Yep, I was soon to be seen walking past the chippy, through the market square past the pick-and-mix shop, through the shopping precinct and to the benches outside the library, blasting music at the squares out of my 'ghettoblaster'. A couple of years before, I'd been on first name terms with the kindly library staff, who'd let me browse in there for hours at a time and often overlooked the occasional late fees (although I soured on them a little when they called my parents to tell them I was attempting to borrow a spin-off book from the film *Monty Python's Meaning of Life*, which had pictures of actual naked female breasts in it). Now I was stood outside like John Cusack in *Say Anything* holding my portable hi-fi aloft.[20]

Not that they noticed. This was less a ghettoblaster than a suburb-wheezer. Whereas the New Yorkers on the telly were wielding metre-long things with two tape decks, packed with subwoofers, tweeters, knobs and dials, mine was a paint smeared radio-cassette player I'd found in the garage. It had one deck, was about 10 inches long, and had an output that scarcely drowned out my own breathing. It would be ideal for listening to *The Archers* while you filed your stamp collection or did some scrapbooking; not so ideal for attempting to subvert the outmoded musical norms of your dead town. So it didn't have quite the impact I was hoping for, but it was a start, and I was still spreading the gospel of hip-hop by playing cassettes of obscure electro to the heathens of Bingham's

[20] *Say Anything* is a 1989 film directed by Cameron Crowe and starring John Cusack and Ione Skye. The sweet romance at the heart of the film has lasted pretty well, and while John Cusack may look pretty risible in his trenchcoat, holding a ghettoblaster aloft pumping out Peter Gabriel's "In Your Eyes", it's undeniably an iconic 80's film moment. I certainly didn't play Peter Gabriel out of my ghettoblaster, although I did have "Sledge Hammer" on 7 inch vinyl, a school disco staple.

pedestrianised shopping area. Well, to those of them that strayed within two feet of my cassette player when there was a lull in all other ambient noise.

It was through my ghettoblaster that I had one of my first brushes with racism. In 1984, there were very few black people in my market town. There was only one black kid in the entire school, who – shame on us – was nicknamed Sambo. I don't think I'd ever really thought about race at that stage of my life. I wasn't from a family of racists – in fact, I can say with some certainty that I never heard a single racial epithet or comment from my parents or siblings ever – but I suppose I was casually racist in the way that many people were and are. I unthinkingly went along with calling my schoolmate Sambo, not realising how it would make him feel, not realising how many people called him that, how much it would hurt, not even realising where it came from. I was a stupid kid, in a sea of them, and I thank my lucky stars to this day that hip-hop changed my life, and taught me differently. I called my radio a ghettoblaster – a name which, I'm aware, has its own racial overtones – but when some local moron had a go at me in the market square and said, "What you got a wog-box for?" I was still shocked. But to many people that's what they were – wog-boxes. Even though I was a white boy in a white town, clearly this hip-hop music was a real threat.

By 1985, MC Melody Ski and DJ Touché weren't threatening the charts, but we were getting somewhere: We'd started to rap along to other people's records. Both of us were short of pocket money, so our Saturday trips into Nottingham to buy vinyl were fraught with difficulties. We'd get the bus 12 miles to town, passing through endless small towns and villages, slowly drawing nearer to civilisation. We'd alight at the Victoria Centre bus station then make our way to Arcade Records. This wasn't the only place to buy hip-hop records in Nottingham, but it was the coolest. It was where Pete

Littlefair went. Falco and I were too cowed by the atmosphere to ask them to play anything before we purchased it, so we spent ages thumbing through the racks, weighing up what we could get, what might have sold out before we got our next instalment of pocket money, what we'd heard of versus what looked amazing based on the cover art.[21]

We could usually afford one record each, and tried to maximise the music per pound by buying albums instead of singles. An import

---

[21] I don't want to come across too, 'Oh, music was better when everything came in 12" gatefold sleeves with iconic artwork and in-depth liner notes' about this, but as the author of a book about hip-hop cover art (the Ronseal titled *The Book of Hip-Hop Cover Art*, out of print book fans), I can't just drift past this topic without saying something. What has disappeared, to a large extent, is a way of buying music based entirely on the cover art and the contents of the sleeve. This was pre-Internet, so every release didn't come out pre-hyped, each label or artist didn't have their own websites, there was no YouTube on which to listen in advance, no leaks, no torrents, no Wikipedia or Google to find out about these artists. Many people didn't even have access to a hip-hop radio show, so the records that turned up in the likes of Arcade and Selectadisc were totally unknown.

You might buy something by happy accident because it was racked at the front, or in proximity to another artist you liked or, very often, you just liked the look of it. The songs would just have titles that appealed. The blokes on the cover might be wearing a sports brand you liked, so you'd buy it. One of my first purchases in Arcade Records was Doug E. Fresh and the Get Fresh Crew's *Oh my God!* LP from 1986. I bought this partly because I'd heard of them – they'd had a hit with "The Show" in 1985 – but also because they not only wore Fila tracksuits on the cover (and borrowed the Fila lettering for the artwork) but Doug E. Fresh also had Bally trainers on, which I'd heard him rap about. This was the total package – and I lusted after Fila and Bally apparel from then on without, it has to be said, ever actually owning any in the rest of my life to date. Regardless, this was a win – it turned out to be a classic album.

But there were losses too. I also bought records by the British rap crew Three Wize Men in Arcade. These looked perfect: They had graffiti on them, one of them had a "Warning: This Record Contains Language That May Offend" sticker, they'd used a 'z' instead of a 's' to turn 'wise into 'wize' – suck it, you squares! Unfortunately, like much very early UK hip-hop, the output of the Three Wize Men was utter horseshit. Looks can be deceiving and, of course, many a great record would have a dreadful cover and awful sportswear as well. We were shooting in the dark.

single could cost as much as £5.99, while an album, for a couple of pounds more, was a guaranteed 40 minutes of music (any modern hip-hop album that is less than two hours is now deemed an EP). Occasionally it'd be a quiet day and we'd go to Our Price instead, but they put big price stickers directly onto the record sleeves, which were hard to get off without leaving marks.[22] We were already record anoraks.

On our trips into town we'd see flyers and posters for hip-hop nights in Nottingham. We were only just starting to realise how popular it was in the city as a whole and, at the same time, that the world didn't revolve around Toot Hill School. There weren't gigs, so to speak, because only a couple of rap artists had the international profile to tour Europe, but there were 'jams'. Jams would kick off in the early afternoon and run on until the early hours. Fans from out of town – Derby, Leicester, even Birmingham – would come on coaches to breakdance and listen to the latest DJ's. It was mostly just people playing records, scratching and cutting them up, but with a few local rap performances as well, and lots of breakdancing. Falco and I were 13 when we went to our first jam at the legendary Rock City in Nottingham and, once more, we were shitting ourselves. Cassettes of Rock City jams circulated at school, they were fixtures in my – ahem – boombox. But we didn't really know what happened at them, and perhaps wouldn't have been quite so nervous if

[22] Our Price, which died in 2004, was a retail chain that was second only to Woolworths (also, RIP) in terms of shifting records and cassettes in the mid 80's. They had hundreds of branches, but would go on to be superseded by the hipper likes of Virgin Megastores (with whose corporate history they are intertwined). Early Our Price stores were known for being importers of otherwise hard-to-get records from the US, and occasionally you'd get a branch with a savvy buyer or two who made sure they stocked good stuff you'd never see in other stores. This also applied to HMV, Tower and Virgin. I met my good friend Mike Lewis through his stewardship of the surprisingly excellent hip-hop section at Oxford Street's HMV in London.

someone had said to us, "Yeah, it's basically just a load of standing around and nodding your head to music."

The Rock City Crew were the local breakdance outfit, and we revered them before we even set eyes on them. They didn't disappoint. They made our little playtime dance sessions look parochial and tiny. And while we recognised a lot of the songs being played, DJ's like Mongoose and Graeme Park would drop the needle on stuff that blew our minds, the freshest imports getting a spin before they were even in the shops.[23] We'd see Pete Littlefair there, but he knew everyone and we knew no-one.

What really opened our eyes was a) how black the events were and b) how easily black kids mixed with white. As two of the youngest there, we'd occasionally get 'taxed' – a group of five or six lads would come up to us and ask us for some money. It wasn't a real shakedown – they were usually happy with 50p, leaving us just enough for bus fare home – we were just clearly a soft touch. It didn't put us off. We went back numerous times, slowly growing in confidence, getting on nodding terms with regulars. But we were still kids, and whether we were at Rock City, Bojangles, or the scene of any other amateurish but enthralling jam, we had to leave early. But all the time we were there, we felt like we were involved in something exciting. This isn't something worked out with the benefit of hindsight – I remember feeling at the time that we were doing

[23] There are lots of DJ's, who are probably more associated with dance and house music, who first started out in the hip-hop scene. There was a definite bleed over from the late breakdancing and electro era of hip-hop to the early Chicago house sound. Graeme Park is indelibly associated with the Hacienda in Manchester and is a legend in house music circles, but he started off working in Nottingham's Selectadisc and playing hip-hop at jams. This is probably hugely unsurprising to most readers – many people went from soul to hip-hop to house to indie to EDM and can enjoy them all simultaneously – but as someone who has personally stayed rigidly in his hip-hop box since 1984, I thought it deserved a hat tip.

something edgy, and even if I didn't know the word 'subcultural' then, if I had, that's how I'd have framed it. We were dabbling in something cool and unusual, but self-consciously, like we were looking for something cool to be a part of.

At the time, my pocket money was entirely dependent on my working in my dad's shop. He had a taxi business next to the train station (my sister's diaries, which she has kindly allowed me indirect access to for date and fact-checking, conscious of the fact I used to fruitlessly scour her bedroom in search of them at the time, tell me that in in February and March of 1983 she, her friend Fiona and myself walked door to door delivering advertising leaflets for the taxi service – one of many dull, soul-crushing things I've managed to conveniently forget), and in the early 80's had the idea of using the premises as a video shop as well. VHS was just taking off, and our shop – the excellently named 'Insomniacs Video Club' (so called due to the late opening and the customers who'd come in for a late taxi after the pubs shut and grab a VHS of *Scanners* while they were at it), was one of only two in town (I'd occasionally get sent to the other – L. R. Mees – to do a recce on what new films he had in stock). I'd do a shift after school to give my mum or dad a rest, and the occasional Sunday as well. My sister bore the brunt of it, often working on her own into the early hours, having to serve *Electric Blue* videos to local 'viewers' when she should have been revising for her O-Levels or gushing about Billy Idol with Fiona.[24]

My shifts were easier – there were those *Electric Blues*, after all, if the shop was particularly dead. Taxi drivers would lounge in the office, but there weren't many working on Sundays, so I could watch what I wanted – video nasties, American frat comedies and – at last – films about hip-hop.

1984's *Beat Street* is a revered film in hip-hop circles. It's certainly not for the plot – a clichéd love story with some risible acting – but for some phenomenal set-pieces. A breakdance battle between the Rocksteady Crew and the New York City Breakers, glimpses of performances by Afrika Bambaataa, Shango, Two Sisters, The

---

[24] *Electric Blue* was a long-running video series (it also became a Playboy Channel TV show and a softcore magazine) that provided the first exposure to pornography for many 80's boys (and girls). It was a compilation of US footage and more cheekily toned UK-shot material, often 'hosted' by an adult star. It was softcore (eventually – the first few uncertificated releases were actually more explicit), it was naff, but to the average 13-year-old boy it was erectile gold. Your average episode would have some grainy US NTSC footage of a famous porn star – Marilyn Chambers or Seka, say – a feature on topless trampolining, a nude *Charlie's Angels* spoof, a rude cartoon, then some more grainy footage of a rare Joanna Lumley nude performance from a forgotten movie. This was *Electric Blue* at its creative peak. The post-1984 entries grew progressively worse. Still, the opening credits and theme tune are as amazingly 1980's as that Athena print of the bloke holding the baby and should be YouTubed at least once.

Treacherous Three and a youthful Doug E. Fresh. There's also a tragic subplot about a graffiti artist that refreshingly sides with the artist against the authorities and points up the symbiotic relationship between early hip-hop and graffiti art. For the 11-year-old me, it was *Citizen Kane* (if I'd actually known what that was). It was also a sign that hip-hop was coming, forcing its way into the wider culture. It was a film studio cash-in, of course, but they don't do those unless they see a ready-made market for it. When people said to me that it was a fad and wouldn't last (Jesus wept, if only any of us had realised how wrong they'd come to be), which they did all the time, I'd point them to *Beat Street.*

I loved working in the video shop, especially when there were no customers in. But 1984 was also the year of the Video Recordings Act, when we had to strip the shelves of all unrated films.[25] The video nasties that have given me a lifelong love of horror were gone overnight. No more *Nightmares in a Damaged Brain* or *The Evil Dead.*

[25] If you wanted to – and I do want to – you could draw some tenuous parallels between the moral panic about video nasties and the moral panic about hip-hop. Perhaps the hip-hop one lasted longer – off-the-mark front page headlines about The Beastie Boys in the late 80's were mirrored by off-the-mark front page headlines about Snoop Dogg in the late 90's. The urge to 'ban this sick filth' was again largely tabloid led and didn't really reflect any tangible public outcry, and again hip-hop, like the video nasties, would come to be seen as a major art form. Most of the films that were banned in a rush of blood in the 80's have crept back into certification (some were back on the shelves months later when they'd actually been watched and found to be bland, harmless and largely shit), many uncut, and while a few remain hard to see (or impossible to purchase, legally), many are regarded as genre masterpieces, and we're all a bit embarrassed about the silly fuss that was made. Releasing those films in the digital age hasn't led to a spate of depraved copycat murders, which was one of the original fears. Most newspapers and media outlets have already come to terms with hip-hop's worth and staying power, and those Beastie Boys headlines have the same taint of Mary Whitehouse-esque misplaced outrage. The papers can still have their fun with whichever rap artist they deem sexist/violent/a danger to 'our children', but along with video nasties, video games and countless other things that make life richer, this is a battle they've already lost.

No more porn (although at age 11 I only liked boobs, and didn't understand the downstairs bit), and thus the shop was never the same to me after that. But at least they left *Beat Street* behind. That would only have been a problem for the BBFC if they wanted to ban stilted acting and ridiculously predictable plot arcs.

Five
Travelling at the Speed of Thought

With Falco, I knew I could talk about and play whatever hip-hop I liked. With my family, it was different. While Susan was moderately open to a bit of it, she couldn't exactly be called a fanatic. And my parents? Like most parents when their child adopts a music that comes with its own subculture that they don't understand (punk or death metal, for example), they were slightly horrified. This mostly manifested in me not being allowed to play my music at home. Plus, my dad wasn't exactly delighted that I'd used large parts of his record collection to practice scratching on our hi-fi.

It wasn't until later, when I came to know DJ's personally, that I learned about balance, weight, tone arms, use of the fader and specialist needles and cartridges – all of the things that mean you can create a wonderful scratching sound AND not damage the records you're using in the first five seconds. All I'd seen from my vantage point on the floor of Rock City were DJ's going back and forth on a record to create the trademark hip-hop scratching sound which is now so familiar as to no longer be incredible. But back then, it truly was something new. It had an air of vandalism to it – taking records and dragging them back and forth against the needle to invent a new sound – but of course it was one of the actions that invented hip-hop.[26] The joy of grabbing a record and scratching with it remains, both for true DJ's and we amateurs, but even if I learned to do it, studied all the dexterous techniques and mastered the turntablists' art, I don't think I could recapture the joy I felt when I was fucking up my dad's records, aged 12.

Of course, I denied it at the time, and I'd freeze in panic if he decided to play – for the delectation of the family, obviously – a record I'd been practicing on. Such was my clumsiness, there was scarcely a record I'd used that didn't have a skip where there'd never been one before. I'd sit there willing the needle to ride the grooves gracefully, my body wracked by nerves. My father was not a particularly temperamental man, at least not with me, but there were certain signifiers of displeasure – most notably a tell-tale twitching of the cheek – and I knew how to spot them and make myself scarce. I imagine he was delighted when CD's came along and my opportunities to trash his prized music collection were limited.

Around the time that I was losing myself in music, my dad was trying to set up a business in Portugal. Similar schemes had come and gone before. In April 1983, my dad told us that we may be moving to Torquay to run and live in a pub. This was mentioned only once and never reared its head again. We had a trip to Oporto in

---

[26] When the first rappers graced the mic in the Bronx, New York in the late 70's, they didn't have their own instrumentals to rhyme over. Instead, DJ's would take two copies of a popular record and play the 'break' – the funkiest bit of the tune – on one while cueing the same bit up on the other turntable which they'd then slide to, creating a constant loop of that killer moment for the MC to rap over, or just for people to dance to. In the process they invented the whole musical genre. Scratching was an addendum to this, and through time it became an art form in its own right, with its own competitions, awards and highly-regarded experts. Personally, I don't plan to dwell on 'turntablism' as it's now called (by some), because for me it has become too divorced from the music that gave birth to it. It's now a series of clever but ultimately empty tricks that is no longer umbilically linked to hip-hop.

1984 and then my Dad started going regularly to the Algarve in 1986. He took me with him in August of that year. My dad being quite the local businessman and friend to publicans, we had a big going away party in The Chesterfield pub. We were waved off in the night by well-wishers galore. The big end of my dad's van then died a death somewhere around Grantham and, after a cold night in a lay-by, we returned home sheepishly the next day.

I'm not sure if the long term aim was to move the family out to Portugal – I certainly was never privy to such a discussion, but would have probably had to like it or lump it – but it did mean we had a couple of trips a year to the Algarve.

It's not enough that I was a graceless, spotty boy who picked on his big sister. I also had to be travel sick to a terrible degree. There were few motorways that were not speckled by my projectile vomit, no matter how many Joyrides or Dramamine I necked. A plastic bag was always to hand, no matter how short the journey. One of the taxi drivers who worked for my dad once ran me the mile from the video shop to our house in his car. I plastered my trousers and the floor of the passenger side en route. Happily, music gave me a distraction from the nightmare that was being in a moving vehicle. If I sat there with my Walkman on, I'd be snapped at for being anti-social, if I took it off, I'd be heaving into a bag. But as I got older, brasher and more confident in my musical taste, the car cassette player became the new focus of family tension.

A drive to Portugal, via a stop-off in Spain, would take several days. That's a whole lot of vomiting, napping, arguments in the back seat between me and Susan, and lulls where we'd play a game – each choosing a letter of the alphabet and scoring a point every time we overtook a car with that letter on the license plate, to cite one thrilling example. It also meant a lot of music. Dad was largely in charge of the tape deck and would mostly play rock and metal, stuff we knew and could tolerate, but occasionally he'd nonplus us with a left-field choice. To this day, Susan and I can remember our shared bafflement as he played us Herb Alpert's *Tijuana Brass*, a captive audience in the back of a car hurtling past Pamplona or Javea. It didn't help that he prefaced it with a lecture telling us how much we'd love it, meaning we'd already made our minds up not to. I believe a terse silence accompanied us for the next 100 miles of the journey after mine and Susan's joint hilarity over the farting noises of Herb Alpert went down like a lead balloon in the front of the car. I don't mind a bit of Herb now, but at the time it was like having supermarket music piped into the back of a car.

As I grew older and bolder, I wanted my music played in the car as well. But, I pride myself on saying, my musical tastes were no longer the typical tastes of a young white Anglo-Saxon male. I was part of a cool music scene, and some of the stuff I liked – the same two minutes of a brilliant electro classic by Chris 'The Glove' Taylor` endlessly scratched and mixed into one continuous, hauntingly repetitive 30 minute segment – wasn't really going to cut it as the soundtrack to a jolly holiday.[27] No, when allowed access to the hallowed portals of the car cassette deck, I had to choose my offering wisely, lest it be yanked out unceremoniously, unspooling all the while.

My dad, to this day, keeps an open mind on music, bless him. He'll ask what I'm into these days, and likes artists as diverse as

---

[27] Chris 'The Glove' Taylor was an early pioneer on the West Coast hip-hop scene, a member of The Radio Crew along with other artists who would go on to varying degrees of fame and success, but who were all influential – Ice-T and Egyptian Lover being the most prominent. He'd later go on to have mixing credits on Dr Dre's monumental *The Chronic* LP, but to rap fans he'll always be known as the guy who released the cut-and-paste masterpiece "Itchiban Scratch" in 1984 and as the man whose name and gimmick were entirely derived from him wearing a glove on his scratching hand.

Christina Aguilera and Rammstein. He's forever flicking through the music channels on TV, before calling me up to ask if I can give him an mp3 of Robin Thicke, or something. And there was certain hip-hop he really liked, and that I could play in the car. It fit a very clear pattern, however – it usually sampled rock guitar. So I could put on the Beastie Boys *Licensed to Ill* LP, because it has "Fight For Your Right To Party" and "No Sleep Till Brooklyn" on it, which were rock-rap. I could put Run DMC on because of their "Walk This Way" collaboration with Aerosmith. And LL Cool J could pass muster as he used Chuck Berry's "Roll Over Beethoven" on his single "Go Cut Creator Go". If I tried to go too far out of these never verbalised but tacitly accepted constraints, I got short shrift. I vividly remember getting a tape in of one of my all-time favourite records, "Cracked Out" by Masters of Ceremony, a stunning piece of New York anti-drug rap which interpolates George Clinton's "Atomic Dog" and features Grand Puba Maxwell, a cult figure in hip-hop history. It got 30 seconds, tops, before my Dad said, 'What is this shit?' and ejected it. My Dad rarely swore at us. He must really have hated it.

Portugal had a lot of appeal for me – it was hot, and it wasn't school. I got bullied quite a bit at Toot Hill, and retain some anger that the headmaster did nothing about it, even when I presented him with the names of boys from older years who'd hit me repeatedly and threatened to kill me. I used to take circuitous routes to classes to avoid the areas where I knew they were, and had flashes of fear every day when I sighted them, so being hundreds of miles away was a joy. It also helped that my Dad had got in with a few expats who ran a place called White's Bar in Lagos, so we had a social hub. On the later trips, Susan was 16 and 17 and flirted outrageously with the guys who ran the bar (but, as she'd told me when she was 16, "I'm a woman, and a damn good one at that". I still remind her of that gem), while I male-flirted with the DJ's.

One, called Spike, was a Brit with a Def Jam Records hat (an iconic label, home to the first Beastie Boys LP, and riding the crest of a cultural wave with signings such as LL Cool J and Public Enemy) who dropped plenty of hip-hop into his sun-drenched set of party classics. The poor bastard must have wished he'd never played any in front of me, as I was there every day for the whole holiday, pestering him in the DJ booth, flicking through his records and telling him how much I knew about LL Cool J. As he was a 20-year-old British DJ in an Algarve bar, it doesn't take much of a stretch of the imagination to work out what he was probably more interested in, and I wasn't it. With my sunburnt cheeks, wavery teenage voice and backwards baseball cap, the ladies who wanted to talk to the DJ probably thought I was his mentally-challenged brother, there on a coach trip. Spike, wherever you are, I'm sorry for cock-blocking you so effectively. It wasn't me, it was the music.

Photographs of me as a child tell a story that most of us are familiar with. A cute, tousle-haired beginning gradually blurring into spotty, gawky adolescence. I love my parents deeply, but I don't think they helped me very much sartorially (or tonsorially, or dentally), and I was never the sharpest dresser. This is important because hip-hop is a music that didn't just deliver a radically new sound, it also came with a radical new look. It's a look that is taken for granted now, because urban sportswear is the default mode for young people to dress in these days, but in the mid 80's, it was relatively fresh. It wasn't just about wearing trainers with jeans – if that was the case then hip-hop fans would wear white Reebok Classics with Levi 501's and be done with it, and no hip-hopper worth his salt would ever wear that cursed combination – it was about wearing a certain kind of trainers, and certain labels, and in a certain way.

As hip-hop is primarily an urban US culture, fans around the world have largely taken their lead from trends in the States, whether it be a matter of music, clothing or slang. I'm happy to see that British urban culture has developed its own strong identity as well, but we still quite cravenly follow the US in many ways.[28] One of the ways is that people in hip-hop circles tend to call trainers 'sneakers'. As I write this, in my early 40's, I'm a very moderate 'sneaker freak', as they're sometimes called. I've got about 65 pairs. This may seem outlandish to the average person, who probably rotates a couple of pairs until they wear out and then replaces them, but when I say I have many friends with hundreds of pairs, and a couple with thousands, this puts me in the small-fry category. But even having been part of hip-hop culture for 28 years, I still find it quite hard to say 'sneakers' instead of trainers. I feel very self-conscious and a little ridiculous. I might occasionally truncate it to 'sneaks', but sneakers just doesn't sound right coming from my mouth. And I'd never say 'kicks' as some do. No, generally, I stick with trainers, but as I'm writing this rather than saying it, I'll go with sneakers.

Hip-hop and sneakers are deeply intertwined. Any book about rap music can't help but touch on it. And there are many, many books dedicated to sneaker culture itself. I don't want to overstate the case – I know hip-hop fans with no interest in sneakers, and serious sneaker heads who don't listen to hip-hop – but for me the link is

---

[28] The word 'urban' has become quite problematic. It's now a bit of a radio station and TV catch-all for 'black', even though the boundaries between most musical genres have somewhat melted away in recent years and pop music has always had a large 'black' element anyway. Maybe it's a response to the success of artists like Eminem in hip-hop so that they think they can't really call it 'black music' when so many white people are involved in it. In a literal sense, urban refers to music from large towns or cities, and its opposite would have to be 'rural', but I've never heard of 'rural music' or a 'rural radio station'. Or even 'suburban'. It smacks of panicked presenters and programmers going, "Oh, is this rap? R'n'B? Soul? Fuck it, let's call it 'urban'."

significant. There are rap tracks specifically about footwear – Run DMC's "My Adidas" is probably the most famous, but I have to also mention "Read These Nikes" by The Geto Boys, Busy Bee's "Converse", The Pack's "Vans" and The Original Lee Love's "Get On The Troop Tip" – and that's without mentioning the dozens of songs about particular types of sneakers, rather than just brands. Plenty of artists have gone into the booth purely to express their love of Nike Air Force Ones or Jordans, and rightly so.

When Run DMC were at the height of their fame and powers in the late 80's, they were synonymous with Adidas, and even got a sponsorship tie-in after they released the aforementioned ode to their favourite kicks. They pioneered wearing sneakers without laces. This was seen by many people as a) silly and b) impractical, but a little context is needed to truly understand it. Hip-hop is a music of reinvention, and an earlier trend had been to wear sneakers with 'fat laces'. Run DMC weren't just delivering a harsh new sound that shrugged off the hip-hop of the past, they were wearing their stuff differently as well. At least, that's one romantic notion – another is that they were wearing their sneakers 'convict style', as prisoners often weren't allowed to use shoelaces in prison. Whatever the reason, it stuck, and is just another evolution in the use, or otherwise, of shoelaces in sneaker culture.

This continues today – I have friends who will criticise my lacing style and tell me I've gone through the loops in the wrong order (FYI, I rarely have my laces tied – I am truly a dangerous, subversive individual), whereas some people will tie their laces into huge bows. And some still insist on the fat laces people wore in the early 80's. The point of all this? To drill home just how important footwear and fashion is to hip-hop people. I've always scoffed at couture fashion, and the self-importance of fashion journalists who cover that world. They may know more about stitching than I do, but they can only spot fashion trends that will be worn by people who read *Vogue* and don't realise that the *Evening Standard*'s puddle-deep *ES Magazine* is a harbinger of the apocalypse. They can tell what handbags will be bought by 3000 people. What I can tell you, is that the most influential fashion movement of the last 30 years, worldwide, has been hip-hop. It's so mainstream now that maybe it's not as noticeable, but throughout time, hip-hop fashions have been the biggest trendsetter in terms of what real people wear.

A case in point: As I write this, one of the most vivid recent trends was for people to wear big headphones. The earbuds that were everywhere a couple of years ago were consigned to the drawers, and people were and are dropping big money on (not particularly good, so audiophiles say) massive headphones. The same kinds of headphones that hip-hop fans have been wearing publicly for twenty years – I still remember a guy I used to see in Leeds in the late 80's whose headphones were almost as big as him, and I admired him heartily for it. I'd advise you not to scoff at hip-hop fashion; we invented wearing hooded tops, we invented radical lacing concepts, we invented wearing baseballs caps and basketball boots, even when we'd never even watched those two sports on TV. And that's before we even get to customised jewellery, gold rope chains, four finger rings, bootleg Gucci sweatsuits and fake gold teeth. I've loved watching the shifts from copying the US pioneers to adopting and adapting some UK terrace casual culture. I've gone with the flow as the streetwear trend morphed into the rugged urban trend and everyone put on Timberlands. I've enjoyed the labels that have come and gone in hip-hop hotness, from British Knights to Polo, Hilfiger to Helly Hansen.[29] Hip-hop's fashion game is deep. Unfortunately, mine wasn't.

As a kid, I hadn't cared less about trainers. They were just something I played football in. Once I got into hip-hop, I cared immensely. It didn't help that some of the boots that pupils were wearing at my school were highly covetable. Hi-Tec 'Tecs', were one of the first sneakers I fell in love with, and it just goes to show how out of touch Bingham was that when the trend for basketball boots came in, everyone I know referred to them as baseball boots. Chunky, white with red detailing and a big flappy tongue, the 'Tecs' were soon being worn by all the coolest kids at school, and I fell to pestering my mother endlessly to get me some. She was probably a bit surprised, considering I'd never shown any interest in how I was shod before, but now I knew what I wanted, I was hell-bent on getting them. Mum didn't want to take me all the way into Nottingham just to get some trainers, so I knew that we'd have the slim pickings of Bingham's shopping precinct, and the only sportswear shop in town, Eliv Pele.

I'd walk past Eliv Pele on a daily basis, pressing my nose up against the glass to lust over some of the trainers on display. The latest, trendy styles that could cost as much as £29.99 – imagine! They even had Hi-Tec 'Tecs', and the Nike windcheater that was de rigueur in the playground (even Falco had one, as well as his Campri

---

[29] In later years I'd flick through *The Source* magazine's pages to see what the next fashions would be. Often they'd have rappers wearing stuff that was only available in NY boutiques or chains, adding to the allure. Rappers then became the go-to models for labels targeting the hip-hop audience, so you'd see Snoop Dogg wearing Cross Colours, or Erick Sermon from EPMD casually tying his Lugz boots. Their endorsement almost made some of these items desirable. Almost. The fashion story culminates in rappers launching their own labels, with generally dreadful results. Puff Daddy's Sean John label, Jay-Z's Rocawear, Wu-Tang Clan's Wu-Wear – stuff that would generally turn up heavily discounted in TK Maxx shortly after launch.

jacket, the lucky bastard). I couldn't wait until my mum took me into this Aladdin's cave. Unfortunately, while I had developed an interest in clothes, my mum had not developed a complementary interest in dressing me. I wasn't allowed a windcheater, and £29.99 was an extortionate amount of money for trainers. No Hi-Tec 'Tecs' for me. My joy curdled. The £14.99 white Le Coq Sportif 'baseball' boots we could afford were duly tried on, and my surly 12-year-old response to my mum cooing that they were nice went no further than a grudging, "They're okay, I s'pose.".

There's a scene in Shane Meadows' brilliant film *This Is England* where wannabe skinhead Shaun is taken shopping for shoes by his mum. While he's after Doc Martens like the rest of his new gang, his mum and the shop assistant conspire to try to get him into safer, cheaper shoes with the promise of them being 'from London'. It resonates so much because we've all had our parents resort to such cheap tricks to keep in check our expensive desires. My new boots were so ridiculously white that they didn't last five minutes, and they drew precisely zero praise from my friends at school, as I'd predicted. Even Falco – my very own DJ – didn't comment on them. Et tu?

This was to be my path through hip-hop fashion. Until I was an adult with disposable income, I was always late to the party and, when I arrived, I was wearing the wrong stuff. As I grew older and felt at home at hip-hop concerts and in large groups of fans, I always knew that my gear was inferior, that my sneakers were last year's thing and that my wardrobe smacked of discount. Hip-hop fashion moved on so quickly that it was unforgiving, and I don't think I've ever been on the cutting edge of it. It was impossible as a teenager, simply because we didn't have the money, and being stuck out in Bingham – and, even worse, Barnstone when we moved there – in a pre-internet age, meant that in hip-hop fashion terms we were like those Amazonian tribes that have only recently been discovered and fire arrows at passing helicopters. Although they still probably had better sneakers than me in 1984.

Six
This is Something for the Radio

For reasons that have only recently become clear to me, the fortunes of our family had taken a bit of a nosedive around this time. The gas was cut off in our house, shortly prior to the whole kit and caboodle being repossessed. In August of 1984 we moved from our lovely detached house that was on the same street as my primary school – a street that rejoiced in the comforting-sounding name of Nursery Road – to a flat that was above a butcher's shop, and only accessible by a long, dank, rat-haunted alleyway that smelt like you'd imagine the back of a butcher's would. This was in Bingham's main shopping precinct, and my memories of this place are fleeting and sketchy. Perhaps this is because it was such a small place – and my bedroom ceiling would occasionally leak directly onto me as I slept – that I spent increasing amounts of time outside of it, hanging out with friends or alone. It was close to Toot Hill Comprehensive, so I could go home at lunchtime, sitting in the lounge with a tray of chips and gravy and watching telly. Hardly the stuff of Proust, but perhaps pointing up the fact that this was not a place of happy years in the bosom of my family.

We were there for a couple of years. By then, Susan had finished her O-Levels and was looking for work. My father, meanwhile, was furthering his Portuguese adventure, while my mother (and sometimes I, but mostly my mother), kept the taxi/video shop going. As we'd downgraded from a nice, spacious house to a poky flat steeped in blood and offal, I assumed that our business wasn't exactly setting the world alight. My dad, in pursuance of his Mediterranean dream, was trying to establish a satellite TV company on the Algarve. Satellite dishes are commonplace now, small, sensitive things attached to the outsides of homes, about the size of a baby. In the mid 80's, that was not the case. The dishes that my dad was trying to sell to wealthy ex-pats in Portugal were big enough to bathe an elephant in. It was a two-or-three-man job to erect them, and unfortunately for my dad he only had himself. I spent the better part of a summer holiday helping him out in this, time I'd rather have spent furthering my investigations into onanism, playing on my Spectrum (yes, that again. But honestly, it's far too late for me to be getting product placement money from Sinclair Research, if that's what you're thinking) or writing 'world-changing' lyrics.

A further downside of this then nascent technology was that bloody massive metal dishes + Algarve sun X pasty Brits = heatstroke. We cut such pitiful figures toiling in the sun that one retired businessman we were putting a dish up for took pity on our parched souls and let us use his outdoor pool, then his indoor table tennis table, and dozens of man hours were lost as we spent day after day at this house ostensibly working but actually holidaying. Obviously we didn't tell my mum. Don't read this bit, Mum.

Returning to England was bleak. At the time, I was a 13-year-old with all the endless hours of navel gazing that entails. I didn't realise how much tougher it was for my mum until much later. We'd now moved to a rented cottage in Barnstone, a village outside Bingham. This was away from all the friends we'd spent the previous seven years building relationships with. It was a village that, on a weekend, was served by a total of two buses, if they bothered to show up at all. Susan had moved there with us, but in 1987 saw sense and left to become a nanny just outside Leeds. All week our house and hot water was heated by coke that I had to shovel in endlessly to remove the single-glazed chill caused by the wind whipping in from the bleak fields behind us. At one point I took on the newsagent's paper round, a round so small I earned the sum of £2.50 per week. For 5 night's work. The only thing Barnstone was even vaguely known or remembered for was that comedian Duncan 'Chase Me' Norvelle was supposed to own the social club there.[30] But I never saw him. I imagine that, no matter how low you are on the evolutionary scale of camp comics, the minute you get on primetime ITV, you swear never to return to somewhere like Barnstone.

My mother's husband was in Portugal, her daughters were all in Yorkshire. She was stuck in a shit village with a pretty unpleasant son whose main interests were rapping into a hairbrush and Samantha Fox.[31] If I'd been a little bit more savvy and a lot less self-obsessed,

---

[30] I am unable to verify whether or not Duncan Norvelle did indeed own the Barnstone Country Club, or whether it was just a rumour after he once played there. Google is curiously reticent on this matter. If the latter, can I put this forward to be considered the most inept, useless and incredibly 1980's rumour of all time? Norvelle's entire act was a hugely stereotypical, mincingly camp homosexual charade of the type we were tiresomely familiar with in the 70's and 80's. In fact he's heterosexual, has three children and has been married several times. Norvelle's IMDB credits – an episode of *3, 2, 1*, several episodes of *Blankety Blank* – capture his career with a minimalist beauty I can only be jealous of, but the amateur darts player in me doffs his cap to the time he scored a record 281 as a celebrity guest on *Bullseye*. That's champagne darts.

[31] It's entirely appropriate that Samantha Fox – who rose to fame baring her 16-year-old breasts in *The Sun* for the delectation of their smudgy-fingered readership – is now a lesbian. The very likeable Sam was a figure of lust for many in the mid 80's, although viewed through the fog of time it now seems ridiculously naff, like getting an erection at the stockinged Hill's Angels as they chase Benny in speeded up footage, or Cleo Rocos' permanently tumbling and spilling cleavage on *The Kenny Everett Television Show*. Sam went on to release numerous albums, having success in far-flung parts of the world, but will always be linked with Page 3. I had a Sam Fox calendar tucked away in what I thought at the time was an

I might have noticed the glaring signs of fractures in my parent's marriage, what with them spending large parts of the year in different countries. My sisters were more aware of the issues this caused and either a) cared enough to shelter me from it or b) found talking to me actually unpleasant. Either way is understandable.

I cringe in thinking of the trials I put my mum through, but the biscuit-taker must have been when she was told I'd been shoplifting in the Co-Op after a friend of hers actually caught me in the act. It was only a Fry's Five Centres, and we'd have been home free if Steven Lovett – a vicar's son, note – hadn't emptied his coat sleeve of stolen sweets before we'd even got outside the shop. What an amateur. He was also born on 25th December which was either a lie perpetrated by Reverend Lovett to drum up business or entirely spooky (aka coincidental). But this – and similar incidents – were the perhaps inevitable result of spending so much time making my own entertainment. After school, I'd get the bus home, and most days my mum was still at work. Alone in a remote cottage, I'd simply stoke up the boiler and then indulge in whatever hip-hop record I'd bought that week. Or further 'research' Sam Fox.

So monomaniac was my focus on music at that time, I got a reputation among my small group of friends as being the one who knew all the lyrics. I would play tapes and albums again and again and again, using my Denman hairbrush as a microphone, my arms gesturing in the way I'd seen rappers do on TV (and is now tedious shorthand whenever someone – invariably white – attempts to do a 'funny' portrayal of a rapper). It helped that my music collection was so small, but I also had the ability so soak up the lyrics of a song

---

ingenious hiding place but, thinking about it, it was just under a pile of clothes in my wardrobe, and as my poor mother did all the washing and ironing, I can't imagine it escaped her notice. This is one of the many reasons why MI5 have never approached me to be a spy.

after only a couple of listens, something my tired middle-aged brain would struggle to do after 30 repetitions of the same verse today. On the bus to school, I'd sit at the back mumbling these lyrics to myself. And then on the way home. And then for most of the evening.

If someone had been making recordings of those recitals, and those recordings had survived to this day, you'd be struck by how many of the words I was getting wrong. I wasn't alone. The frame of reference of rappers based in the South Bronx (and by now spreading to Boston, Los Angeles and into all nooks and crannies of the USA) was so different to mine, it's no surprise that I didn't get every reference, didn't parse every piece of slang. Rappers would routinely refer to streets, cross-streets, clothing labels and people that simply weren't on my radar. References to US politicians, sportsmen and TV shows abounded. They'd even rap over the theme tunes of popular US sitcoms, but as we didn't get those, we didn't know. Sometimes I'd hear the name and make a mental note to look into that further (fuck knows how – this was long, long before the internet, and I doubt there was much knowledge about hip-hop stored on microfiche in my local library), sometimes I'd just get it wrong, mishear a lyric and for years later still not know I was in error. I wasn't alone. Everyone did and does this, in all musical genres. As I write this I'm still discovering that lyrics I've been reciting for over 30 years are entirely wrong. Hideously so.[32]

---

[32] I asked some of my friends which lyrics they had got wrong over the years. This reinforced my view that I was not alone and even made me feel better because about six respondents all cited one track in common, one that I'd never got wrong. Losers. Chris Aylen, who runs a hip-hop website and record label and should know better, says he thought that Sugar Bear's 1988 hit "Don't Scandalise Mine" went, "Don't steal our rhymes!" My good friend Rob Pursey (labelled by many as London's finest hip-hop DJ) says that, "I know most people thought of that as 'Don't steal my rhymes!'" and DJ and podcaster James Hamlin says, "I agree with Rob, it was always 'Don't steal that rhyme!'"

My thirst for hip-hop and my lack of funds – my pocket money was always delivered sporadically, tending to longueurs where I didn't actually get any for months, and no backlog was ever acknowledged by Dad – meant that I wasn't buying and hearing as much music as I'd have liked. Falco was also permanently skint, being from a single-parent family, so even our preternaturally mature policy of only buying records that the other didn't have wasn't really cutting it.

It's around this time that I discovered the radio. Lonely nights in the Barnstone cottage had led me to twiddling around on the family midi system, not searching for anything other than some novelty. One night I chanced upon the distorted echoes of a rap song, one I'd never heard before. It was on crackly medium wave, and it took minutes of steady-handed tweaking and twiddling to refine the broadcast to one that was vaguely listenable. I was out of my seat with delight – had I discovered some hitherto unknown hip-hop radio show? Shit – was this beaming straight out of the one and only NYC into our isolated, windswept cottage? Had I tapped directly into the source, something that would ensure me not only an endless supply of bleeding edge, up-to-the-minute body-rocking sounds, but also shitloads of playground kudos as I knowingly intoned to my acolytes the artists that were about to blow up – ones that they hadn't even heard of? No, it turned out I hadn't. The record ended, I heard a dull, flat, slightly sardonic monotone voice, and then a track came

---

Names can be misheard too. DJ Superix (who I only found out years after first meeting him had also gone to Toot Hill School in Nottingham. Thus with its alumni of him, DJ Ivory and me, it was pretty much the hip-hop centre of the universe, only no-one knew it) and his friends thought that the UK top 10 hit "The Show" was by an artist called Doggy Fresh, rather than Doug. E. Fresh and, "someone gave me a bootleg copy of the first Public Enemy album and referred to them (and wrote on the tape) as 'Paul Academy'." Public Enemy's influence is seen again in this anecdote from Rob Pursey: "At a Public Enemy concert a mate of mine heard everyone shout 'Terminator X!' He said, 'who's Jim Latex?'" A question that's never been satisfactorily answered.

in that was so far away from what I wanted to listen to that I was crushed. I listened on, perhaps for two hours, and in that time the grand total of two more hip-hop songs were played. I was actually delighted, eventually. That's still more than I could ever hope to hear on any other show. And these weren't the songs that had made it to the charts, to the Sunday Top 40 on radio, to the school disco. These songs were a million miles from that.

I know now that the song after the first one I heard on that radio show was probably by the Dog-Faced Hermans, or the Bhundu Boys or perhaps Crispy Ambulance. Most likely, it was The Fall. Yes, I'd discovered John Peel. Peel's reputation as a broadcaster among the musical cognoscenti remains untouchable. Even Radio One didn't cast him off during the dreadful era of roadshows[33], Bruno Brookes[34] and Adrian Juste[35], such was his aura and his devoted following. Ever the musical explorer, Peel was early on electro, early

---

[33] The Radio One Roadshows finished in the late 90's, after kicking off, much like myself, in 1973. They were summer events, with DJ's from the station playing outdoors at beach resorts, handing out Radio One goodie bags and introducing acts. My passion for these events can be guessed at from a typical line up – the largest ever Roadshow event in 1992 featured Del Amitri, The Farm, Status Quo and Aswad. I'd rather be boiled alive. My extensive legal team, led by one Mr Tulkinghorn, have advised me not to attempt any broad Operation Yewtree links at this point in the book.

[34] Bruno Brookes might seem like your typical naff 80's Radio One DJ – and to a large extent he was. He hosted a teatime show and the Top 40, was a Conservative supporter, dated Anthea Turner – but did Steve Wright or Peter Powell ever play Humanoid's Acid House classic "Stakker Humanoid" twice on one show, as Bruno once did? Did they fuck.

[35] Adrian Juste's Saturday lunchtime show on Radio One might be my most hated thing in the history of broadcasting. This might seem a tad unfair to fans of his – at the time – slightly forward-looking combination of classic comedy clips spliced with his own skits, jokes and routines, but even as a kid I found it nauseatingly unfunny. The forced bonhomie and relentless wackiness grated and also forged a template for all those self-consciously 'bonkers' DJ's who can't help but interrupt whatever they're playing with catchphrases and silly noises. He makes Alan Partridge sound like Alistair Cooke.

on hip-hop, early on house music. He was committed to certain strains of African music, fringe elements of rock from the deep south of the USA, avant-garde Scottish poetry. Every show was an education, even if it stretched your patience to the absolute limit. And even on a good night, over two or three hours, he'd only play two or three hip-hop songs. I would wait, my fingers poised on the record button, a blank C30 or C90 cassette (ask your grandad) ready, tissue stuffed into the holes at the top so it would record. And when I heard the opening bars of a rap, or the tell-tale Electronic drum sounds of the music I loved, I'd record every distorted second of it.

Some veteran B-Boys, of a similar age to myself, will tell you that their formative years in hip-hop were spent in clubs, at jams or at early breakdance events. I've spoken to genuine hip-hop legends and pioneers who were there when the music was still foetal, and then helped to deliver it kicking and screaming into the world. People who were actually present when the holy trinity who formalised the sounds and conventions of the music at its actual birth – Afrika Bambaataa, Grandmaster Flash, DJ Kool Herc – were doing their thing for the very first time. Yet for me, if I think back on what shaped my hip-hop life, I can't really go beyond my time huddled in my bedroom, listening to John Peel. He opened up the world to me, not just with his wonderfully open-minded approach to what he played, but in his attitude to it as well.

I went from cutting off the recordings I made the second the track ended, to leaving in his deadpan reflections on what he'd just played. He approached rap like an indulgent but world-weary uncle. As I head toward the age he probably was (or at least sounded) when I was listening to him, I feel the same way. He was often caught out by the tricks hip-hop records played, by their abrupt endings. Peel was no stranger to dead air, still cueing up the next track when one had already ended. His saving grace was his usually pithy, deadpan response to his own cock-up. These were, again, moments to be cherished on tape.

Peel was also famous for his Peel Sessions, with both new and established groups coming in to record for his show. You wouldn't know it from the Peel Sessions subsequently released on vinyl (obviously put out by some rap-hating indie doofus, such is their seemingly wilful ignorance of all black music), but he didn't neglect hip-hop here either, giving airspace to the struggling UK scene. Early sessions from Brit legends like Overlord X and MC Duke were a shot in the arm for them and their small independent labels, and a delight for listeners like myself.

Eventually, being of a left/liberal disposition, Peel got a bit tired of some elements of hip-hop. He issued an unofficial ban on tracks that contained the word 'bitch'. The Beeb were already sensitive about the use of the word 'nigger', which crept into rap in the mid 80's, before becoming pretty much ubiquitous in it to infinity and beyond. He played less and less. House music took its place although, Peel being Peel, he played the cutting edge, underground hyper-bleepy stuff (you can tell I am not a dance music writer), and was ahead of the curve as per usual. I'm not trying to be the 'voice of a generation' with this book, but meeting people later in life who shared the exact same experience, who had their own stash of 'Peel tapes' (many of which, to my delight, have been digitised and uploaded to the internet) drives home how much this isn't just my story, but the story of many, many hip-hop fans in the UK.

But I'm getting ahead of myself, and here we are still in the mid-80's. I've bought a Mongoose BMX bike from a boy called Craig. Craig's uncles and cousins have a reputation around Bingham as being a bit 'tasty'. What I mean is that they were actually a bunch of thugs and petty criminals, and if your warehouse got knocked off, the police would be paying them a visit, usually too late. What I therefore really mean is that my buying a pretty sweet Mongoose BMX for £30 might not have been a legitimate transaction. But in the no-horse village that was Barnstone, it was badly needed. Down one long, narrow, twisty and completely dark country lane lay Cropwell Bishop, and my mate Falco, aka my DJ, Touché. Down another long, narrow, twisty and completely dark country lane lay Bingham, school and the video shop. I spent a lot of time on these lanes on my BMX, somehow avoiding being mown down by people drunk driving their way back from Duncan Norvelle's club.

As I turn 13, I am your genuine teenager: Obsessed with a few things to the expense of everything else. Unpleasant to my family. My voice wavering and my body developing in strange ways. Discovering the joys of 'titting up' in the bike sheds at school. Hip-hop, New York's greatest invention, has turned me into a lover of all things American. I have started following American Football. I have even started playing American Football. I BMX to practice in Bingham every Sunday, and play every lunchtime in the coach park at school. I am all set to waste my teenage years as a hip-hop listening, BMX riding, radio taping, American football statistic collating waster. And then my dad comes home from Portugal and tells us that we're all moving to Leeds.

SYNDICATE

Seven
My Vinyl Weighs a Ton

My Dad's Portuguese experiment has come to an end with someone breaking into his car and stealing thousands of pounds worth of satellite equipment. While he's understandably disappointed, I'm just relieved I don't have to say goodbye to my friends and go to some international school, full of kids whose parents are all ex-pat racists (I'm generalising wildly, but also in a 100% accurate way). Instead, it soon transpires, I will have to say goodbye to my friends and go to some school in Leeds. Balls. I don't want to be too unfair to my parents, who surely had their reasons for moving us back to West Yorkshire – to be nearer their parents, my sisters, for my dad to make a fresh start on his career – but I was not in favour of the move. It didn't help that it was presented to me in this way: "We might move to Leeds, but as you're already a few months into your GCSE's and this will disrupt your schooling, the final decision is with you." I said I didn't want to move. We moved. The illusion of choice.

To be honest, I didn't really care about my GCSE's. I didn't really care about my education at all. I hated my current school, except for my friends, girlfriends and the small hip-hop circle I'd built up. Would I ever again get to kiss Heidi Peploe, Maria O'Hare, Katie Hunter, Julie Spibey or Claire Gilbert? Would I get to go record shopping with Falco again? That's what I didn't want to say goodbye to. But we'd sold the video shop and taxi business – I assume for a knockdown price based on our future prospects – and at the age of 14 I was going to Leeds. No offence, but this wasn't exactly a hip-hop Mecca as far as I knew, and I felt the split with my DJ, Touché, keenly. Who knows what might have happened if we'd stayed together? What sonic wonders we'd have created if we'd actually ever got around to, you know, making ANY music. We could have been the great Nottingham rap group that got away. No, I'm not even convincing myself here, never mind you, the reader.

The move to Leeds wasn't exactly seamless. We didn't have a house to sell, so we fell upon the hospitality of my Grandad Ramshaw, my maternal grandparent. Harry Ramshaw was a truly lovely man, a fantastic father to my mum, a brilliant grandfather to us kids. He was endlessly funny and kind, playing the comic foil to my somewhat grumpier grandma, Mary, until her death. He was very tall and very slim, a gentle giant in many ways. But he was also, when we moved into his small home, in his 80's. There we were, in his two bedroom flat, my parents unemployed, me a stroppy teenager. I had to sleep on the sofa in the lounge when we first moved in, a real comedown for someone who'd always had his own room. I'd even had a double bed in Barnstone. Also, the flat was in Gipton, an area of Leeds with a dismal reputation that it entirely lives up to. It's a bleak shithole of a place, with a high crime rate, dozens of boarded-up houses and pubs from hell. And this was my new home.

The first school my mum took me to visit in Leeds was also hellish. Even though I was at my monosyllabic worst as we toured it, the headmistress divined the fact that I'd once read a book or two in my past and told my mum that I was too intelligent for her school, I'd be better off going somewhere more academically inclined. This wasn't a school so much as a storage unit for Leeds' most feral children. I can only assume (and hope) that Foxwood School has turned itself around a bit since then, but I later found out I'd dodged a real bullet. It was the Gipton of schools. Instead I started at John Smeaton Community High School, and on my first day a teacher put me in the care of a couple of boys who were charged with looking after me. I'm happy to say that one of these boys – Paul Chatterton – took the commission seriously enough to remain my firm friend to this very day.

New schools are intimidating places, but Paul and a few others – Simon Gledhill, Richard Silvey – made it as easy as it could possibly be. Unfortunately, none of them lived near me, and none of them were into hip-hop. It looked like I was all set for a solo career.

Even with my new friends, I spent an awful lot of time on my own at this point in my life. The radio was my only companion at home, and in class after class I sat on my own. But this solitary life suited me. I was doing better at school – I sincerely doubt I'd have gained more than one or two GCSE's if I'd stayed in Nottingham – but I was also throwing myself into something I'd never done before: writing lyrics.

There were areas of the curriculum that were of no interest to me, and at which I had no aptitude. Let's call these areas 'science' and 'anything that involved any practical or physical skills', especially P.E. So what I did in these lessons was scribble lyrics into my notebook. At first I was just writing the lyrics of my favourite groups and sketching their logos, but I also started to craft my own 'songs'. Most of the hip-hop I consumed at this stage was of the braggadocio variety, so that's what I wrote myself. Whole notebooks were filled with idle boasts of spectacular inaccuracy.[36] I'd fill them up so

---

[36] I no longer have the chemistry and physics notebooks that would have had most of these in, but other, later notebooks will give you a flavour. A future civilisation – if for some reason they had no other evidence to sift through and

rapidly that soon I was writing in the margins and in between the lines, while my classmates learned valuable lessons about the periodic table or, I dunno, refraction.

Once I was home, I'd put on the instrumental versions of some of my records, grab my hairbrush, and do my best to fit my lines to the beats of my heroes. I didn't know it, but I didn't really measure up. There's a big difference between the powerful flow of LL Cool J, and the indistinct, weedy voice of a 14-year-old going through some hormonally influenced changes. But Ladies Love Cool James himself must once have been a teenage bedroom MC, a rapper without portfolio, desperate for someone to hear his voice, to give him his chance. I was a late starter, but I was determined I was going to make it.

I'd also started to find things that I liked about Leeds. There was an NFL shop on the main shopping street, Briggate. I could go in there and buy myself a Chicago Bears mug or a keyring. I'd also discovered that there were plenty of record shops that stocked the latest hip-hop, and I began to hang out in these. A lot. Jumbo

---

somehow gave a fuck about the parcel of ephemera I'd left behind – could work out what kind of person I was and my passions and interests from how many rap group logos, doodles, snatches of lyrics borrowed and original, were in each part of the curriculum's notebook. Science? Actually more hip-hop than science. But in all my English notebooks I could only find a couple of snatches of rhymes and a few fantasy records sketched out on the back of some notes about "Twelfth Night", because that was a lesson I was rarely bored in.

The earliest lyrics are barely worth recording. They're just straight copies of stuff my heroes were doing – LL Cool J, Rakim, Doug E. Fresh – but without any of the wit, verve or originality. I'm not saying my lyrics would get better, but at least they'd start to get topical and then personal later on. It wasn't until I was actually in a group that I realised you needed to stamp a bit of your own personality on your lyrics, and that a bedroom-bound Leeds boy imitating LL Cool J was not what the world wanted. The aforementioned future civilisation, or perhaps our alien overlords, would look upon these works and probably surmise that we deserved to die out if this is what we did with our time.

Records in the St John's Centre was pretty good, with lots of bargains, but Crash Records on the Headrow was even better.[37] They're still there today, even in this digital age, and I'd like to thank the stereotypically stroppy and elitist staff there for helping me indulge my mania for collecting records over many years.

I spent hours and hours in Crash Records, dropping in on Saturday to see what the latest imports were, before rationing out my money as ever on the one or two I could afford. It's in Crash Records that I'd meet the friends who'd help me get as near as I ever would to hip-hop stardom.

As well as developing some new friendships and finding some places to hang out, a couple of other things changed life for the better. Tempers had become frayed in Grandad's little flat, and we were moving out. My dad was still unemployed, but my mum had found a job, and we had enough to strike out on our own.

We moved to the other side of Leeds, two bus journeys away from my school, but near my oldest sister, Tracy, and her family. Susan was going to move back in with us as well, and my journey to school was made easier by the fact that Paul Chatterton also lived in our new area – Beeston.

If you've heard of Beeston, it's probably for one thing. A couple of the suicide bombers who attacked London on 7/7 were from there, one worked in a local school. My mum knows people who were evacuated from their houses and streets when that news broke. But Beeston is a big, big place, and it contains lots of lovely people as well. It has character. It also has lots of Leeds United fans, as it's adjacent to Elland Road, but let's not hold that against it. It's still better than Gipton. While I didn't realise it at the time, being an

---

[37] Jumbo Records' bargain box of promotional records is still displayed in the same place on the counter today as it was in 1987. Bless them for being a rare constant in a sector that isn't what it used to be.

obstreperous teen, the move to Beeston was good for me. My three sisters were a positive presence in my life, as they still are, and I got to be near my niece Hayley. There is little in this world I would recommend unreservedly – Public Enemy's 2nd album, the combination of eggs and chorizo, marrying the love of your life, Charles Dickens, having a dog, Billy Wilder's *The Apartment*, a day at the cricket with friends, that's probably about it – but being an uncle makes it onto the shortlist. You should give it a try. Or be an auntie. Your choice.

My record-buying funds were soon boosted when I found a little evening and weekend job for myself. This isn't a book about how cricket changed my life, so I won't dwell on it too much, but I started as an indoor cricket umpire at a place called 'Cricket Wicket'. I'd never liked, watched or played cricket before, but sitting up in a box and scoring as company teams played each other in a relaxed environment really got me into it. I've loved it ever since. But what I actually loved then was the £50 or £60 I was getting every week from working there, which I turned into a rapidly growing vinyl collection.

I write this at a time when most music is purchased and consumed digitally, and I never leave home without my iPod or smartphone. Yet for myself and most of my hip-hop friends from the 80's until now, buying vinyl was how we expressed our love for the music. I have a collecting instinct anyway – books, DVDs, posters, press packs, memorabilia – but I've been an obsessive hoarder of records since I first had disposable income.

There's a tipping point, different for everyone, where buying records turns into collecting records. By the time I was 18, I had two crates of records, maybe 160 bits of vinyl in total. At its peak, my collection reached 4000 records. My best friend probably had around 8000. I know a few collectors with twice that. These collections are constantly honed and refined, but they are never complete. There is always something out there still to be discovered, or hunted down. I've had things on my 'wants list' for 20 years without ever finding a copy, and every week I buy records I've never heard for the weakest of reasons – they share a label with something I like, they once performed on a track with another artist I love, the picture on the cover is nice. Once upon a time I only collected records from New York, the home of hip-hop, but as it spread, so did I. Now I'll spend a couple of months tracking down stuff from Houston, or from Philadelphia or Texas. A producer credited on the back of the sleeve of one of those records will lead me onto something else. I know one guy who pursues test pressings of records, early promos pressed so that the group and label can check everything is okay before they proceed to make the whole batch. Despite the fact that the track listings are almost always identical to the finished release, he'll pay £50 for something that has the exact same audio as the finished product that costs £2. There's a bloke who wants every hip-hop record that has a picture of a car on the cover. He can't drive. I know someone else whose thing is acetates, an even earlier stage in the production process. He has thousands of them, many of which never even made it to the test press or full release stage. What gives them a fragile beauty is that they decay with each play – your average acetate starts to fall apart after ten listens. Collecting never ends. And if you think it has, I can authoritatively inform you that you haven't got everything. It's just that you've grown tired of collecting records.

All the collectors I know have their own filing systems. We go online to discuss the best shelving for our collections (Ikea's Expedits are a firm favourite, FYI. A recent story about Ikea possibly ending the manufacture of said shelves sent small, highly specialist parts of the Internet into a right tizzy. It turned out to be a false alarm) and how we sort and file. Alphabetical is common, but do you do it by surname or first letter? Do you separate artists from different areas and countries? Some file their records by label, others chronologically. An acquaintance of mine justified the latter by saying he'll sometimes be in the mood for something from 1992, so he knows exactly where to go in his collection for that. We're a strange breed.

I won't mix my smattering of jazz, soul, funk, metal, pop and indie records in with my hip-hop. I used to keep British hip-hop separate from American hip-hop, then I merged them, and later I de-merged them. I couldn't tell you the thinking behind any of this, the justifications that drove me to spend hours and days tinkering with my collection elude me entirely – and if I could it'd probably give you an insight into my brain that I'd be uncomfortable with you having. There are even differences of opinion on how they're put onto the shelves. I have them so that I can see the spine with the artist and track information on them, but I know people who have the open side of the sleeve facing out so they can get to the record quicker. Imported records usually come with a shrinkwrap, which I zealously preserve, but some tear theirs off. If I have a record that's worth a lot, I'll add an extra plastic sleeve to protect it.

To be honest, I'm only skimming the surface of record collecting here. I haven't even addressed the people who'll only buy second hand records that are in a certain kind of condition, or those that covet sleeves and shrinks with stickers on (I do actually know a bloke who goes by the nickname 'Stickered Steve'), or those people who buy old records that are still sealed and leave them sealed, never to be played. Or even those that avoid sealed records because over time the shrinkwrap tightens and can warp a record. And if you'd told me in 1987 that, 25 years later, I'd spend hours a week interacting with these people online, I'd have told you to fuck right off – not least because 'online' didn't exist then. No, in 1987 I was just starting to accumulate records, I wasn't yet a collector. I wasn't yet a crate digger.

What I was, however, was a big nerd. I wasn't just jotting lyrics into my school exercise books, I was crafting an entire hip-hop fantasy world. I'd start by thinking of a new hip-hop name for myself, then think of a name for the group I was in. Let's say 'MC Tremendous' for me and the group could be called 'R.I.S.K' aka the Rhyme Imperial Strength Kings. I was big on acronyms, and big on randomly threading what I thought were typical hip-hop words together. I'd then think of imaginary tracks for this group. I'd write out flyers for their 12" releases, with B-sides and remixes. And then once they'd 'released' three or four 12"s, I'd give them an album. Then there'd be spin-off groups, collaborations, solo careers. I still have some of this stuff, it makes me chuckle, but it also reminds me of just how all-consuming this passion of mine for hip-hop was.[38] I needed an outlet for these ideas that were spilling out of me onto the page, but my attempts to form fledgling groups at my new school were going nowhere. Until I met Brett Dickinson and Steve Mason.

[38] I file this mentally in the same category as other ephemera I might chance upon in the loft – statistics from imaginary NFL and cricket games, played out with dice with elaborate scoring systems and bits of paper as counters, featuring my friends and I playing alongside legends of the respective games such as Walter Payton and Ian Botham, but also my heroes from the music world. That time I compiled a double century with Grandmaster Flash is one for the cricketing annals. And who knew Mr Lawnge from Black Sheep had such a probing away-swinger? Clearly all of this is me wanting to be part of a world I manifestly wasn't part of. It also goes some way to explaining my middling performance at school.

Eight
Rebel Without a Pause

I had finally met the two other hip-hop fans at my school. Brett wanted to be a DJ while Steve wasn't really anything in a hip-hop sense – he didn't want to be a rapper or a DJ.[39] He just liked the music, but even then only a little bit. And yet despite his complete inability to say one or two rap lines in anything like a vaguely intelligible way (I hope he forgives me for saying this, but he was even more useless than me, and knew it. He stopped trying after about six minutes of his rap career and never tried again), I was still so hell-bent on having a 'crew', that I made him part of it. Thus the Rhyme Imperial Strength Kings were born (I knew I'd find a use for that name), my second group, and the second one in a row that would do precisely zero in the way of making any music. We didn't even practice, or have any songs.

Only three tracks have survived on tape from anything I ever wrote or recorded before meeting the rest of the P.A. Posse. Three little songs recorded in my own bedroom, which meant me sticking a record on the turntable, recording straight to tape, and rapping

---

[39] From Brett: "If I remember correctly I went by the name of the one and only DJ Destiny, which was even cooler without a turntable! I can't remember Mason's alter ego. I know he was heavily into Ice-T so it was probably pretty hard sounding, MC Concrete or something."

through my headphones. These sound dreadful. Not just 'the quality of the recording' dreadful, although they are very distorted due to the DIY recording method. I remain someone who couldn't wire together a turntable to a mixer without a manual, the help of several other people and repeated consultation of step-by-step YouTube videos. No, they're also dreadful in every other possible way too.

"Ace in the Pack" is, mercifully, just over a minute long. In it I point out why it would be foolish to diss me, diss DJ Destiny (Brett) or diss Mase (Steve Mason). And that's it. "Kings Thru and Thru", meanwhile, clocks in at over three minutes:

I move over a groove to prove I'm a hot one
Known as the top gun, you're just a pop gun
You can't match the best of the batch
Beats at the front backed up with a def scratch
Never called a fake, your microphone I take
The prophet's in the studio, on the master tape
Have no fear, I will drop science
Overseas first class to form a def alliance

It's standard brag fare, and no more true than pretty much any brag rap. If you wanted to pick holes, you could start out by pointing out that I've never been known as the 'top gun' by anyone, then continue by remarking upon the complete absence of a 'def scratch' on the track, that I'd never taken a microphone from anyone, that I wasn't in the studio and that I'd never flown first class, and certainly hadn't formed any 'def alliances'. But other than that, spot on. I think the only thing on this entire track that has any basis in reality is that I mention that myself and DJ Destiny wore Troop trainers. We did.[40]

The second verse is just nonsense – almost literally as I can't decipher most of it. It's like listening to an alien rather than myself. But the third verse has stirred up some memories and brought some things into focus – I think at this point I was trying to turn R.I.S.K. – the brilliantly named Rhyme Imperial Strength Kings, remember – into P.O.D. – the Prophets of Dope. That's the group I seem to mention the most in this verse, as well as "the B-Boy prankster MC Dizzy" which I assume was Steve Mason's actual rapping name at some point. I keep making repeated reference to the dope beats and crazy music being created by DJ Destiny, but must reiterate I was just rapping over records I'd bought by the likes of YZ and the Demon Boyz.

The last track, "Stop Dissing and Listen", is so awful it has just made my penis retreat inside my body in shame. It's not the lyrics (although they're bad enough, one long, broad swipe at anyone who listens to pop music or hip-house), it's the little bits of mic filler that I do between verses. "Time to drop knowledge!" I say before the track kicks in, then, "I'm out like Mandela!" at the end. I must have thought I was the man. I don't think anyone other than Brett aka DJ

---

[40] The Troop line of sneakers and clothing had a moment of sunshine in the late 80's, helped in no small part by their sponsorship of LL Cool J. They were all over the UK and US and vintage Troop jackets still go for decent money on eBay. However, they went bankrupt in 1990, their demise in no small part attributable to an entirely false rumour that did the rounds that Troop was owned by the Ku Klux Klan and that it was marketed to black people so that they'd fund their own demise. MC Shan aligned himself with Puma and alleged that the Klan made Troop clothes on his 1988 track "I Pioneered This", while it was also rumoured that Troop was an acronym – To Rule Over Oppressed People. It was, as these things often are, 100% untrue. Troop was owned by two Jewish guys and a Korean partner. It just goes to show how quickly a rumour could spread if a popular rapper decided to make a record incorporating some guff he'd just heard in a shop from some bullshit artist.

Destiny ever got to hear these, which I can live with. They certainly didn't inspire him to go out and buy the equipment to become the producer I seemed to claim on every track that he was. So in a way these three tracks, with their technically inept rapping, saved him a whole bunch of money. You're welcome, Brett! Me and Brett – and a reluctant Steve – merely acted as if we had a crew. The rest was just lived out in my exercise books. As it would be until I met a person who was then known as DJ Hype.

My obsession with hip-hop was by now so all-consuming that, when asked by my Geography teacher to carry out a piece of research for my GCSE coursework, measuring urban temperatures, I immediately took the necessary piece of equipment to Crash Records and asked them if I could leave it there. When asked by my Human Geography teacher to carry out a retail survey for my GCSE coursework, I again went to Crash Records. I wasn't really fulfilling the remit of the project – something about retail patterns, blah blah blah – I just stood in the record shop and asked customers what music they liked. When they said 'hip-hop', I said 'me too'. I was adding nought to the sum of human knowledge, but at least it was a tolerable way to spend time.

About the fourth or fifth fan I met that day was a lad called Dan. He mentioned that he was on his way to Jumbo Records as they were getting some new imports in that day. As I'd finished my exhaustive research into the slow death of the British independent retailer, or whatever it was I was supposed to be doing, I tagged along.

Dan didn't look like your stereotypical hip-hop fan, but then neither did I. He was tall, gangly, with a head like the bloke out of the Tefal adverts, and glasses that looked like they'd been stolen from the face of *Coronation Street*'s Deirdre Barlow (he has since become a charismatic man with very fine eyewear, albeit sat on a head that is increasingly like the bloke's out of the Tefal adverts). He did, however, have cooler sneakers than me. As we walked from record shop to record shop, it was clear he knew more about what was coming out than I did, was more plugged into the local scene, had a bigger record collection and, basically was like a less boastful Pete Littlefair. I'd got to know one or two of the staff in Crash – he was on first name terms with pretty much everyone in every shop. Had I heard of De La Soul? Sir Fresh and DJ Critical? Queens Brooklyn Connection? No? Well, he'd do a tape for me.

It took some time for me to get this tape. I didn't bump into Dan again for months, and when I next saw him, he said, "Ah, I promised I'd do you a tape. Sorry". But eventually I got it. It was De La Soul's debut LP, the game-changing classic *Three Feet High and Rising*. He'd filled up the rest of the C90 with tracks by the other artists he'd mentioned, all of them detailed on the inlay card in red ink, credited to 'DJ Hype'. The reason I can recall this tape from 1989 over 20 years later is that I still have it. It's in the loft, gathering dust with the rest of my tape collection, the plastic cases cracked and splintered, nestled with recordings of John Peel shows and the demo tapes we were to later make. If there's one lesson I've learned about hip-hop, it's never to throw anything away. One man's shit is another man's gold. Although, to be fair, most of these tapes are actually just shit.

That was the last I saw of Dan for quite some time, besides the occasional encounter in a record shop. But he'd soon be back in my life, changing it like Kirky or Touché before him. In the meantime, however, I was still forcing lyrics and song titles on my somewhat reluctant school crew. Written out in my dreadful longhand, I was accruing quite the sheaf of songs. I was following the three verse pattern, with each verse averaging about 24 lines. Hip-hop is quite intensive, lyrically – your average love song or pop ditty doesn't contain 72 completely different lines, does it? Lazy bastards. When people criticise hip-hop lyrics, I always point out that, whatever the shortcomings of the particular track, at least they're putting the graft in. They're conveying a lot of information in those lines, even if it's not all nuggets of gold. Of course, you could counter by championing brevity, and the wonderful way some lyricists and songwriters can encapsulate a mood or an emotion in a mere line or two, or even with a wordless instrumental, but at that point I'd just put my fingers in my ears and talk over you.

Looking back on these pages and pages of lyrics, it might perhaps have been wise for me to spend a bit more time honing them down. It turns out that 16 lines is the optimum length, not 24. But I had ideas to burn, and the raps just spewed out of me onto the page.

The stuff I was writing had changed as well. While I'd still pen the occasional brag song, I was now specialising in portentous, pretentious, well-meaning liberal topics. Hip-hop had started to politicise me. It's almost impossible for me to fathom large chunks of my life without the influence of this music and its culture, but one of the earliest things it instilled in me was an awareness of racism. As I mentioned earlier, my family weren't racists. But nor were we actively anti-racist. My family as a whole wasn't particularly political and didn't talk about Thatcher or Mandela or Reagan or anything. I'd been massively scared of nuclear war, reading books about it in the library, watching *Threads* on TV and pretty much trying not to shit myself about the impending catastrophe of mutually assured destruction, but I didn't know anything about what might cause it. I knew who the protagonists in the 'Cold War' were, but I didn't know why there was one.[41]

---

[41] I'm aware that I can tell people who live in war zones or who are fleeing oppressive regimes absolutely nothing about living in fear. But I can most definitely sit in my rocking chair (NB. I don't have a rocking chair) and tell those born in Britain in the 90's and more recently just how bum-clenchingly terrifying it was growing up with the spectre of possible nuclear war and the ensuing apocalypse. Cold war tensions in the 80's had gone beyond DEFCON One up to

Hip-hop was now starting to fill in these gaps, and prompting me to fill in the rest myself. Public Enemy were the catalyst. They're still going, the old war-horses, but the original line up of Chuck D, Flavor Flav (or 'Timey Time' as my sister used to call him when she couldn't remember his name, because he always wore a giant clock around his neck for reasons that have never been adequately explained), Professor Griff and Terminator X was the one that thrilled my every nerve from 1986 onwards. Their 1988 masterpiece, *It Takes a Nation of Millions to Hold us Back*, released on the iconic Def Jam Records, remains my favourite LP of all time. After years of groups putting out LP's that were just collections of their singles with some filler, a token love rap track and an instrumental or two to truly pad it out, rappers were now starting to act like actual artists.[42]

'Christmas Day in Albert Square' levels of drama. I used to pore over books about nuclear devastation in the library, full of descriptions of what life would probably be like after the mushroom clouds came. But it was truly brought home by the amazing and frightening *Threads* which screened on the BBC in 1984. It depicted the impact of a nuclear strike on Sheffield, complete with Reece Dinsdale getting killed very early on, a woman weeing herself outside of a shopping centre and the years and years of darkness and drudgery that followed as we reverted to a medieval state of living. The film ends on a cheery, uplifting note as a character screams at the site of the deformed baby she has just given birth to, largely as a result of eschewing folic acid and Mumsnet advice boards and just eating radioactive rat instead. It was harrowing but also brilliant. So brilliant that we can forgive the director, Mick Jackson, for going to Hollywood and making the dogshit Whitney Houston vehicle *The Bodyguard* later in his career. We can regard that as a palate cleanser after the stressful rigours of showing an apocalyptic Sheffield.

[42] I mentioned the love rap earlier when writing about rock/rap crossovers. Often an album of brutal, hardcore boasting and threats of violence would grind to a halt while the rapper delivered a treacly dedication to his girlfriend/wife/mum. On the plus side, these songs showed another side to most rappers, and proved that hip-hop could do more than just brag, boast and talk about itself. It also threw up wonderful songs like Kaos' "Do It Again", Rated X's "Be Cool To Your Girl", Positively Black's "Ebony Princess", Method Man's "You're All I Need" and Donald D's "Letters I'll Never Send". On the minus side, these tracks were the exceptions and most were utterly execrable. LL Cool J pretty much invented the

Nation of Millions contains multitudes. A track about police and prison brutality, a track about refusing to serve in an army for a land that 'never game a damn', a track about how the media misrepresents hip-hop, a track about mindless TV, even one by group clown and comic relief Flavor Flav that is almost complete nonsense. All of these served over radical music overseen by the group's in-house producers, The Bomb Squad. Instead of the repetitive loops and simple drum lines most groups thought adequate, they were throwing the kitchen sink at it. And then the rest of the kitchen as well, including the Formica worktops and tea towel holders.

Sample layered upon sample, squalls of horns grabbed from James Brown records, pieces of jazz, elements of spoken word down in the mix. Some aspects didn't reveal themselves until the 5th, 10th, 20th listen. I was already on my 20th listen after owning this stunning piece of vinyl for three days. You'd need one of those boards with dozens of post-its and lots of pieces of string like TV detectives or 9/11 conspiracy theorists have to properly map it out. Lead rapper Chuck D's lyrics were fiery, righteous and shot through with references to Black Power icons and freedom fighters that would have had me Googling them immediately if Google – or indeed the Internet – had been invented. I couldn't even Ask Jeeves.

Instead, I went to the library. Not that this was a perfect solution, apparently. Public Enemy, and my other favourite political rapper of the late 80's, the previously mentioned KRS-One (Knowledge

---

sub-genre with the success of his "I Need Love", but to me it still sounds dreadful. Not as dreadful as the 1989 *Cat Got Ya Tongue* album from LL associate Bobcat, however. That album saw Bobcat take the unique, brave and ultimately idiotic decision to reverse the normal balance of things and make the album one almost entirely full of love ballads, with a token hip-hop track. It remains an unwanted staple of bargain bins in record shops the world over. Hip-hop has famously been terrible at addressing women for most of its existence, and the tracks that take a genuinely feminist perspective are few and far between.

Reigns Supreme Over Nearly Everyone[43]), would refer to a library as a lie-bury, where they bury the lies. Television was 'telling lies to your vision'. Hardly subtle, but meat and drink to a 15-year-old hungry for information, ripe for influence, eager to rebel. All I was likely to find in a library was the white history of the world – 'his story' – with little information about Rosa Parks, the Underground Railroad, Steve Biko or Jesus being black.

If I'd come from a political family, there's a good chance I'd have known all this – as it was, hip-hop was now my teacher and guide to a world of information I didn't know about. Naturally, being a teenager, I became immediately tiresome on these subjects, despite not having fully digested or understood (ahem, in hip-hop you 'overstand' not 'understand') them. I was also guilty, as so many of us were, of believing everything rappers told us, which is problematic to say the least. I swapped one set of beliefs about the world with another, one that sounded radical both in content and form.

I was now officially left wing and an anti-racist. I thought Jesus was probably black, although in later life, I'd come to realise that Jesus' colour isn't the real issue there – it's that it's highly fucking unlikely he was the son of God. But I wasn't there yet. I was just beginning my shift to the left, and I was doing it with a patchwork of ideas put together from records that I was then feeding into my own lyrics. I'd still write the occasional boast-filled verse, but now I was penning songs with dull and worthy titles like "Gates of Freedom" and "History", that sounded less like cool tracks and more like public service documentaries. I was regurgitating things I'd learned from hip-hop, and adding a few splashes of white liberal guilt

---

43 To this day he's yet to make clear exactly which few people knowledge doesn't reign supreme over.

into the mix. 'Sorry about that whole racism hoo-ha', was the abiding theme of many things I wrote at that time.

The downside was that I still had no outlet for this stuff, except for in my bedroom on the Parkwood Estate in Beeston, which by now was entirely decorated in American Football posters. I felt a little bit trapped. I felt trapped by my skin colour – why couldn't I be black? I felt trapped by geography – why couldn't I live in New York, the home of hip-hop? And most of all I was perhaps trapped by my own ineptitude as a rapper. My voice, a weedy mix of Nottinghamshire and West Yorkshire, just didn't have the rich, fearsome timbre of Chuck D's or Rakim's or Melle Mel's, no matter how much I copied them, trying out different voices in my bedroom. I was stuck with a voice that would later be described by a future colleague of mine as 'the sound of a man lifting a fridge'.

The first non-home recording of this weedy rapping voice I have is taken from a radio show in about 1989. I'd started to search for local pirate radio shows in West Yorkshire, and had chanced upon a couple that served up hours of rap at a time. PCR – Paradise City Radio – was based in some attic in Bradford and played soul, reggae, hip-hop and a lot of Asian music. The hip-hop show was presented by DJ Shock, who played some fantastic stuff but also took requests. I'd phoned a request in, but when Shock read it out, he took the piss out of my name. I was incensed. And what do you do when you're angry and someone is mocking you? Why, you ring up their phoneline and record a diss rap to them. Which is what I did.

Your rhyming is wack, DJing sloppy
Why write a rhyme, having to copy?
Not yourself, having to emulate
You're boring, while I stimulate
I'm dope, you cannot cope

Mess with me I'll hang you out on a rope
I know the time don't need no clock
I'm gonna take you out Shock
Dedication to Paul and Sly
Peace, I'm out of here, bye.

Bless DJ Shock for playing this on air, rather than just deleting it (perhaps it was a slow day). It's hardly stunning, original or even clever, but it was the first time I'd ever heard my own rapping voice outside of my bedroom. In the long, uphill struggle that was my rap career, this was a great leap forward for me. I was thrilled and excited to be part of a live rap battle, no matter how weak or stilted. Not only had I engaged with someone who was part of the actual hip-hop community in Yorkshire, it was coming out over the airwaves to the whole Leeds/Bradford conurbation. Next stop, the world.

Nine
Hip-Hop Hooray

If hip-hop had been the flash in the pan that everyone – friends, family, enemies – constantly told me it was going to be in the mid to late 80's, then my failure to be a part of it wouldn't really have mattered. It would have been a footnote in my teenage years. But hip-hop by the time I was 15, in 1988, was huge. It was huge in terms of record sales, huge in terms of profile, huge in terms of influence. That it is way, way bigger now is unavoidably true, but 1988 was when hip-hop had broken through to the mainstream, its first flush of global success paving the way for it to seem like it does now – like something that's always been here. Like fucking Lulu or Shirley Bassey. And it hadn't broken through on the back of terrible commercial crossovers, or ersatz versions of the real thing. Run DMC and Beastie Boys might have been the household names and mums might have known LL Cool J best for his sappy "I Need Love", but they weren't the only people kicking in the door. Rappers were now on *Top of the Pops*, they were now touring the UK and were even finding their way into once stale, white magazines like *NME*.[44]

[44] A magazine I once loved and would read from cover to cover but, let's be honest, where was their 80's and 90's coverage of some of the great R'n'B and soul being made in those decades? They were just excited by the newness and threat of hip-hop and never really managed to write anything interesting about it.

Hip-hop had also influenced other genres, with Blondie dropping into rhyme on "Rapture", complete with references to hip-hop luminaries like Fab Five Freddy. This was rapping on a new wave record, rapping moving beyond its small corner. Pop musicians started to drop little raps into their songs, borrowing some cool.

Shops dedicated to selling only hip-hop vinyl were popping up in the UK, storied retailers like Groove Records in London, a focus for the scene, a place of far-away dreams for us Northerners. And it wasn't just finding space in publications like *NME*, *Melody Maker*, *Record Mirror* and *Echoes*, dedicated magazines were being launched to chronicle it. In 1987, a premium rate 0898 phone line called The Hip-Hop Connection was established, hosted by DJ Dave Pearce, which invited amateur rappers to call up, listen to rhymes from their peers, and then record their own.[45] Its success led to the launch of a monthly magazine, *Hip-Hop Connection*, the first of its kind in the world (the much more famous US monthly *The Source* likes to think it was the first, it wasn't. Anyway, much more about *Hip-Hop Connection* later). Clearly, a marketplace for the culture beyond the music was being established in the UK.

The music's influence was widespread, and its unusual, unique customs and habits left it open to lampooning. Over-serious rap fans like myself were dismayed by the number of cash-ins, genuinely awful novelty records and the general air of disdain from people who

---

[45] Dave Pearce, another DJ best known for catering to clubbers on Radio One, Radio Six and in countless clubs up and down the country, was the host of *A Fresh Start to the Week*, an early hip-hop show that launched in 1986 on Radio London 94.9FM. Pearce would be a mover and shaker in rap; both managing artists and promoting shows, plus he also had a hand in the creation of the Hip-Hop Connection phone line. But his greatest achievement, in the eyes of myself and many others, is that his voice is captured for posterity introducing Public Enemy to a noisy audience on their 1987 tour of the UK, a moment the group used on *It Takes a Nation of Millions to Hold us Back*. Being sampled on the greatest album ever recorded isn't a bad claim to fame.

didn't think this music was here to stay. Novelty rap wasn't that new – Adam Ant (a genuine, early fan of hip-hop) had released "Ant Rap" in 1981. Murine TV star Roland Rat had tasted success in 1983 with his "Rat Rappin" single (with keyboards by Errol the Hamster, guest vocals by Kevin the Gerbil and backing from Glenis the Guinea Pig – a potent combination).[46] But in 1988 it became more frequent, and much worse.

Liverpool FC released "Anfield Rap", which as a Manchester United fan struck me dumb with its melding of shit rappers with football players I hated, while Morris Minor and the Majors (which included Tony Hawks – the British fridge-transporting comic rather than the American pro-skater) sold 220,000 copies of their Beastie Boys knock-off "Stutter Rap (No Sleep Til Bedtime)". You could see such attentions as flattering, but I was too po-faced for that and saw it, depending on the time of day you asked me, as either ignorant guff from people with no music taste or just straight-up racism. But it wasn't so much these records – they could be turned off and ignored – as much as the endless bad impressions that riled hip-hop fans.

Actually this hasn't changed. People still do it. Hang out with someone culturally naff for long enough and they're almost certain

---

[46] Anyone who has kept rodents will tell you that asking a rat, a hamster, a gerbil and a guinea pig to co-exist in peaceful harmony is a big ask. Roland Rat was a kid's TV character introduced to *TV-AM*, back in the embryonic days of breakfast television (I'll leave it to you to explain to your children that as recently as the 1980's there was often no TV on at breakfast and that someone had to go and invent it). He's credited with turning the ailing show around, drawing in kids and their parents and multiplying viewing figures. He was such a phenomenon that he released an album and had a big money transfer to the BBC. The fame clearly went to his head as he traded in dowdy old Glenis for Roxanne Rat. Perhaps there'd been an outcry about the inter-species relationship from some rodent racists, or maybe he wanted to get involved with hip-hop's 'Roxanne Wars'. Bloody hell, even Kevin the Gerbil had a single in the actual music charts. What were we thinking in the 80's?

to do you their impression of a rapper. In fact, they're on a continuum of time between when they last did it, and the next time they'll do it. It is inevitable. They will throw their hands up in what they think of as a rapping gesture, they will squat down by about 10%, their knees bowed (I don't know why this is, but it's true. Perhaps they think all rappers are small or overly fond of squatting), they will put on a slightly gruff voice and they won't actually rap. What they'll do is say some variation on "Yo, motherfucker". I'd like to be able to tell these people that rappers don't actually say "Yo, motherfucker'", but of course many of them did, do and will do in the future. They just don't do it in such a shit way. Nuance is everything. After nearly 30 years of witnessing this, I've got slightly better at dealing with it. I no longer remonstrate, or try to correct them. But I can't force myself to smile or laugh either. I just fix them with a look of utter hatred and contempt.

So, yes, it was a bit all over the place. You had hip-hop cementing its place in the world with mainstream sales and the arrival of accoutrements that other, more respectable and established musical genres had. And yet you had relentless piss-taking of it, coupled with a slight whiff of moral panic. MTV had to be lobbied to include more hip-hop, back when MTV actually played music videos all day long. It was still seen by many as an ignorable sub-genre of black music, rather than the cultural behemoth it so clearly was. In living memory, it was treated like an interloper, whereas now hip-hop style, argot and inflections are second nature not just to 'urban' youth, but to kids everywhere, and to lots of their parents as well. The generation I was part of felt like we were in a struggle for the survival of our corner of the musical map and we had to fight for every little bit of recognition, scrap for every inch of territory. Now that generation is one where I know people who have named their children after DJ Jazzy Jay, Rakim and Big Daddy Kane and where my mum, in her 70's, will use the word 'diss' correctly.

Another sign of hip-hop's growth was its splintering. This had been going on to some degree ever since its birth, but by 1988 it was incredibly rich and diverse. While the mocking outsiders might have seen it as just one thing – rap – to us it contained many facets. It had already evolved from disco rap to electro (which gave birth to house) to drum-machine rap to the sample-heavy stew of its Golden Age.[47] But within that there were all kinds of sub-genres and tangents and angles and regional differences. Some of these already gloried in names, others would be attributed years later, and others were still to

---

[47] The term 'Golden Age' is even more contentious than 'urban'. Whatever you're talking about – music, TV, vacuum cleaners – people all have different ideas of when the Golden Age was. If you're the typical hip-hop fan that I grew up with, it's any time except now or in the future. I've long argued, however, that hip-hop's Golden Age is set in stone. It doesn't even matter if you were born after it and your favourite hip-hop era is 10 or 15 years later – think of a different name for that. For me – and for many others – the era of 1987-89 (give or take) is when hip-hop took a great creative leap forward. This was helped in large part by the advent of sampling, which opened hip-hop up to more than just drum machines and synthesisers. It was also helped by the arrival of rappers with interesting things to say and increasingly interesting ways of saying them. KRS-One, Rakim, Chuck D, Big Daddy Kane, LL Cool J, Kool G. Rap – all of these rappers arrived in that time period and made, arguably, their finest records and contributions to the genre then. It felt like a time of riches.

Of course, more riches were to come, but that period unlocked the door for hip-hop, it afforded a glimpse of the future, and hip-hop lurched into it. As radical as its early days had been, this promised us an even more radical future. That's why it's The Golden Age. I'm not saying it's called that because it's the best time in the genre's history (although in some ways it is) and everything after will disappoint (it definitely won't). I'm saying it's called that because many people call it that and why don't we all try to rub along with that and not say, well, 94-98 was even better? For me it's like trying to say the Victorian age was in 1664, or the Mesozoic period is due in 2050. If you have an era you prefer (and sometimes I love the early 90's music more), or that you think was more radical (you're wrong on that one), then you can have 'The Platinum Age' or 'The Fandabidozy Era'. Just leave 'The Golden Age' alone.

come. From my vantage point in the second decade in the 21st century I can look back on that aforementioned disco rap and electro but also on melody rap, crossover, underground, independent, boom bap, hyphy, crunk, afrocentric rap, G-Funk, gangsta rap, trap, horrorcore, Miami bass, bounce, ghettotech, chopped and screwed, hip-house, grime, glitch-hop, freestyle and more. I don't like all of these, but for my money it all goes to make this hip-hop lark a lot more colourful than Joseph's dreadful dreamcoat.

In the 80's, especially in the UK and New York, you were likely as not to align yourself to a particular kind of hip-hop. New Yorkers were known for being sniffy about 'regional rap', protective of what they saw as theirs. Most UK fans only listened to east coast American music (except for a wise few) and a bit of our home-grown scene. Such alignments are less common these days. The breakdown of rivalries and the coming of the Internet means that now you can (and should) listen to everything, unless you're a sad old man who only likes Golden Age rap. I know this, because I know plenty of them.

Many of these genres didn't exist yet, and I didn't know all of the ones that did. What I did know was the UK rap world, and I genuinely thought I could be a part of it. I've mentioned a couple of our home-grown artists already, but there were plenty more, and some were great. Cash Crew, Krispy 3, Hardnoise, Hijack, Demon Boyz, Unanimous Decision, Blue Eyes, Blade, Cookie Crew, London Rhyme Syndicate, Katch 22, Huntkillbury Finn (now that's a name to conjure with) – UK hip-hop may have had little international profile, but the domestic scene was buzzing. Derek B actually made the charts. MC Duke seemed like he could have been a star, if everything would only fall into place for him. Americans at the time (with a notable couple of exceptions including the always wise Chuck D, who paid attention to the world at large, and Ice-T, who actually signed London's Hijack to his label and took them on tour with him) thought of British hip-hop as a bad joke, full of people trying to sound like them and who couldn't do any of it properly.

There was a strain of thought that told many New Yorkers that only the particular set of circumstances they lived in could give rise to true hip-hop. They invented it and they intended to keep ownership of it. Anything from anywhere else was fake, a sham. This has obviously been thoroughly debunked because it turned out the whole world could make compelling hip-hop, but I'll be honest and admit I once believed this myself. Yet UK rap did find its place, and did throw up great artists, records and albums. While there were rappers from Britain who adopted a US accent to try and fit in, the vast majority didn't, and many added a truly British touch to their music. Even if that British touch was drawn from the musical heritage of places that were part of the Empire or the Commonwealth. British musicians sounded a lot more comfortable than their US counterparts when it came to marrying reggae with rap. They also talked about domestic politics, about Thatcher. They looked to the world and attacked Apartheid. There was much to be proud of. And it wasn't all worthy – some of it was just funky. I'll be in my deathbed on the moon after a jetpack accident before I stop tapping my toes to Demon Boyz' "Rougher than An Animal" or Caveman's "I'm Ready".

Leeds had its own scene too, tiny as it was. A bloke called Paul who worked in Crash Records was part of a group called Breaking The Illusion along with a lad called Tommy. They made honest music, perhaps influenced early on by the likes of De La Soul and other groups that were comfortable talking about emotions. They were just about to put out a self-funded 12" and Paul mentioned to me that they were supporting an American act at a club called The Warehouse. I thought I'd go along and show my support. I did, and ran into Dan again. And that's when I became a proper rapper.

AND I'D RATHER GET A BUS THAN A BENZ
POP OUT TO MY FRIENDS OR MY DADS AKA LENS
I PICK UP COLOURED PENS AND I'M WRITING
JOURNALIST STYLE WHILE I FEEL MY CHEST TIGHTEN
COUGH-COUGH,GET MY INHALER FOR MY ASTHMA
[illegible]KE A PUFF,I'M OKAY,NOW PASS THE
SCAM,DAN CHECKS THE SWATCH AND IT'S 4
SO THE BLACK COFFEE GOES ON THE BOIL ONCE MORE
WHILE BLUE NOTE JAZZ SOOTHES THE ROOM
I WONDER,IF I BLUNDER,WILL MY LIFE BE CONSUMED
SHOULD I PONDER OR WANDER OFF ON A PATH
LIVE IN THE HERE AND NOW,OR THE AFTERMATH
OF A LIFE THAT'S TWENTY,PLENTY
TO CHOOSE FROM NOW AND I HOPE IT'S NEVER EMPTY
LET MY SENSES BE STRETCHED TO THE LIMIT
FROM OLD SCHOOL TO NEW AND ALL THAT'S WITHIN IT
NAVIGATE THE STRESS AND THE MESS AND AVOID THE STRIFE
....TO LIVE A HIP-HOP LIFE

[illegible] LIVIN' HIP HOP FROM MY SOUL MY GOAL
AIN'T A GOLD RING THING 'COS THAT'S A SLIPPERY POLE
A MEANS TO AN END BUT THERE'S NO END TO YA MEANS
FOR A SELLOUT PHASE WHERE YOU JUST DROP OFF THE SCENE
LIKE THEY SAY I AIN'T GOING OUT LIKE THAT
[illegible] NOT TRYING TO HEAR IT,NO HIP HOP YES I FEAR IT
TAKE THE WHEEL AND STEER IT ANOTHER WAY
PROGRESSIVE AGENDA TAKE THE PARALLEL PATHWAY
NO NEED TO BE A RAP STAR
JUST COLLECT RESPECT AND SAY CHEERS TA
SPIKE LEE'S ON THE BOX SO I AIN'T FLICKING CHANNELS
GLUED TO THE SET WHILE PEPSIS CHIP TOOTH ENAMEL
OR WE MIGHT JUST DIG IN THE CRATES
SPIN A PROMO PLATE,AN OLD SCHOOL GREAT
SOUL-JAZZ ARE COOL BUT THE RULE IS THE REBEL OF THE RHYME
TOAST YA HOT LIKE BREVILLE
PHAT BEATS ARE LIKE SWEETS BUT NOT SICKLY
AS I FLY PAST WELL THE RHYME FLOWS QUICKLY
STAY TRUE AND THE REACTION IS AFFIRMATIVE
UNLIKE EAZY-E HE IS A PERMY DIV
REJECT THE CURLS AND THE GANGSTER STANCE
DO THE BIZ DANCE WITH NEW FLESH 4 OLD WE ADVANCE
SO SHUT UP,YOU'RE NOT TOO BIG FOR A SWIFTY
A SIMPLE LIFE....IS THE LIFE I LIVE SIMPLY.

SCAM.PA.1993.

Ten
Me and my Posse

This was not your typical audition. I'd bumped into Dan and his friend Martin at The Warehouse, all of us there to show our support for Breaking The Illusion. Martin was also known as DJ Countdown and had been making music with Dan for a while. They were looking for a rapper, and they'd heard on the grapevine (I still haven't a clue what grapevine this was, but such was my limited rep in Leeds at that time, I assume it was a withered one. I can't imagine I'd mentioned to Dan that I was an aspiring rapper, as I found how plugged in he was to the Leeds hip-hop scene more than a bit intimidating) that I was one. They even mentioned they'd heard my radio diss of DJ Shock, who was a friend of theirs. I don't think they knew how excited I was. After years of being in non-group groups, ones that existed in name, on paper in countless school exercise books or in my over-active imagination only, I had a chance of actually joining a trio with two other lads who actually seemed to know what they were on about. They had equipment, a four track, ways of sampling music and making beats, turntables to scratch on. They did pirate radio on the thrillingly named Lethal FM. They bought jazz, soul and funk records from charity shops to pore over for possible samples.[48] Martin had a car. Christ, they even had a mate, Foresight (not his real name), who talked about being the group's dancer. I really, really wanted to be a part of this.

---

[48] You can't write a book about hip-hop without mentioning sampling. For the absolutely uninitiated, it means to take a portion of an existing song and rework it for your own song. It might be a few seconds of a drum beat, a snatch of trumpet, a bit of organ or maybe even the vocal itself. By piecing these bits together, you create your own track. A producer may chop up the sample in a way that makes it impossible to detect the original, or it might be glaringly obvious.

Sampling makes sense within hip-hop. As discussed earlier, the very first hip-hop events saw the DJ's scratching the same portions of tracks repeatedly to create a long groove, which is proto-sampling. And early Rap hits like Sugarhill Gang's "Rapper's Delight" had session musicians borrowing an already well-known groove (Chic's "Good Times") and replaying it. Hip-hop moved away from that form of sampling in the early to mid 80's, as it shifted into an era heavily reliant on drum machines, although it cropped up from time to time. In 1986-1987, and the advent of The Golden Age, sampling became more prevalent and more creative. Albums like Eric B & Rakim's *Paid in Full* were chock-full of samples, both obvious and obscure. The floodgates were opened, and it seemed to be open season on the back catalogue of James Brown. His funk-filled coffers were raided by hundreds of rappers and producers. He provided lyrical inspiration, especially when hip-hop was in a more racially conscious mode, and he provided musical backdrops both wholesale and spliced together with genius. In fact, the whole James Brown sampling thing got so big so quickly that there was already a backlash by 1988, with the group Kings of Swing releasing the song "Stop Jockin' James". But nobody stopped jockin' James.

Sampling did evolve though. Producers started to look to jazz records for samples, and the late 80's and early 90's saw hip-hop enter a Jazz era. And then things got more esoteric. Producers started to compete to dig up the most obscure samples possible, ones that no-one else could find. They'd even blank out the record labels before taking them to the studio so that no-one could copy them – a move already used by northern soul DJ's to protect their pride-and-joy record. Soundtracks, pop, rock, library music, spoken word – these were all fair game. And this gets to the crux of the issue for many people. There are those who see sampling as simply artistic theft. People who decry hip-hop would say it was a music where people rapped over other people's songs. And there is certainly a fair bit of that about. But sampling is most definitely an art form of genius in itself. The genius doesn't lie in finding the rare, untapped samples. No, the genius lies in what you do with the samples, whether famous or not.

Many defences of sampling in hip-hop, especially when it was a bit of a hot potato (again, the late 80's) seek to justify it on the grounds that it shines light on

I'd expected to have to go round to one of their houses and try out for them (I wonder if the dancer did the same?[49]). We're so used now to televised auditions, with nervous youngsters (or the old, weird ones they're exploiting for cheap, pitiful laughs) singing in

some obscure or forgotten musicians. Stetsasonic recorded a brilliant defence of the right to sample in 1988 called "Talkin' all that Jazz" where they pointed out that no-one was really listening to James Brown anymore until Eric B & Rakim sampled him, and that rap was responsible for resurrecting the careers of other artists. It's a strong argument, and while people might not exactly have forgotten an artist of the calibre of James Brown, sampling certainly introduced him to a new generation. There was fresh interest in the back catalogue of hundreds of artists off the back of sampling, careers were revived, and in the same way I discovered hip-hop from a cassette tape, there are those who discovered soul, funk and jazz off the back of a sample. It also make a big difference geographically and culturally. Rappers and producers living in the US may have grown up in a house where they'd hear Stevie Wonder or Marvin Gaye or John Coltrane all the time – a white UK kid was somewhat more likely to be exposed to Genesis, Pink Floyd or *Stewpot's Pop Party*. There was real joy in discovering the history of black music through hip-hop records, a joy that diminished somewhat as sampling became expensive and also because every trendy bar or café playlist is now curated by someone from my generation and they've all rinsed Marlena Shaw's "California Soul" to death.

So, that's one defence. But I don't think sampling even needs that – I think that people like Pete Rock, Large Professor, The Beatnuts, DJ Premier, Dr. Dre, Q-Tip, Kanye West, Lord Finesse and many more like them took hip-hop sampling to such a high level that that's justification alone. Yes, Dr. Dre turned a lot of people onto the brilliant psychedelic rock-jazz musician and producer David Axelrod when he sampled "The Edge" for 1999's "The Next Episode", but he also gave us "The Next Episode" itself in the process, a brilliant song in its own right. Isn't the argument for sampling as a creative art form already won, especially now that legal changes and challenges mean that artists now get paid (and so do legions of lawyers, naturally) when they're sampled? It could be argued that Elvis Presley and the Rolling Stones 'sampled' the black artists they were so heavily influenced by. Hip-hop just does it in a different way.

[49] In the 80's and part of the 90's, rap groups seemed a bit pre-occupied with wanting to present the complete entertainment package, so in addition to a rapper and a DJ, they'd have dancers. But not just unnamed guest dancers – their very own dancers. Big Daddy Kane had Scoob and Scrap Lover, Heavy D and the Boyz only featured Heavy D on the microphone – the Boyz were dancers Trouble T-Roy and G-Wiz. Steady B had Thick and Thin, Masta Ace had Big Steps, MC Lyte had Leg 1 and Leg 2 and even Public Enemy has the S1W's.

front of a panel of twats. This was nothing like that. All they wanted from me was some of my hand-written lyrics to read. This was pre-email. In fact, it was pretty much pre-laptop and pre-home PC. I didn't even have a typewriter. So after the night at The Warehouse I went home, sat in my bedroom, and sifted through my piles and piles of lyrics. I was not short of material. In fact, due to me also 'ghostwriting' lyrics for someone I'd met through *Hip-Hop Connection* magazine, I had stacks and stacks of lyrics ready to go.

Hip-Hop Connection was more than just a magazine full of interviews with rappers and DJ's and reviews of the latest releases, it was also, as the name suggests, a way for like-minded fans to get in touch with each other. A page called 'Connections' was full of little adverts from people in London, Nottingham, Glasgow, Portsmouth and elsewhere, all along the lines of 'Hardcore hip-hop fan into Ultramagnetic MC's, Public Enemy and Run DMC wants to swap tapes'. I'd written to a couple of people who had cassettes of London-based radio shows entirely dedicated to rap that I fancied getting hold of. I'd even corresponded with a few girls, where our talk of rappers we liked was a gossamer-thin meniscus obscuring the roiling sexual tension below. Well, it was from my point of view.

Eventually I took the plunge and put my own advert in.[50] The response was decent. I was trading tapes, but because I'd also mentioned I was an aspiring rapper, I got an unusual request from a guy in Ireland.[51] He was a rapper too, but hated writing his own

---

[50] It was printed, complete with a typo that may have been as a result of my shaky scrawl, as 'Andy Emey aka Scam would like to hear from anyone interested in swapping tapes and lyrics, as well as writing letters. Likes Kane, Biz, Ultramagnetics.' My taste was flawless.

[51] I was trading albums I had, for albums I didn't, all copied on my double tape deck in my bedroom. I feel free to mention this as I think the statute of limitations has passed on this piece of home piracy and I'm unlikely to have a

lyrics. Would I ghost-write for him? Well, why not? So I was in the unusual position of being a rapper no-one had heard rap, writing raps for a Belfast rapper I'd never heard rap and would never meet. I crafted him some standard brag-raps and avoided all mention of 'The Troubles'. However, it did mean I was now well equipped with lyrics.

I didn't want to overwhelm Dan and Martin, so I had to choose three or four of my best songs. I wanted to give them a bit of politics, a bit of humour, but also some stuff that was about hip-hop and how much it meant to me, and how I wanted it to be 'real' and not 'sell-out'. The type of guff most rappers used to write in the late 80's and early 90's, basically. I was also aware of the fact that my handwriting is pitiful, so I spent hours and hours copying out my couplets in my 'best' handwriting, my left hand cramping. And when I'd done all this, I was to meet them again, in Crash Records.

I handed over the lyrics, expecting them to take them away and analyse them, scratch their chins and give me feedback, umming and aahing. In fact, they just had a quick shufty there and then, which took all of about 20 seconds, and declared themselves delighted. Why didn't I come and rap for them? I played it as cool as I could, but I was both elated and incredibly nervous. I got the bus home, hardly believing it. It eventually sunk in... After six years of hoping and wishing, I was finally in a real rap group. I was the rapper in the P.A. Posse.

It didn't really bother me that I didn't get to name the group. Despite my notepads and diaries being full of imaginary posse names I'd hoped to one day form, I was just so pleased to be part of something that I went along with what Dan and Martin already had.

SWAT team at my door for taping someone I never met a copy of Doctor Ice's *The Mic Stalker* album onto a Scotch C90 in 1989.

When I'd first met Dan, back when he made me that tape, he'd gone by the name of DJ Hype. But there was another DJ Hype out there, and Dan's habit of wearing mostly green clothing had led someone to call him Greenpeace. It stuck. I was Scam by then, simple and plain.[52] I thought it denoted a craftiness, sounded a bit on the margins, a bit dangerous. Entirely fitting for a 16-year-old schoolboy who worked as a part-time indoor cricket umpire. DJ Countdown had had his name for a while.[53] And the P.A. Posse? It stood for Prehistoric Ages.

Even in 1990, hip-hop was already looking backwards. The aforementioned novelty records, hybrid forms like hip-house and the proliferation of populist, crossover chart rap had already turned a lot of us into rabid purists eager to man the barricades to defend the music we cared so passionately for. We were still, technically, in hip-hop's Golden Age, but we weren't deterred from harking back to some lost era that, in the way of these things, didn't actually ever exist. Because, from the birth of hip-hop, there were people involved trying to record music that would make it into the charts. And, with the benefit of hindsight, what's so wrong with that? But as teenagers

---

[52] Other rappers would later use this name. A bloke called Skam dropped a single in the US in 1989, later on there'd be another Skam who actually recorded with Eminem, while the UK's Richie Rich put out a megamix called "The Scam" and there's a rare US independent EP called "The Scam". Clearly great minds think alike. Sadly, while I'm aware of all these other Scams/Skams, they were never aware of me. OR WERE THEY? No, they really weren't.

[53] "Many people have thought it was because I had an uncanny resemblance to the late great Richard Whiteley, or that I had a crush on Carol Vorderman," says the man himself, "but I got the name Countdown because there was a DJ electrical shop in Chapeltown called Countdown Electronics. I used to pass it on the number 36 bus going to town. The shop had a neon sign which my plan was to acquire and put on my wall. Before Countdown I was DJ Batfink, and for a bit I changed from DJ Countdown to DJ Fresh as the word Countdown was too long to make a stencil for my T-Shirt. Then finally I ended up with Countdown which has stayed ever since."

we were full of piss and vinegar about such 'sell-outs', and Prehistoric Ages was all about taking hip-hop back to more innocent times – and, er, when could be more innocent than the Prehistoric Ages? Honestly, we didn't have a fucking clue. Later on, a much more talented group would go on to have a successful and lauded (if ultimately quite limited) career doing quite a similar thing, their vocals actually taking its cue from the early live performances of rap's founding artists. Their name? Jurassic 5. Spooky.

The P.A. Posse, in 1990, was in full and total effect, as we used to say in the hip-hop world. Two DJ's, a rapper and possibly a dancer. Although we didn't see much of him. Perhaps he'd realised there wouldn't be a lot of dancing to do. Our arrival as a group was even mentioned in the national press. Well, I exaggerate. The now defunct fortnightly teenage girl's magazine *Mizz* used to have a feature where they profiled the 'hot' boys of a particular city. Dan and Martin went record shopping in Manchester one weekend and ending up getting roped in for the 'Mizz meets the Manchester Boys' spread. I still have the issue, and there they are, both wearing camouflage baseball caps, Dan's with 'Prehistoric Ages – Greenpeace' embroidered on it (what teenage girl could resist?). I never went to the expense of getting one of these done.

Dan's caption in the magazine reads: 'Daniel is also a student of business studies, and doesn't have any idea of what he wants to do when he leaves. He likes hip-hop music. "Ultra Magnetic and most American MC's. I don't like Derek B." He does like clubs, though, and clothes by Adidas or Hi-Tech. He also likes reading, watching *The Simpsons* on Sky Television and seeing films like *Die Hard 2*.' Right below him is Martin's. 'Martin is a mate of Daniel's, and he likes hip-hop music too. "KRS 1, stuff like that. In fact we've got our own group, we're called Prehistoric Ages (?!) and we do DJ-ing. We've also just found someone to rap for us and we're working on stuff now.

I'm not actually interested in anything except for music and clothes." He does have a job though – he works as an accountant for Asda's head office. He does have an interest in girls as well... "any with dark hair and skin"'.

There you have it – the birth of a hip-hop legend captured for all time in a journal of record. The question mark and exclamation are entirely theirs. *Mizz* used to forward letters to the boys from readers – I believe Dan and Martin received one between them. Courtesy prevents me from saying who it was addressed to. They were probably unlucky to share a page with another Manchester boy, Kieran O' Brien, 16, who doesn't mention in his brief bio that he'd actually been the star of kid's TV show *Gruey*, and nor does he predict a future where he plays *Cracker*'s son, pops up in HBO's *Band of Brothers* and then is the only actor ever seen ejaculating in a mainstream UK feature film, in Michael Winterbottom's *9 Songs*. That's some tough competition.

Finally, I was getting to do some actual rapping. I'd head over to where Dan and Martin lived, on the much nicer north side of Leeds. If we were at Martin's, we wouldn't be disturbed but his bedroom was snug to say the least. If we were at Dan's, his two younger brothers Robert and James would be all over us and his mum would shout at us. But it didn't matter to me – I was rapping. Dan would play us some beats he'd been messing around with, and we'd start to actually try and construct songs. I wasn't short of ideas. Dan would loop something, and I'd pick up the mic and rehearse my lyrics. I'd suggest possible vocal snatches from other hip-hop records for Countdown to scratch into the chorus, stuff that fitted thematically, and he also brought plenty to the table too. We'd slowly start to piece together tracks, limited as we were by some pretty shonky equipment. Microphones kept breaking, the four track kept getting borrowed by other local musicians that Dan knew, the turntable jumped. But tracks were gradually taking shape. They'd take some moulding, and we were still in the early stages, but these were tracks we thought would really shake hip-hop up. Well, at least in Leeds…

Eleven
Just a Friend

Hip-hop wasn't a full-time job… yet. I was in school, Dan at college, Martin working a 9 to 5. So the little time we could get together to make music was precious. We still wasted it as best we could. On some days – usually it was a Sunday – we'd just mess about. Martin would cue up some instrumentals or breakbeat records and we'd all just rap nonsense over them. Most of this stuff was disposable, but just occasionally it would feed into our actual music. One of us would summon a couple of lines in the middle of a rambling verse largely consisting of nothing usable that were worth honing into something bigger.

To get to either of their houses, I had to catch two buses from home. There is a distinct lack of glamour about this. While it gave me time to read, or to polish up the latest killer verse I was writing, it was also tedious. The rappers revolving on my turntable were talking about their amazing cars – a Benz, a Ferrari, a Jeep – and driving down legendary New York streets blasting music through their pumping Alpine system.[54] I, however, was at the mercy of the

[54] Of all the many bragging-related hip-hop subgenres (jewellery, girls, guns and so forth) cars is a particularly rich one. From Public Enemy's "You're Gonna Get Yours" to Masta Ace's "Jeep Ass Niguh", LL Cool J's "The Boomin' System" to Paul Wall's "Sittin' Sideways", Outkast's "Benz or Beamer" to The Lost Boyz'

West Yorkshire public transport system, making sure I had my bus pass so I'd get half fare, picking up abandoned tickets for my sister Susan's 'Bus Bonus' collection, trying not to be sat next to the pissed wino or the Leeds United fan who sat with his legs so aggressively far apart you could drive a tank between them.

I think I first felt a real, solid part of the group when, one weekend, I turned up with a rap that they'd never heard before. I'd written it on the Saturday, and rehearsed it repeatedly over one of the fastest instrumental tracks from an old UK album called *Skool Beats*. It was at a real breakneck pace, but at that age I was pushing myself to have more in my locker than just wordy, worthy songs. I wanted to prove I could be a fast rapper like Big Daddy Kane on "Raw" or Rakim on "Lyrics of Fury". Martin let the track go and I was all over it, spitting venom into the microphone that I was holding like my heroes would.[55] Dan and Martin were obviously impressed.

"Jeeps, Lex Coups, Bimaz & Benz", Devin the Dude's "Lacville '79" to Dr. Dre's "Let Me Ride", all of these are wonderful songs that make driving an automobile sound alluring, glamorous and sexy, and I speak as a non-driving, *Top Gear* hater who owns zero pairs of stringback driving gloves.

[55] It may seem silly – and indeed it actually is – but there are right and wrong ways to hold a microphone. For starters, and somewhat stating the obvious, you need to be holding it. The only people who can get away with head-mounted mics are people with ridiculously energetic dance routines (Madonna, vintage Bobby Brown) and stage magicians who need to pretend that there is magic coming out of their fingertips and who need both hands free in case their trick goes tits up and they find themselves drowning in a glass box or trying to fight off a lion that has suddenly decided to eviscerate them in front of a studio audience that, deep down, really wants to see those things happen.

The worst crimes against microphone holding occurred on 80's TV when all the channels ('all' being 'four') decided to move to silly, slimline mics that looked a bit like Doctor Who's sonic screwdriver, but thinner and less effective against Daleks. Worst of all was the *Blankety Blank* wand-like microphone, which looked like some horrible, probing torture device from the future. Kenny Everett famously bent one being wielded by Terry Wogan in half. Happily, despite mini-mics being available, most people seem to have realised that butch, chunky mics look best. Rappers tend not to hold their mics toward the bottom, but at the top,

They made the 'bo' sounds of approval while I was still going.[56] As an asthmatic this verse pushed my lungs to their limits (something the great rapper Percee P summed up brilliantly with his track "Lung Collapsing Lyrics"), and I came out of it breathless, but thrilled to my core, charged up by the pats on the back my fellow posse members were giving me. While we worked for months on actual songs, this would be my trademark verse, the one I'd fall back on to show them what I could do when I applied myself.

I wasn't alone on the microphone, though. While I was undoubtedly the lead rapper, flying solo on most tracks, Dan would flex his skills on the occasional track as well. Martin didn't seem interested then, and didn't need to, he was absolutely brilliant at cutting and scratching, but later on he, too, would want his time on the mic. It didn't matter to me, I wasn't precious about hogging the limelight. My schoolbook dreams of being the centre of attention with a DJ or two at the side or back of me had been only that. Once in the real world of an actual group, I knew it wasn't going to be that way. Dan's verses added variation and texture to our music and, strangely, all these years later, I find it easier to recite his old lyrics

---

partially covering the bottom of the head, with the mic itself sticking upwards at an angle of about 45 degrees. It looks brilliant, but pretty much like when people hold guns sideways, it's not particularly effective. It probably riles sound engineers as well.

[56] The 'bo' sound being that noise that some people make to replicate the sound of a gun going off. It derives from Jamaican dancehall behaviour, where people would actually fire guns in the air to show their appreciation of a record. You couldn't move at hip-hop clubs in the late 80's and early 90's for people awkwardly lifting their fingers in the air to imitate a gun and going 'Bo! Bo! Bo!' when a DJ put on a popular record. It seems to have morphed into 'Brap', which is probably a more accurate rendition of a machine gun sound, although Michael Winslow from the *Police Academy* films could undoubtedly do you a better impression.

than I do my own. Slowly but surely, as we got to know each other, we started to record what would become our first demo tape.

For us, demo tapes were still how you became known. Hip-hop might have been radical in many ways, but the approach to trying to get signed to a label was still the same-old, same-old. I'm certain many artists got signed off the back of live performances, and a wise few pressed up their own records and controlled their own careers, but we were all about trying to get signed to a real-life label by sending them a C30 cassette in the post. It's strange and interesting how disparate individuals ally themselves to do these things. Music history is littered with tales of groups of friends who grow famous together and then grow to hate each other, but largely, from my experience, groups are held together with spit in the first place, weak agglomerations of people with a common musical interest, but no real deep friendship or affinity. 'Does that mate of yours want to play bass in the band?' 'Know any singers?' It's a temporary, pragmatic relationship often thrown together randomly.

Like many, many groups now and forever, we were developing a friendship in tandem with developing a musical career together. I was the rapper in Dan and Martin's group before we'd even spent time together as mates, which means you rely heavily on trust. You trust each other to do what you've all claimed you can do – rap, scratch, produce – and you trust each other to try and get along with each other. Happily, we all got along fine. Dan and Martin had known each other longer, but Dan and I were soon getting close, and when Dan wasn't there, Martin and I rubbed along great as well. But I never, at that stage, felt confident about mixing groups of friends together. My school 'crew' of Brett and Steve were 'mates', and as they weren't particularly ambitious about hip-hop, they didn't seem to mind me swanning off with a new posse. My good friends at school – Sarah, Paul, Richard, Vanessa, Simone – weren't remotely interested in hip-hop, although they had to put up with me banging on about it all the time and doing silly things like posting up 'Top 10 hip-hop tracks of the week' lists up on the notice board in the 6th form common room, something that interested nobody. My ability to waste educational time on day-dreaming about hip-hop was undiminished.

I don't know why I was so reluctant to mix school mates with hip-hop friends. Maybe I thought the resulting Venn diagram would be too horrible to contemplate. More likely, I didn't want my hip-hop friends to see how uncool I was at school, or my school friends to see how stupidly and childishly me and my hip-hop friends behaved much of the time, giggling over the microphone and farting in confined spaces. Also, I couldn't imagine the event that would bring all these people together at once. Where would it be? What would be happening? It's a strange contrast – the cocky, aspiring rapper telling people what they ought to be doing and attempting to set the world straight in verse after verse of rap, simultaneously worrying about social death in a very teenage way.

With my school friends I went to the pub, talked about books and poetry, teachers, hopes for the future, possible jobs or universities we might go to. Dan, Martin and I didn't really do that stuff. We talked incessantly about hip-hop, and occasionally girls. We also went to London together. That was a thrill in itself. While we loved our local record shops in Leeds, the ones in London were famous for being cutting-edge, for having the latest records first, and for having UK artists actually hanging out in them. It was joyous to troop up to Groove Records on Greek Street in Soho and walk out with a couple of fresh imports within their trademark carrier bag. There was other stuff about London that reminded us how small Leeds was as well. You couldn't get *The Source* magazine anywhere at home, but it was stocked up and down Oxford Street in London.

We'd also make a pilgrimage to window shop in Four Star General, the best place for hip-hop clothing. Originally in Carnaby Street, later relocating to Camden, it was the main stockist of B-Boy brands like Troop, SPX, British Knights, Starter jackets and Triple Goose leather coats, while they also did custom graffiti T-shirts, name belt buckles and four finger rings, in addition to fake Louis Vuitton and Gucci merchandise. Run by George, people came from all over Britain to get the latest street fashions at Four Star General, before getting the coach back to their somewhat less happening towns and villages. On one visit, laden with records, magazines and a T-shirt or two, we saw Normski on the streets of Camden outside Four Star.[57] He was already a bit of a celeb and a few people were catcalling him. His car was parked on the other side of some railings and he attempted to vault them with somewhat studied nonchalance. He totally misjudged it and fell flat on his arse, to even more abuse and laughter. At that point, he was the closest thing I'd ever seen to a celebrity, apart from the one time me and my Dad ran into Roy Kinnear in Portugal. He didn't fall on his arse though.

As well as joining a group, the other thing that had made life much more tolerable in Leeds was entering 6th form. I so nearly didn't. I sleepwalked through my GCSE's, failing to apply myself properly, and managed to fail Technical Drawing by losing my coursework on a bus the week before the deadline. I was particularly gutted as I'd designed a record shop called 'Public Records' which

---

[57] Normski is best known to many people as the presenter of BBC 2 music show *Dance Energy*, part of the short-lived but fondly remembered *Def II* teatime strand, which also included stuff like LL Cool J and Public Enemy concerts, *Rapido*, *Behind the Beat* and *The Fresh Prince of Bel Air*. From 1988 to 1994 it was the best hip-hop TV you could get in the UK. The strand was produced by Janet Street Porter who, coincidentally, was going out with Normski for quite a while. He's also known in rap circles as an excellent photographer who captured indelible images of much early UK hip-hop, as well as visiting American stars.

used the logo of Public Enemy. Talk about a one-track mind. As I was sick of being skint, I was thinking of leaving school and getting a job – god knows what – when the kindly Miss Smith, head of 6th form, intervened. The 5th year had been invited to visit the separate 6th form area of the school for a talk about what you could do if you stayed on. Afterwards, my English teacher Mr Slater (a man who once generously wrote on a school report that I had 'infinite potential' and, while he was wrong, certainly ensured that that was the only school report I ever kept) set a creative writing assignment about our impressions of the 6th form. Still not thinking of actually joining it, I wrote something silly that was all 'hallowed portals' this and 'Miss Smith's reign of terror' that. It obviously tickled Mr Slater's funny bone, and he showed it to Miss Smith, who wrote me a letter, aping the tone of my piece, saying that if I was capable of writing such prose, I shouldn't waste it and should allow it free rein in the 6th form.[58] Like the day Richard Kirk played me electro music, this was an event that would shape my life. I applied for A-Levels.

It was in January 1990, only a few months into those A-Levels, when my dad left us. The move to Leeds had proved, ultimately, not to be so great for him. He'd failed to find a job he thought befitted his experience and seemed a bit lost. My mum had become the primary bread-winner, enjoying her job at Burton's and becoming more independent as a result. Their marriage was disintegrating, and the house was becoming increasingly tense and unpleasant.

---

[58] I still treasure this letter, which reads in full: To Andrew Emery, 5W2, a mere 5th year. From: Miss Smith in the hallowed portals of that area from which all lesser mortals are banned. Mr Slater, that most casual and elegant of deputy heads has passed your assignment to me to read. I would like to add a 10th commandment, which I was obviously remiss in omitting during my speech. Commandment No. 10. If thou hast the gift of wit and skill in writing satirical literature thou shalt, nay thou must enter the Sixth Form of John Smeaton Community High. I hope that you will obey.

Christmas 1989: Dad bought Mum an eternity ring. A couple of weeks later, he was gone.

I was the first to find out. I came home from school, Mum and Susan still at work, and walked into a maisonette with a lot of furniture missing. It took me a minute to realise we hadn't been burgled. Whenever I hear 'family values' idiots on television or read them delivering an encomium to marriage and the importance of families staying together through thick and thin in a newspaper, I laugh. As much as I love my dad, his leaving was the best thing he ever did. The best thing for him – he obviously found life as it was intolerable – and the best for us. The horrendous atmosphere of simmering resentment and unspoken grievances lifted immediately. I'm a firm believer in broken families calling it a day before someone gets hurt. It's not a failure, it's just something that happens.

The three of us left in the house rallied round, and got on better than ever. We didn't have to watch what we said. There was less tension around what we could watch on telly, or who we could bring home with us. Mum gave me the latitude to be myself at the time when I was starting to have proper, long-term girlfriends. And while I wouldn't see Dad for some time, I also believe that our relationship benefited in the long-run from his leaving us. It makes a big difference to be able to go and see your father when you don't owe him anything and you don't need anything from him, and you don't have to apologise for yourself and you can see why you really love him. You start to see each other for the right reasons, and find common ground, rather than negotiate your relationship as a go-between between two warring parents, or as a piece of territory in a broken marriage.

Life in the 6th form was much more laid back than school had ever been before. And, let's be blunt, a large part of this was down to the fact that all the stupid, aggressive thick twats who'd bullied people in the playground had left. I no longer lived with the daily threat of being hit because I was from Nottingham/a tall nerd/had curly hair/liked rap. Instead I could dress more casually, could try out naïve and embryonic political views on the 6th form committee, and spend time in the common room between lessons with my friends. Also, I could sneak into pubs into Leeds with these friends for underage pints. What bliss.

I also got to put my new-found confidence on the microphone to use in the school's 6th form talent show. I pretended to be reluctant to join in with this, but secretly I was delighted to be asked. People would be doing magic tricks, comedy, dance routines, singing. And me? Rapping, obviously. The thing is, I didn't want to do it on my own, and no-one else from my school group was really a hip-hop fan (or at least not one prepared to humiliate themselves in front of their peers). Which is why I ended up performing the best song in recorded history – Public Enemy's "Rebel Without a Pause" – with back-up from certified non-hip-hop people Paul Chatterton and Dave Goodwin. I kept it somewhat real – I had on a Public Enemy T-shirt, a baseball cap, some shades – but these two were something else. In order to perform this song, I had to do it with two people tricked up in full novelty rap regalia – garish hoodies, backwards baseball caps, the clichéd works. I might as well have been Morris Minor and them The Majors. Albeit Morris Minor rapping potent, politically-charged lyrics.

It was a performance of two halves – me prowling the stage in full Chuck D mode, word-perfect (if I do say so myself), trying out rap moves I'd want to do in the real world, in front of real fans. And then these two behind me, two rhythm-less idiots (no offence Paul, Dave) in fancy dress, waving their arms in stereotypical hip-hop ways and doing that 10% squatting down thing I hate. It has to be said, it went down a treat. And it has to be said that we wuz robbed. Looking back, it's somewhat typical that my only live performance at that stage had been a cover version performed to a bunch of schoolies and teachers with comic relief as back-up, rather than anything with my actual proper crew, The Prehistoric Ages Posse. But that was soon to come.

Twelve
It's a Demo

Having been together as a group for a few months, we were now earnestly recording tracks for a demo. And, as is often the way, we spent a long time doing everything except that one thing. We spent a lot of time thinking of 'clever' names for our tracks. We wasted far too much time talking about getting personalised T-shirts and custom name-belt buckles made (neither of which ever were, vintage merchandise fans). And I wouldn't like to count the hours we pissed away turning our good old fashioned hip-hop names – Greenpeace, Countdown and Scam – into pretentious acronyms. Because now that we were Prehistoric Ages, with everything that was supposed to represent, our names had to chime with it. So Scam became S.C.A.M. - Speaking Critically About Mankind. Oh fucking yes! Ladies might Love Cool James, but my naming game was next level.

Greenpeace was obviously going to be tricky to turn into anything wieldy, not that that stopped dozens of rap groups, so he expanded his name to Greenpeace the B.O.M.B – Bringing Our Messages Back.[59] We were obviously very serious about this whole

[59] If you think our names were dreadful, you've seen nothing. Some rappers made their names into acronyms that actually sounded cool – so Big Daddy Kane was 'King Asiatic Nobody's Equal' and Kool G. Rap was the 'Kool Genius of Rap'.

'transmitting from the Prehistoric era of hip-hop' thing we'd concocted. Martin wasn't so sure, and cleverly turned Countdown into The Count Doing Only What's Necessary which in hindsight is much cooler than the names we chose. So, with our full names good to go, and patiently explained to everyone who kept asking us about them, and also tediously explained to people who didn't ask about them but we wanted to tell, it was time to stop procrastinating and lay some world-changing music down.

Our first demo was to contain such gems as "Get the Sell-Out Of Town", "Pretty Boys Don't Survive Up North" and "Street Pilgrims". Don't fret, dear reader, I will dwell at length on all of these. We already had a trademark sound. Trademark to us, anyway. Dan was big on the use of organs, sampling Jimmy Smith on every other track, and we all had record collections from which we'd tease snippets for Countdown to scratch dextrously for the choruses.[60] Because we were 'hardcore' and 'real', we wouldn't have actual choruses, just a load of scratching. On a later demo, thinking we were being brilliantly cutting and sardonic, we actually had a chorus that

---

However, I was never convinced by K-Solo's 'Kevin Self Organisation Left Others' but groups in particular were really terrible at it. Ed OG and the Bulldogs sounds like a decent rap name, until you find out it means 'Every Day anOther Girl and the Black United Leaders Living Directly Off Grooving Sounds.' I would be prepared to lock them up, starve them of food and see exactly for how long those Grooving Sounds sustained them. Black Moon – menacing, pithy, atmospheric. 'Brothers Lyrically Acting Combined Kicking Music Out on Nations' – less so. I actually take my hat off to JVC Force's 'Justified by Virtue of Creativity For Obvious Reasons Concerning Entertainment' and the Goodie Mob's 'The Good Die Mostly Over Bullshit' just for sheer contrivance.

[60] I don't want to get too dewy-eyed about the late, great jazz musician Jimmy Smith, but it says something about how amazing he was that he built his entire career out of instrumental records recorded largely on the Hammond organ, which sold shedloads. That takes some skill. We sampled the hell out of him and we weren't alone, with many other groups including The Beastie Boys doing so.

consisted of us going, "Catchy chorus, catchy chorus, it's all about a catchy chorus". Biting, non?

At the time I was a big fan of a Queensbridge, New York rapper called Tragedy the Intelligent Hoodlum. On one brilliantly angry political track called "Arrest the President" he used the phrase "Pretty Boys Don't Survive Up North". In NY hip-hop parlance, 'up north' generally refers to prison, as that's where many of the prisons are in New York State. Tragedy was clearly discussing the likelihood of 'pretty boys' getting bummed or shanked in prison. We decided to take that in a slightly different direction. Despite not actually – in pretty much any way or to any noticeable degree at all – being the victims of the North/South divide in the UK, having been subjected to zero discrimination whatsoever, and definitely not from the UK hip-hop fraternity, we decided to make a track about how unjust all the stereotypes of the North were. Bear in mind I actually grew up in the Midlands.

This is a message to the blind
People in London have closed minds
They think up North is where the wind blows
High unemployment, broken windows[61]

---

61 Some clever readers might assume that with the phrase 'broken windows' I'm alluding to the famous 'Broken Windows' theory of crime. I'm not, but bless the couple of you that may have thought so. I didn't know about that back then. So, the first purpose of this footnote is to point out the error of ever attempting to read too much into my one-dimensional lyrics. What you see is almost always what you get. Secondly, the Broken Windows theory is of interest to the hip-hop generation in several ways. Put insultingly briefly, it posits that there's a link between things like broken windows and small petty crimes and larger crimes in general. If a window is already broken, criminals are more likely to break another one. If the windows are intact, they're more likely to be left intact. This theory was put into practice by New York mayor Rudolph Giuliani, with the belief that by targeting squeegee merchants, petty criminals, fare dodgers and subway graffiti

That used to be true, I suppose
But since then there's been overthrows"

That last line is particularly clunky, I realise. What the hell are

---

artists, they'd stop larger crimes from happening. And, if you believe that correlation is causation, it worked.

Harsh crackdowns on petty crimes coincided with a large drop in homicides and other serious crimes. But this didn't happen without 'stop and frisk', which has always, wherever it has been implemented, targeted black people disproportionately. To cut a long story short, a generation of young black people, mostly male, were criminalised, this in a country with a huge private prison industry which relies on exactly such a thing happening to safeguard its profits. With New York being the home of hip-hop, rappers didn't take kindly to Giuliani or his policies. I visited New York for the first time in 1991 when the 'clean up' had started. Years later, you could see the difference. For tourists, it was cleaner and safer, there was less harassment on the streets, fewer muggings. Times Square had been purged of its porno palaces. But something was also missing. I worked in London's Soho for 12 years and the same thing happened there – the area was tamed but simultaneously lost something of the grime, grit and sleaze that made it special in the first place.

So much of the hip-hop of the late 80's and early 90's is a reaction against the Broken Windows policing of the NYPD and no surprise. Their generation was being targeted for minor drug use, and entering a correctional system that didn't give them much chance of ever getting on in life, while cocaine use by white people on Wall Street (in fact, everywhere) received scant attention. It was anger about such things that strengthened my bond with hip-hop. Giuliani built a successful political career, one that involved talk about a tilt at the presidency, from incarcerating black people for petty crime.

Was Broken Windows effective? Most studies are immensely sceptical and say that the drop in serious crimes also happened to coincide with a 39% drop in unemployment in New York, an economic upturn and the end of the crack epidemic that ravaged black communities and fuelled crime. There was a nationwide drop in serious crimes of similar levels, often in places with no such Broken Windows policy. Critics also point out that arresting people for petty offences isn't usually a great way of getting them not to commit other crimes. Once they have a criminal record, the chances of them getting a job that would keep them out of trouble are drastically reduced. Let's just say that Broken Windows has the neat smack of something that would excite Malcolm Gladwell as a theoretical exercise but doesn't stand up to much scrutiny. Or, to echo many of my rapping heroes, 'Fuck Rudy'.

'overthrows'? But that – and the subsequent 66 lines or so that I rapped over three verses, conveys the point clearly. We – the Northerners – were not going take it from them – the Southerners – anymore. Even if we actually hadn't been taking it from them in any way, ever. I could put a gloss on this and say that I was attempting an analysis of how milk-snatcher Thatcher was cutting the North adrift through her free-market economic policies but, to be truthful, that didn't even cross my mind.[62] As was often the case, I heard a vocal sample that I liked, and forced a song into that gap.

We had decided that, because the rappers we loved always dropped in references to US TV, film, sport, food and so on, some of which we understood and some of which left us baffled, we'd do the same. "Pretty Boys" is full of our attempts to be demonstrably northern and British.

Be original, to gain credit
My dues were paid by direct debit
So like Harry Gration, Look North
Stay on course as we roll with force

Over 20 years after writing these lines, I'm glad to report that veteran BBC presenter Harry Gration is still going strong on Yorkshire's *Look North*, and sad to report he's never had me on to interview me about my amazing rap career. It's never too late, Harry.

"Get the Sell-Out Of Town" was our track about sell-outs who, as you can tell, we wanted to get the hell out of town. See what we

---

[62] It turns out our milk wasn't the only thing Thatcher had her greedy hands on. US rapper Chubb Rock, in his 1990 song about apartheid, "What's the Word?" called her "crumb-snatcher Thatcher". I don't drink milk, but if I'd known she was also after our crumbs, I would definitely have written a rap about it.

did there? We had a sample of Ice-T saying 'sell-out', and this was our opportunity to attack those terrible artists who wanted to actually have their music heard by real people and perhaps be paid a decent amount as recompense for the time they'd spent making it. Our argument does, of course, seem petty and silly with the benefit of hindsight, but we did feel a keen hatred for over-commercialised hip-hop at the time. I like to think we've grown out of it, but I know dozens of hip-hop fans from that era who are still stuck in the same mindset, all with stories to tell about their times in the hip-hop wars, like they're Vietnam veterans suffering flashbacks.

I see the situation coast to coast
The ones who boast seem to sell the most
Talkin' bout bitches, guns and ho's
...but that's not how it goes
For the PA, it must be scholarly what we say
So those with some taste will give us a replay
So cut it out I plead in this prophecy
Modern day rappers deserve a lobotomy

What strikes me most about this verse is that I'm pouring scorn on pretty much all of the hip-hop I've ever loved and listened to. Public Enemy and De La Soul are perhaps the only artists I can think of among the people I was into at the time who don't fit into this category. 'The ones who boast'? I had the cojones to condemn LL Cool J, Big Daddy Kane, Kool G Rap and countless others rappers I adored. I'm not even making sense, to be honest, because they weren't the target for my ire – I was really getting at the likes of MC Hammer and Vanilla Ice, and one thing those guys didn't make their money from was songs about bitches, guns and hoes. Still, I hope you enjoy the irony of my attempt to be 'scholarly' before I spectacularly misuse 'prophecy' two lines later.

I've just listened to the next song on the demo – "Caught In The Essence" – four times in a row. I've then perused the printed lyric booklet we produced to accompany the demo (an act of hubris, perhaps, but many of my lyrics are so unintelligible and baffling on tape that this guide would actually have come in handy for anyone trying to decipher it. Think of it as a *Cliff Notes* for gruff Northern rappers). And yet despite these labours I can't really fathom what this song was supposed to be about. There's a bit of a pop at sell-outs again, some stuff about corporate sponsorship, and then poor old MC Hammer gets it in the neck once more. I take time out to condemn 'new schoolers' who are 'coming fake', spoken with all the authority of a man who'd been involved in hip-hop for all of seven years at this point and was recording his first ever demo tape. There is a reference to Dusty Bin from game show *3, 2, 1* because, well, why not? Most jarring is the fact that Dan performs the last verse, and manages to match me for pointless meandering.

So here we go, a little mellow, but not too slow
Ulterior motive, respect not dough
Or dosh enough cash to take a wash
Buy cold Pepsis or orange squash
Buy my Timbys, nothing flimsy
Big Timberland coat, mmmm, give me

Dan has gone from condemning material greed to basically dry-humping a Timberland coat in mere seconds. But he does then get back on message with perhaps my favourite lines we ever committed to tape, a simple encapsulation of what we were trying to achieve, one of the few times where our aim – to be down to earth rappers from the North but not to be seen to be trying too hard about it – found an artistic output that captured that essence.

No need to be a rap star
Just collect respect and say cheers, ta

It's not much – and it irks me somewhat that it was delivered not by me but by the 'back-up' rapper – but it has a certain charm that still makes me smile when I listen to or think about it.

What lacked that charm completely was another song on the original version of our demo, before we tweaked it and re-recorded it, adding a couple of tracks and polishing others. This song, "The Steppages of History", was such a heavy-handed attempt to be clever and political that I honestly can't bring myself to write much about it or quote any of the lyrics without a therapist present. It was 6th form politics of the worst kind, with me basically apologising for lots of historical calamities and problems that were, of course, nothing to do with me.[63] Listening to it is cringingly, painfully embarrassing. In an essay about a terrible piece of science fiction writing that the otherwise brilliant John Updike produced near the end of his career, David Foster Wallace writes about something that, "ends up being embarrassing in the special way something

[63] Occasionally our government will formally apologise for something terrible it did or didn't do in history – slavery, genocide, overlooking historical abuse, the existence of Noel Edmonds – and that is very right and proper for it do so, as elected representatives of the people, expressing our collective culpability and shame. It's less right and proper and totally disproportionate for a random 16-year-old boy to do so, when he should in fact be apologising to his mum for not making his bed and calling his sister a 'twat'.

pretentious is embarrassing when it's also wrong".[64] That encapsulates perfectly how I feel about this.

When I think back on the awful moments in life that I wish I could change – from things as trivial as jokes delivered to a group of people that died on their arse, those I offended when in my cups, misreading sexual moments as a teenager, right the way up to the time I nearly drowned my non-swimming mum by accident on holiday – I think making this song was the worst. It is a snapshot of a naivety it pains me to think I ever had. The only thing positive to come out of this was that Dan also managed to produce one of his worst tracks ever to accompany it, so deleting it from the demo, if not entirely from history (ideally I'd like to delete all memory of it, and am hoping for some kind of *Eternal Sunshine of the Spotless Mind* type scenario in the near future where I can make that happen. I'd probably also delete that time I shat myself right down to the socks on the school bus when I was 15, but as I've now written it down in this book, I'll have to get all the copies of this burnt as well), was a fait accompli.

That naivety also found outlet in a typed sheet that accompanied the first, dreadful draft of the demo. On it we break down our names in their full acronymic glory, and provide the kind of information we must have thought someone wanted to know.

The Brief:
Recorded live at Green Lodge (Dan's bedroom)
Produced by the Street Pilgrims aka the P.A. Posse
Overseen by the founders of rap. Don't sleep on the old school.

---

[64] *Consider The Lobster: Essays and Arguments* by David Foster Wallace (Abacus, 2007)

The P.A. History:
The Prehistoric Ages have been together for 14 months. Before this Greenpeace and Countdown had been DJ's for several years, while Scam rapped for various crews [you, the reader, are already aware we're being economical with the truth here]. We hooked up through a concept – The P.A. – this means moving back in time metaphorically to a time of peace, no racism, no sexism. The manifesto has been set, follow or be left in a future that has no future. Ecologise, be wise, harmonise, strengthen ties, rationalise, civilise... and don't sell-out.

A little bit of me dies typing that out again, curiously mixed with a little bit of pride that we cared so much about what we did and what we were trying to mean. It mattered to us that we weren't just making beats and rhymes, even if it mattered to nobody else. The Prehistoric Ages concept was dead in the water from the start, and here you can see why – what the hell era is this with peace, no racism and sexism? To be honest, it must have been some time before the first fish left the sea and set up shop on the land. In our defence, we're not the only rappers to not think things through, and it's clear that we meant well. This stuff also makes me very happy that we now live in an era of hip-hop when artists don't feel it's necessary to get the typewriter out and cobble together a 'manifesto'. Although Kanye West is probably typing one right now.

There is no life in music as minutely examined as that of the rapper, by the rapper – and we followed our heroes by attempting to chronicle just about everything we ever did by turning it into songs. Our enjoyable shopping and bonding trips in Countdown's Ford Fiesta found their theme tune in "A Day Trip in the PA Craft". It's a silly song, inspired perhaps by A Tribe Called Quest's "I Left My Wallet in El Segundo", although it's not like we had any kind of narrative to propel the track. Instead, we get three simple, pointless, fun verses about going shopping in Manchester and other Northern destinations.

Hop in the craft and go to Wetherby
Explore the world no matter what the weather be
Tag up bridges and take the pictures
Countdown graffitis on many fixtures

We take time out to namecheck various record and clothes shops, from Afflecks Palace to Powercuts, Crash Records to Trax, all as part of the same project that inspired "Pretty Boys Don't Survive Up North" – we wanted to capture our world, no matter how small and parochial it was, in music.

So we take a trip to the side of the sea
Blackpool, Morecambe and Filey
The beach ain't played so take a bucket and spade
The rain comes down, hit the arcade
Money in slots, 10ps we got
Buy my gal a stick of Blackpool rock
Sugary sweet to rot her dentures
Return to Leeds after funky adventures

If we'd managed to keep up this kind of jaunty tone for our entire career, we might have had something. Other groups from Britain managed this, such as Bristol's Parlour Talk. I might not be a big fan of most British hip-hop, but I can see and appreciate that other groups had similar ideas – and often executed them better. The same New York hip-hop had inspired them, but what were kids in the South West or North of England going to say about racial politics in

Harlem? Unfortunately, that's not the kind of group we were at this stage. I was still convinced that the only way we were going to be taken seriously was to deliver deep political content. So, after our pleasurable little trip to the seaside, we get back to the stodge of "Basic Beliefs".

The bureaucratic pages
Are incinerated by the Prehistoric Ages
'Cos in 91 see the government rules
Treating you and I like fools
As the seconds tick by to Armageddon
King Scam gets his thinking head on
And addresses those with open minds
As I speak critically about mankind

Bloody hell. Much of this song makes we feel the same way as "The Steppages of History", but at least Dan managed to find a nice Jimmy Smith sample to enliven matters. Despite being a teenager, I come over in this song as a middle-aged Disgusted of Tunbridge Wells, or a dismal leader writer for the *Daily Mail* or *Telegraph*. I have a go at people for watching TV instead of doing something with their lives (when all I ever do is watch TV these days), I have a go at skyscrapers (no idea why), I have a go at...

Violence, racism and ignorance
Prejudice, sexism and beligerence

Good god, who wants to listen to that? The strange thing is, I didn't really write much of this sort of stuff before I met Dan and Martin. This Prehistoric Ages/Basic Beliefs thing must have come out of conversations we had, especially as those two had the P.A. Posse thing in mind before I even joined up. And yet I can't remember a single political discussion between the three of us, ever. I'm no firebrand, as you can tell, but I can't think of two less political people than Greenpeace and Countdown.

We were more into the kind of larks captured on "Day Trip in the PA Craft". We talked almost exclusively about hip-hop records and girls. I'd always been a brag rapper, they were producers and DJ's, and yet when we got together, stilted inconsistent diatribes were the non-sexy result. I'm aware that some of this seriousness came from me – as I said, I thought we needed to be taken seriously while retaining some of our sense of humour. I actually say that on this track...

The mental craft is the PA ship
Look at the serious side of life, but on the comical tip

But the comedy kind of dies once each track starts and I start joining together random thoughts about the end of the world, people reading crap books, pollution and, in one bizarre couplet, the concept of making music with electric implements. This on a track recorded, as our typed information sheet helpfully informs the listener, with a 'Cheetah Sampler/ Atari ST sampling program and sequencer, one turntable, Gemini Scratchmaster Mixer, one borrowed mic, recorded on a battered tape deck'. With all that, we were hardly banging bones together in a cave.

The demo ends with "Street Pilgrims". It's well produced, mercifully brief (just two verses – clearly all the righting of the world's wrongs I'd done on the other tracks had exhausted me mentally) and once again full of contradictions that might suggest I was making it all up as I went along. At one point I'm talking about punching someone in the mouth and fucking up their teeth. I then retract this and say I only hit with a 'mental fist', and then at the end I talk about beating up a fascist, making it very clear that it wasn't with a mental fist but with a flesh and blood one. This really is idle talk, but encapsulates the confused thinking that suffuses this entire demo tape.[65]

Not that confused thinking in any way undermines great music and great art. It can be an essential part of it. My favourite Marvin Gaye album is *Here, My Dear*, famously an album he recorded as part of his divorce settlement with Anna Gordy, daughter of Motown boss Berry. Initially Gaye intended to toss off a sub-par album, as he resented the fact that Gordy would end up with the proceeds from it. But it took on a life of its own, and became a compelling exploration of a crumbling marriage, all wrapped up with some stunning production and beautiful songs from the sweetest voice in the history of recorded music (other opinions – wrong ones – are available).

Gaye would sit in divorce court humming melodies to himself and then proceed to the studio to lay them down. This immediacy and the emotional honesty are what make *Here, My Dear* so incredible and rich an album, but it's also because Gaye's mind is all over the place. He'll move from tender evocations of their love in its infancy to complaining about why he has to pay attorney's fees within moments. This kind of confused thinking takes the album to a new level – it's a masterpiece because it veered so off-script, and captured

---

[65] The only punches I've ever thrown as an adult were at a moronic former colleague who broke my glasses, threw wine over a girl and attacked a friend, all in the space of two minutes. And I once squared up to the actor Woody Harrelson in a Soho pub, but that's a story for another time (suffice to say I find it difficult to watch and enjoy anything he's in now, as I have first-hand experience of him being a bit of a prick and calling the same girl who had wine thrown over her by the other bloke 'a cunt'. *True Detective* was great though, as hard as it is for me to write those words)

something almost unknowably real about life and love. The confused thinking you'll find on our demo isn't this – it's just three young blokes scratching around for something to say and, not finding anything interesting or new, saying it anyway.[66] Still, at least by writing the preceding paragraphs I have succeeded in having my first ever proper rap demo discussed in the same passage as an indelible soul classic. So that's something, even if I had to do it myself.

66 At the time of writing, none of the original P.A Posse have gone on to get divorced. However, in a legally watertight mutual pact, we've agreed that should the unthinkable happen and we cast aside our marital vows, our spouses are welcome to the proceeds of our first demo in its entirety.

Thirteen
Please Listen to My Demo

Our first demo – re-recorded, re-edited and with the track that dare not speak its name excised from the running order – was now in our hands. It was accompanied by, first, its typed sheet and then by a full deluxe lyric booklet (which thanked Dan's mum, whose house it was entirely recorded in, with a credit for 'Power supplied by: 'Turn that shit off' Nagging Mother), the front cover of which was a nightmarish collection of floating heads.[67] It had been good practice, it had let the three of us get to know each other better, and to discover our strengths (few) and weaknesses (many). We'd developed a working relationship. But at

---

[67] A Tribe Called Quest gathered lots of their favourite hip-hop peers and heroes to don headphones and be photographed for the iconic cover of their classic 1993 album *Midnight Marauders*. They had the Beastie Boys, Afrika Bambaataa, Grandmaster Flash, P-Diddy (then simply Sean 'Puffy' Combs) and more. Most esteemed rap journals and websites have failed to accord us our due for beating them to it by a full two years, although they are excused as I imagine precisely zero esteemed rap journals or websites have ever even seen our demo booklet. In an early piece of design genius, the heads of Countdown, Greenpeace and myself float at the top of the A5 page, while below are the heads of some our peers and heroes: Harry Gration, Terry Wogan, Roy Walker from *Catchphrase*, Dawn French, Anneka Rice, Lenny Henry, Edwina Currie, Russ Abbot, Woody Allen, Cary Grant and, er Gloria Hunniford. Okay, they're not wearing headphones, we don't like some of them and we probably just cut their pictures out of *Radio Times*, but we were still there first.

the end of the day we were left with a demo that sounded like it was recorded by three amateurs in a bedroom while the woman who owned the house slammed doors and cupboards deliberately loudly downstairs. And not three gifted amateurs, either.

Yet we were still prepared to send this demo out into the world – why else would we produce that lavish photocopied and stapled booklet? And so I dug out all my UK hip-hop records, copied down the label names and addresses from the back, and sent our work out there into the world.

Amateur musicians the world over will be familiar with the feelings of excitement, anticipation, impatience and trepidation that accompany sending off your demo. Okay, things are done differently now – there aren't so many cassettes doing the Royal Mail rounds these days – but whether you're posting a CD or a memory stick, uploading stuff to YouTube or emailing over a dropbox link full of MP3s for the intended recipient to download, the emotions are the same. I'm not going to pretend that the old way was better, it was just how it was done then. The stacks of post that the record company intern would have laboriously opened have merely been replaced by stacks of emails and tweets for them to sift through. What the artist feels doesn't really vary, even if degrees of confidence in your ability and the finished product vary widely. Obviously you're hoping for success, but bracing yourself for failure. You try to inure yourself to the bruise to your ego that will come if you're ignored, you steel yourself for the criticism that may come your way if you're lucky enough to get any feedback. And even for the worst pessimist there's a thought, dancing away like a tiny, flickering flame at the back of the brain, that this track, this demo, could be the one that gets you signed. The one that opens up a world of artistic validation or untold riches or whatever it is that you dream of.

The reality is often never as black or white. In truth, all music sent on spec to labels or people you admire exists along an infinite curve with infinite gradations of success and failure. You're not just filed into yes or no, your music is somewhere – anywhere – on the spectrum between absolute defeat and total triumph. Indifference, hatred, needs more work, unpolished, unpolishable, we should sign these, we can't sign these, no-one will sign these, love the music hate the rapper, love the rapper hate the music, hate the rapper and the music but love the booklet they've thoughtfully sent us. All this and more, multiplied by the endless variations and prejudices of the people who listen to it. It's a wonder anybody ever gets signed, noticed or championed, but that flicker keeps us hoping.

At this point you might expect that we wouldn't hear back from anyone. That the response would be deafening in its silence. But not so. I'd anticipated that myself, but still rushed to meet the post's thud on the doormat every day with the keen expectation of the child on its birthday. While a few of the independent labels that we thought were our bankers didn't even bother to reply – that means you, Kold Sweat – plenty of others did. There was a polite refusal from East West Records, a similar one from Music of Life.[68] A couple of others said something along the lines of, "Thanks for thinking of us, but this just isn't right for us at this time" (in other words, 'This would never be right for us at any time ever, from the time the first mammals developed rudimentary hearing cells through to the inevitable fiery ending of mankind. Why did you even think of us, for fuck's sake?'). But one label did show some interest.

---

[68] I still have this rejection letter. I hoped one day to be able to shove it in their face, to jump on their desks and laugh maniacally at how wrong they were to turn down the PA Posse, but I don't think they're at that address any more. Also, they haven't existed for two decades. And I don't have anything to shove in their face anyway.

Gee Street records was founded in London by Jon Baker in the late 80's, and had a couple of notable British rap groups on their books – Outlaw Posse and Stereo MC's. The latter were interesting because they were three white guys, one of whom looked like Catweazle. We felt convinced this was a label worth approaching – they evidently didn't care if you were white and they weren't that bothered about looks. We got a letter from Gee Street asking us to give them a call, to discuss our demo.

We were thrilled. It was a foot in the door. This was still before the days of mass mobile phone ownership, and because all three of us wanted to be in on this conversation (although Dan led discussions as he was the oldest and was a business student, according to *Mizz* magazine) we made several phone calls to Gee Street crammed into a phone box. I'm not sure why we weren't calling from one of our houses, but I'm sure it was something to do with parents slamming doors deliberately loudly or the worry that they'd barge in at the wrong time to ask if we wanted sugar in our tea just as we were discussing per diems and merchandise shares with a label head honcho.

It turned out they liked our demo and saw some promise in it. They'd hit upon a wheeze where they wanted to release a bunch of double-header records, with different artists on each side, to showcase underground hip-hop from around the country. Okay, we weren't that delighted that we'd have to share our spotlight with someone else, but it was still a start. It's not like the other labels were in a bidding war for us, and all we really wanted was to be on vinyl. But then came the kicker. They wanted our track or tracks to be produced by the Stereo MC's.

With hindsight, this was a glorious opportunity, even if it was a chimerical one made down a phone line that almost certainly wouldn't have happened even if we'd said yes. But our own stubbornness prevented this idea from even getting so far as to be still-born. We flatly refused. Yep, this pretty terrible rap group from Leeds who'd just recorded their first demo – a demo with which you are now painfully familiar (especially if you've navigated your way to the online audio samples of it that I've provided to accompany this book) – was not willing to play ball with the only label with the generosity to offer us an in to the world we longed to be part of. And why? Because we wanted to produce all our own material.

Let's pause for a second to consider this. How much of the great music we've enjoyed, danced to and taken to our hearts would we have to forfeit if artists only produced their own material? For starters, the great producers – from Phil Spector to Quincy Jones – would be stuck being solo artists rather than crafting classics for The Crystals and Michael Jackson. Would Johnny Cash have enjoyed a career renaissance without Rick Rubin to lead him to "Hurt"? In hip-hop, my favourite record label was Cold Chillin', where Marley Marl initially produced each and every artist on the label, to wondrous effect. Nas, a brilliant rapper, has only produced one bona fide classic album, 1994's *Illmatic*, largely because he employed producers such as Pete Rock, DJ Premier and Large Professor who were all at the top of their game. His subsequent career has seen him employ such a tin ear for good production that the mind boggles at what rubbish he'd generate if left to his own devices. The case for using other people to produce your music – especially when you're not particularly well known – seems watertight.

But still we said no. Part of this is because we weren't fans of the Stereo MC's. We weren't fans of them at the time of our demo and we definitely weren't fans when their next album, 1992's much dancier *Connected*, became a worldwide smash. But it was also out of loyalty to our own producer, Greenpeace. We'd formed a group and we all had clearly defined roles. Countdown was the DJ, I was the rapper, Dan was the producer. If we let somebody else come in and make the music, what does that say about Dan? Where does it put him? As enjoyable as many of his rapping contributions were, it wasn't his first passion. He was much happier feeding samples into the computer and manipulating them, playing us new loops every week, many of which we'd then turn into songs. Front men aren't always the core of the group, and I felt this way about the P.A. Posse, most of the time. Dan was the core member. We couldn't nudge him away from the heart of the controls just to put out a one-sided 12" produced by a group we didn't even like.

Of course, in retrospect it's laughable. We were like the guys from the hauntingly on point BBC sitcom *People Just Do Nothing.* Grindah and Beats are very much the Scam and Greenpeace of garage music, unable to see past their own mythical brilliance. The Comic Relief special where they pour scorn on Ed Sheeran – or Ed Shearer, as they call him – when given studio time with the global star, immediately gave me echoes of our arrogance in the face of the Stereo MC's.

I don't think money was on the table, and we never met the label representative in person, but the idea was a non-starter after we'd been so intractable on the phone. I think it was anyway. It wasn't a project that Gee Street went ahead with, even without us. Buoyed by the success of Stereo MC's and PM Dawn in 1992 and 1993, they weren't really the kind of label that was going to experiment with marginal hip-hop, especially since they'd been swallowed up by Island Records. For the A&R man concerned, it was probably a conversation about a vague concept that might one day have been developed into an idea. For us it was an opportunity to get into the record industry, but at the expense of what made us the Prehistoric Ages. The experience solidified us a trio. Hell, we even wrote a song about it that would feature on our next project. And now we were determined that if we weren't going to be signed by a snooty, short-sighted London label, we'd do what many of our peers were doing, and put the record out ourselves.

Fourteen
Enta Da Stage

In the middle of all this, we continued to make friends on the small but solid local scene. We knew both Paul and Tommy from Breaking The Illusion, although for some reason they didn't feel inclined to invite us to participate in any of the independent EP's they released at the time. History has forgiven them. They did invite another Leeds group called Braintax, made up of Joe and Aaron. We thought they were actually quite good – after they split up, Joe went on to have a decent, well-reviewed career as Braintax on his own, running the Low Life label into the bargain – but we never admitted as much, because of the unavoidable fact that Joe was a massive bell-end. Any overtures of friendship we ever made were rejected by this charmless man, and we even once spent an awkward afternoon in a bedroom studio trying to collaborate with them, fruitless and frustrating as it was.

I couldn't bear Joe from then on but Dan, who is more patient and tolerant than me, ignored the snub and throughout his career generously promoted the music of Braintax whenever he had an opportunity to, whether as a journalist or as a radio DJ. He was rewarded when Joe appeared on a 1998 album by the Scottish rapper

Freestyle Master on which his first verse was a thinly-veiled personal attack on Dan. As I say, a bell-end.

Much nicer were New Flesh 4 Old, a group we'd met from York with a line-up in constant flux. At the centre was Part 2, known to his mum as Keith, who was a graffiti artist of some renown and no little skill. He'd passed us some bedroom demos we liked immensely. Keith was occasionally a bingo-caller, and had sampled a night out for a track called "Back to the Bingo Hall" – an indicator that we were looking in similar directions when it came to exploring our backgrounds through our music. He was joined by Ashley, aka The Horny Baker and Boyd aka Ten-4, whose role was and always would be unclear.[69] But, as Bez from The Happy Mondays has proven, you don't need to be an actual functioning member of a group to somehow be an essential part of it. They were just starting to get a night off the ground in York called "No Sell Out" – they truly were kindred spirits. They'd spoken to Breaking The Illusion, who were booked to play, but did the P.A. Posse want to perform as well? We most certainly did.

Our first live show wasn't quite the small scale success that the later one in the prologue was. In fact, it was a disaster. I spent the days in the run up to it practising, practising and practising. And then practising some more. This wasn't the school talent show – it would be in front of a hardened hip-hop crowd, and they were notoriously hard to please. Unless you were a major A-list act, hip-hop crowds would usually give you incredibly short shrift. Even if they loved you and had bought your single, they wouldn't cheer or jump or dance.

[69] I asked Ashley – now a very successful entrepreneur behind some of the best drinking and eating places in Leeds – how he arrived at that name and if he'd had any others: "That was my one and only nom de plume. Keith (Part 2) called me it because I was a pervert at college."

They'd just stand there and perhaps nod their head. This was even worse if you were a British act. In most cases they wouldn't arrive until after you'd finished, and if they did they wouldn't leave the bar to see you.

I've heard the tales of bottles of piss being thrown at punk acts, I've seen a torrent of coins fly towards the stage when all-white rap group Young Black Teenagers took the stage at Docklands Arena. But the indifference of many hip-hop fans to artists performing on stage can be much more cutting. You can run through your repertoire of fantastic songs with a brilliant sound system to a decent-sized crowd and you wouldn't even hear the sound of one hand clapping. The more you try to engage with the crowd or, worst of all, chide them for their lack of engagement, the worse it gets. Things are much better now. Venues wised up and started employing hypemen to support domestic acts.[70] Fans became less concerned with maintaining a veneer of cool and remembered they were at a music event.

[70] Hypemen come in many different shapes and sizes. Many rappers bring their own with them – usually an untalented member of the crew or often a distant relative who needs gainful employ. Said person will patrol the stage with the rapper, chiming in on the big punchlines, filling silences between tracks by asking people to 'make some motherfucking noise' and leading various call-and-response segments. They'll also walk about the stage handing out water to the important people, and reach repeatedly in the crowd to clap hands with those members of the paying audience who wish to boast that they've touched the third cousin of Busta Rhymes or whoever. In common with every other rapper/hypeman in history, they'll also have a pop at the soundman, whether warranted or not, and will occasionally double up as a weed carrier (see Chapter 3). Other venues will just have a general hypeman, who's a bit akin to a boxing announcer, their job being to whip people up into a noisy frenzy just before the arrival of the main act, who they are not actually related to in a complicated way. These are often local DJ's or minor hip-hop names and, unless the act they're whipping us up for is so keenly anticipated that we can't help ourselves, these people are usually on a hiding to nothing.

At least we weren't playing a real gig. This was a 'jam'. The people coming knew there'd be just local acts on, plus a DJ and a bar in the corner. They weren't expecting NWA. But it was still important for us to get it right, to nail our first performance. Countdown was going to man the decks, although they weren't very good and wouldn't stand up to his vigorous scratching style. As Greenpeace couldn't 'produce' live, he was going to join me on the mic, so we chose a couple of tracks where we alternated verses rather than ones where I blathered on for five minutes straight about some politics that I'd failed to understand properly. We'd be on early but the York hip-hop scene had a pretty lively reputation, so there should be a decent turn-out.

As it turned out, they didn't turn out. Perhaps crumpets were half price at Betty's Tea Rooms or maybe the bloody Vikings had come back, but the place was barren. I hesitate to say it was one man and his dog, because if it was the bouncers hadn't let the dog in. We were disappointed, but it turned out to be for the best. Our rectal muscles a-flutter with nerves, we took the stage (i.e. the floor) and launched into our first song.

Listening back to the tape is not an enjoyable experience, but in the interests of diligence I just have. I don't even know what song we were trying to perform. We don't use any of our own beats, and it's not something we ever did a demo of or finished, which makes me think it was one of the first songs we ever tried to write. That might explain why Dan is first to rap on it, as we probably put it together before I'd asserted myself as the group's main rapper. It was hard to tell how it was going down because it was hard to tell if there was actually anyone there, such was the subterranean level of lighting. The sound was dreadful, but good enough so I could hear my own first verse, which I managed to get out there without cocking up. I think I lacked something in stagecraft and presence, but after all it was my very first go, and I was pretty much interacting with the wall ten metres ahead of me. At the very least, this was good practice, and at least New Flesh and B.T.I. would see that we were professional and polished.

All of which thoughts, swimming through my nervous head, vanished when Countdown's chorus full of scratching finished and Dan launched into his verse. I will give him a right to reply – it's only fair – but, fuck me, he was woeful. I'd introduced him on the mic as a DJ who raps, but on this night he did neither. Whether it was nerves, incompetence or the almost complete lack of a crowd I'm not sure, but he lost his flow by the second line of his verse. With a feedback heavy sound system in a downstairs room, it was hard to then get back on track. Dan didn't bother to try. Rather than skip the lines he couldn't remember and move on to some he did, he decided to freestyle. He was no freestyler. I was the P.A. Posse's lead rapper and I was no freestyler. There aren't that many rappers who are actually good freestylers.[71]

---

[71] In a literal sense, freestyling is when rappers improvise lyrics in real time, Throw on a beat, give them a microphone, and they're supposed to make it up as they go along. In reality, this is just as difficult as it sounds and rarely entertaining as a result. Most people who give it a go – and I include some excellent, world class rappers in this – just can't do it. They mumble, they're repetitive, it's hard to think of rhymes so you use things that nearly rhyme or repeat yourself a lot. So, over time 'freestyling' evolved into performing some lyrics you'd already written, or well-known ones from a song, but a capella or over the beat from another person or group's song. Rappers would appear on radio stations, the hosts would throw on the instrumental of a popular record and you'd do something to that, but rarely was it improvised on the spot. And if it was, you could definitely see the joins.

So, this throws up a minor split. On the one side, you've got the purists who say you can't call it freestyling if you're 'kicking a written', and on the other hand you have the realists (of which I'm one) who doff their cap at the rare rapper who can make freestyle into something entertaining but, actually, we'd rather hear some nicely written lyrics any day of the week. Artists have been signed to record deals off the back of a particularly notable or quotable freestyle on a mixtape.

Freestyle can occasionally work in the live arena. A US rapper called Supernatural had a negligible recording career, but toured for years on the back of a knack for turning freestyle into entertainment. He'd stand in the middle of a crowd, microphone in hand, and ask the crowd for cues to rap about. You could hand him anything in your pockets, and he'd instantly rhyme about it, in the manner of *Whose Line Is It Anyway?* It's a good trick, but yet it does seem merely a trick rather than genius. He'd have lyrical placeholders, phrases or words he'd repeat that would delay the punchline until he'd thought of it, gimmicks that gave the brain space to work. But it was still entertaining, seat-of-the-pants stuff. He also did impressions of more famous rappers, another reason why he was a better live prospect than when captured in the studio.

The nearest you can get to genuine freestyling is to attend a rap battle. But again, there are degrees of freestyling on display at these. These are normally run on a knockout basis, and judged on how well the crowd responds. You face off against another rapper, do your material, then he does his, then you go again. It's in the responses that you can see how freestyle can actually work, rappers rebutting their opponents mere seconds after they've heard what's been said. It's like debating, but better, because it has to rhyme. But even then there are seams and stitches, lines that have been par-baked but are finished off in the club with the addition of the opponent's name. Nearly all live rap battle material is pre-written, it's just tweaked in the heat of the moment to be made more specific. Also, most live rap battles are awful. For starters, they often eschew music altogether, at which point it just becomes two people in a room trading punchlines at the expense of each other, which might as well be exchanged in waspish correspondence. Put a beat in the room and most contemporary rap battlers would be lost. They like the space that not having music affords them to think of something new, or to pause for applause.

My friend Rob Pursey – a man whose ridiculously broad musical knowledge and passion I remain in constant awe of – runs a very successful night in London (and beyond) called Hip-Hop Karaoke. I thought I'd canvass his views on freestyling because a) occasionally he'll get a participant wanting to get on the microphone and act as if all the A & R's of all the record labels of the world are present and burst into freestyle, thus freestyling is banned at HHK and b) he knows shitloads about hip-hop.

"Freestyling is definitely a fundamental aspect of hip-hop," says Rob, "and we have to be thankful for it playing a part in getting some of our favourite MC's record deals, which then led to some of their classic recordings. Over the years, however, freestyling has become a bit of an unnecessary and at times, disheartening feature of all rap shows, interviews etc. and in only a very few cases enhances your opinion and feelings towards an artist. In a worse sense it's become the new 'playing "Wonderwall" on the guitar' in social situations and again rarely (if ever) makes you say – "get that man a deal!" The main reason we banned all freestyling at Hip Hop Karaoke is obviously mainly because it wouldn't be true

When you've got a pretty below average hip-hop group performing, and one of them cocks up the rapping, and rapping isn't even the thing he's best at, then you're not really nailing the show. I am reluctant in this memoir to paint myself too kindly in relation to my fellow group members – I was usually the weakest link in the group – but I did the only thing I could do. I realised the song wasn't salvageable, that Dan was all at sea, so I took charge. We had two more tracks to do. One was a solo one, one was another with me and Dan. It had become apparent that Dan was in a dark place.[72] Bless

---

karaoke if not, and to distinguish the event from the hundreds of open-mic nights that are available in London and beyond. However, more crucially so that it follows the tradition of celebrating the recorded works of the artists, rather than a chance for a bit of personal indulgence." Amen to that.

[72] In the interests of balance and (his) self-justification, I gave the much-maligned Greenpeace the B.O.M.B. the right to reply to my account of events: "My memory is inferior to Andrew's so any recollections I have of that night are vague at best. The four things I do clearly remember are firstly forgetting my lyrics quite early into our set. That much is true. I can't say I was nervous, to this day I'm not fazed by large crowds or public speaking, two things that aspects of my subsequent career have called for. Unlike Andrew, I didn't practice at all, but relied on an inherent confidence that utterly failed me. At the time I considered myself to be an average rapper when in the comfort of my home studio. OK, more like bedroom.

The second thing I remember is that when Andrew said I tried to 'freestyle', what I remember doing was an impromptu call and response. Again, incompetently delivered. What I yelled down the mic was "Go York, Go York, Go York" with no sense of timing whatsoever. So rather than saying it in time with our backing track, I delivered it double time, so fast that although I knew what I was saying, it was indecipherable to the human ear. I thought it was funny, Andrew was mortified.

My third recollection was related to my call and response. Wiz from Breaking The Illusion later said it sounded like I was talking Hebrew. Now this could have been a combination of my bad memory and paranoia which conjured this up in my mind over time, but I'm pretty sure he said that. Only he will be able to confirm it. I hasten to add that some years later he chinned me in front of a crowd of lads outside a The Roots concert in Manchester. It's a shame, because I really liked Wiz. We've not really spoken since. My last memory was the pungent smell of aerosol fumes from the graffiti art that was being done while the show was on. In an

him, but I wasn't ready to trust him with another verse. So we launched into a solo track, the same high-speed verse with which I'd impressed Dan and Martin in the latter's bedroom that Sunday. I won't say it went down well – how would I have known in this vacuum? – but at the very least it rescued the situation. It was a track from early 1991 that we never recorded called "Swift with the Gift", and it was pure braggadocio.

Dealing dope, but not a junkie
Scam the Solo rhymes 'cos this tune is too funky
Think like ya enemy, one step ahead
My pockets get fat but not overfed
I'm an artist, but not on paper
If rhymes were constructions mine are skyscrapers
Meaning, they tower above you
If you are down for peace then I love you
...but you're not my Valentine
Get out the way of the mic, this battle's mine
...metaphorically speaking
Switch up the mic while the amp is peaking
Loosely termed this is a lyrical onslaught
Many MC's just rhyme with no thought
Yeah, it's time for a hip-hop uplift
I get swift with the gift

For 90 seconds it sounded as if the man with the microphone in his hand knew vaguely what he was doing with it. I got a rush of adrenaline as it became clear, somewhere two thirds of the way into

---

enclosed space, that wreaks havoc with your vocal chords and so ultimately I blame that for my dreadful performance."

this somewhat overlong verse, that I wasn't going to make a complete tit of myself (and if I did, I'd be a somewhat smaller tit than Dan currently was), and that this live rap thing was actually bloody exciting once you got into it. It goes without saying, however, that we didn't perform a third song. At just over six minutes, our first exhilarating but calamitous performance was over. You're welcome, York.

electric lighting station
46 kensington court
london w8 5dp
telephone 071 938 2181
telex 261425
facsimile 071 937 6645

18/12

Dear Andy

Many thanks for sending us your demo. Contrary to the perennial rumour, every demo that gets sent to record companies does in fact get listened to. Well in our case anyway.

We are returning your demo to you because, despite the obvious time and effort you have put into it, it still hasn't excited us enough to want to pursue any further dealings.

Don't by any means give up on us though. If in the future you get another demo together please let us have a listen to it.

Regards

Hannah Holder
P.P. Charlie Pinder

Fifteen
Girls I Got 'em Locked

While we pursued our dreams of rap stardom at the weekend, at other times we aspired to radio fame. As mentioned before, Martin and Dan had previous when it came to pirate radio, and a new station in Leeds called Dream FM tapped Dan up to do a hip-hop show. Dan would, later in life, go on to co-host a professional rap show on XFM with Zane Lowe, before subsequently hosting it outright. It would broadcast from state of the art studios in London's glamorous Leicester Square and would have international guests such as Eminem and Jay-Z. Dream FM, by way of contrast, broadcast from a selection of shonky sheds and cold-water flats that looked like they'd be ideal locations for shooting up heroin, and the guests were as high profile as me, Horny Baker and our new mate Barrie.

Dan had met Barrie in Leeds – in a record shop, as you do – and as the latter was an aspiring rapper, he came into the fold. Not as a member of the P.A. Posse – you don't tamper with a winning formula – but as a solo artist that Dan was going to produce some tracks for. Our little posse was growing and Barrie would go on to deliver a guest verse on our most fondly remembered track. Remembered by the people who performed on it, that is, because no-one else ever heard it. Barrie's rapping name was S.A.D.E., and in the acronymic way of all things hip-hop, this stood for Skilfully Applying Distinguished English.

The Dream FM studio moved about quite a bit, to try and stay one step ahead of raids.[73] I remember a few of them, outhouses and anonymous brick buildings on the outskirts of Leeds, usually without heating. We'd turn up mob-handed, and Dan would try to maintain an air of professionalism at the helm while we smoked, drank and arsed around in the background. I never had a good voice for radio (but the perfect face for it – boom boom), but we'd still chime in from time to time, announcing songs, giving out the phone number for requests, delivering shout-outs to mates and the odd person who phoned up. It was usually the same two people every week.

---

[73] Pirate radio is, of course, an enduring part of British culture and one that has in no way been permanently besmirched by the awful film *The Boat That Rocked*. The pirate radio I used to listen to wasn't transmitted from boats, but usually from tower blocks in the North, and there were also dozens of pirate broadcasters in London and around the nation. They operated outside of the law. We can have a debate about how they don't pay performing rights for the music they play, but I'd argue that artists played on pirate stations receive more from the exposure they get anyway – I'd buy records all the time based on pirate listens.

The broadcasts were usually so crackly that a tape recording of it was no replacement for the real thing. They provided something that mainstream stations didn't provide (there's anecdotal evidence that Radio Caroline's popularity forced the BBC to restructure into multiple channels) and they gave an outlet to lots of aspiring DJ's. With only the occasional John Peel song or a BBC hour of hip-hop now and then, the opportunity to turn on the radio and hear several hours of a day of the music I loved was too good to resist. Lots of household DJ names started out as pirates, cutting their teeth while dodging the Department for Trade and Industry, which was forever cracking down (a job OFCOM do now) on them. Dan got caught up in a raid once or twice and had his equipment confiscated. It didn't put him off though. Many pirates went legit as the regulatory authorities eased up in the 80's and 90's, but I'm happy to say there are still pirates galore feeding the needs of people who can't find what they want on mainstream stations.

Best of all were the 'freestyle' sessions. After 90 minutes of music, we'd throw on some instrumentals and then kick some of our favourite rhymes. Often they'd be tried and tested verses from our demos, but sometimes, because I was writing so many lyrics, I'd have prepared a new one and I'd unveil it, as would Horny Baker or Countdown, who was now rapping more and more. Very occasionally it would turn into a genuine freestyle session in the truest sense of the word, where we'd all wing it. Of all the tapes that survived from that era, these are the ones I cringe at most. The shows themselves and the written raps? A decent listen, good fun, they capture the era perfectly. The pure freestyles? They're terrible, they're desperate. God only knows how many people turned off during them. People of Leeds, we apologise. Although it does serve you right for supporting Leeds United.

Perhaps the best spell at Dream FM was later, when we weren't all so keen to show off on the microphone. At this stage, the station, which had been doing well – selling adverts and even launching a range of mixtapes showcasing their DJ's (Dan did one) – was based in a foul flat in Leeds' Little London area. It looked like one of those soon-to-be-condemned T. Dan Smith ones that Mary and Tosker lived in in *Our Friends in the North.*[74] We had a graveyard slot, from 2-5AM, often on a Sunday night. Mondays were a bit of a washout for us all. But it was fun. Dan's brother Robert would join us, and we'd smoke weed, drink a few beers and have a giggle while we played hip-hop, funk, jazz and soul to night owls across the county.

---

[74] I'm not exactly breaking new ground by telling you what a wonderful drama the BBC's *Our Friends in the North* was (and I realise I'm being about as topical as someone recommending *I, Claudius* or the Renaissance), although it was fatally undermined by the fact that it covered a generation in the lives of a group of friends in Newcastle without once mentioning the peerless comic *Viz*.

The DJ before us gloried in the name of David Batty, sharing it with a footballer who then played for Leeds United. He was a filthy bugger, and obviously didn't want to run up his own utility bills by using the water where he lived. So, on a Sunday night, he'd wait for us to arrive and take over the decks, run himself a bath, and have a long soak before disappearing into the early morning. Sometimes he wouldn't even wait for us to arrive. He'd stick an album on – something long and ponderous that could be left alone for 25 minutes or so – and then go next door and climb in the bath. Listeners must have wondered at why there was no presenter, why the gaps between songs played out, why the last five songs were all by the same artist. DJ David Batty didn't care – he'd be towelling himself dry as we turned up to relieve him of duty.

I wasn't spending this entire period of my life locked up in sweaty bedrooms and pirate radio flats and in record shops with a bunch of boys. It just seems that way. I was also searching for my first hip-hop widow. I was into girls, but was such an insufferable, self-righteous little shit that I was determined that any girl I went out with would have to know she'd come second to my rapping career. This pompous idea went straight out the window the second I got them into my bedroom and was spending the evening trying to work my hands into their bra. Hip-hop could take a running jump at that point. But my girlfriends of the era – Gail, Andrea and then Sarah – deserve medals for putting up with someone who, when he wasn't trying to feel them up, would be banging on about a record he'd bought, a sample he'd found or a song he'd written, mistaking their glassy stares for genuine interest.

Andrea was my first proper, long-term relationship. I'd got an after school job in a local supermarket called Grandways, stacking shelves. Paul Chatterton worked there, and got me a slot. It was pretty cushy, as it was a 10 minute walk from where I lived and you could work with your Walkman on – which you needed to do as Grandways had one of those soul-crushing in-house radio loops that played the same bland songs and adverts every 20 minutes. If you didn't hate Barry Manilow and the proprietor of 'StayClean Windows' before your shift, you most certainly did by the end. I managed to get off to an inauspicious start by, for some reason that still eludes me, calling the supermarket manager 'Sir' on my first night there. My colleagues ripped the piss out of me while the boss just looked bemused and said, "Don't call me Sir".

Paul and I still went to school on the opposite side of Leeds from where we lived, so everyone we worked with went to Beeston schools. They were a decent bunch, most of whom had their own little Grandways scam going on. One guy had the sweetest job, his sole responsibility to restock the alcohol section, and several bottles of spirits – every night – would find their way into his bag. He'd then sell it on to us. My hustle was much smaller but equally daring – I once stole a tin of Big Soup. I feel the heat from this crime has now died down enough to mention it, but just in case the powers that be decide to pursue it, I'd like it to be known that I'm happy to sing like a canary about the bloke who nicked dozens of Pot Noodles a year. We started socialising with these colleagues, and got invited to a 6th form party for the school many of them went to – Matthew Murray High School. That's where I met Andrea.

I'm not prepared to bad-mouth someone who was the first girl I loved. My family didn't take to her at all – she could be on the moody side – but with me and with her friends she was a lovely, funny girl. However, her family were so dysfunctional that every gathering was like being in that dinner scene in *The Texas Chainsaw Massacre*, and I was Sally, tied up and forced to endure a weird hell. Every single family member seemed to be missing a limb (of which I'm not making light) or permanently injured in some other non-specific way or their teeth had all gone or they were just in a state of physical disrepair. One 'uncle' rocked up once, on a bitterly cold late Autumn day, took off his shoes, pulled off his socks and wrung what seemed like a full glass of water from each of them, straight onto the lounge floor. It was sweat. His hygiene was somewhat questionable, evidently, but it didn't help that the soggy socks had more personality than he. Sometimes, there was a 20-year-old girl there who was six months pregnant to a 70-year-old member of Andrea's extended family.

In the eight or so months I was with Andrea, every single day used to bring news of some fresh familial calamity. One sister was beaten up so badly by her awful squaddie boyfriend that she'd need physiotherapy for the rest of her life. Another sister fell down the stairs and ditto. Once, Andrea's house was blissfully empty and we decided to take a bath together. We'd barely lowered ourselves in when some seven-year-old boy burst in to announce he'd been diagnosed as deaf that day. There were no locks on the bathroom – or indeed in the rest of the house – which makes a kind of sense when it seemed like someone was on the verge of a medical emergency every six hours. Only one sibling had escaped – a brother who'd left to become a reasonably successful county cricket player and coach. He never, ever went home.

Andrea and I split up because I fell in love with Sarah. I'd been at the same school as Sarah since I moved to Leeds, but hadn't got to know her until 6th form, and we became part of the same close-knit friendship group. House parties, going out in Leeds to the few pubs that would serve us, all the stuff that 6th formers do. I thought Sarah was great, but didn't want to do anything about it, partly because Paul had gone out with a couple of members of the same group – including Sarah's best friend, Vanessa – and it had led to a bit of tension. I also didn't want to jeopardise my A-Levels by embarking on a relationship so close to them. But I couldn't help myself and started to wish that our very strong platonic friendship would turn into something more romantic.

Everyone in the group could see it happening – at sleepovers, Sarah and I would share beds, talking into the night – and probably rolled their eyes at our endless procrastination. What they couldn't see was that when I was at home alone in my bedroom I was writing woeful lovesick poetry entirely about her, comparing myself unfavourably to the men I knew she fancied in real life.[75] I was particularly irked that she had a thing for Shaun Ryder of the Happy Mondays, even while simultaneously acknowledging that she found him quite ugly. I was a love-struck teenage boy who couldn't understand the complex mind of a woman, and poured this frustration into doggerel. As bad as my rap lyrics were at this stage, they were like T.S. Eliot compared to my poetry.

The seemingly endless flirtation between Sarah and myself reached a peak on my 18th birthday. I'd arranged to go out with all our friends in town that evening, but was spending the afternoon at my house with Sarah and a bottle of Mouton Cadet (which I thought was very posh wine at that stage in my life). After what felt like an aeon of unbearable tension, the floodgates opened, we kissed, we arrived late for my own birthday drinks and that, a few choppy moments aside, was that for the next five years. Five years where Sarah didn't just have to put up with my many failings as a boyfriend and as a human being, but had to tolerate my hip-hop dabbling too,

[75] Unlike my lyrics, I will not be reproducing a single line of this poetry here. I bundled together and made a gift of these poems to Sarah in what I thought was a grand, romantic gesture. Years later, long after we'd split up, she gave me them back. Re-reading them was incredibly traumatic. Not because of the emotions of love and longing they stirred – they didn't, we'd both moved on – but because they were so shit. I was so upset I didn't try to write another poem for over 20 years, and when I did it was about glaciers.

which she did with admirable stoicism. It also helped that her family weren't like The Munsters gone more wrong, but were lovely. Sarah did get a 'shout out' on a track or two – and what woman could dream of more?

I also got her advice on what we should call our second demo/EP that we were going to release straight to vinyl. I've got a piece of A4 in the 'PA Archives' where she gives each of the six putative titles – *Flick Through the Pages*, *Forward to the Past*, *Looking for Mr Greenpeace*, *Chapter Two: A Different Story*, *Children of the North* and *Outside the System, Looking In* – a mark out of ten (she should really have given them all about one, but she was more generous than that) and some feedback.

While she was being very constructive – "Doesn't relate to subject matter" or "Best rhythm of all, flows well, has all the correct ingredients" – she was probably wondering what the hell she had got herself into. I did actually take her advice, and it was full steam ahead for a while with her favourite, the self-aggrandising and pretentious *Outside the System, Looking In*, although I later thought of something else while we were recording it and jettisoned it in favour of *Headnods and Broomsticks*, which I still prefer. I think that was the sum total of Sarah's involvement in my rap career – apart from her providing endless support – and I think she'll agree it was probably for the best. No one wants to be associated with failure.

I'd been busy writing songs for our next project, and Dan and Martin had been digging for samples and coming up with ideas as well. But progress slowed to a complete standstill when Dan took the opportunity to spend a term in Boston, Massachusetts, as part of an exchange program between Bradford University and Lesley College. I'd finished my A-levels but had decided I wanted to take a gap year out before going to university. I'd actually come perilously close to walking out on my A-levels, flirting with the real world again, sick of being skint and dreaming of earning some money to put towards the Prehistoric Ages projects and my vinyl habit.

My mind-set at the time was so focussed on hip-hop that I was prepared to get a job in order to pay for us to press us our own EP on vinyl. I should have worked out from Dan and Martin – who always had more money than me – not offering to do the same that it wasn't the best idea ever. Wiser heads eventually prevailed and I stuck them out, but afterwards I couldn't wait to spend a year working and travelling and recording music and being self-indulgent before going away to study.

The dream gap year didn't really transpire. After a Christmas spent working in Boots, with special responsibility for the 'home brew' section, I trained as a croupier after seeing an advert in the *Yorkshire Evening Post* for what sounded like an exciting job. This was several unpaid weeks of standing at a roulette table doing maths, stacking and sweeping chips, with the promise of a guaranteed job if I passed. The training was actually enjoyable, as I have a liking for mental arithmetic and it was in the afternoons. The job? Pretty much the most hateful thing I've ever done, and that includes the day I spent shovelling lees out of a giant wine vat for £2.50 an hour while dozens of wasps attacked me. The line I was sold – and I bought it completely – was that British croupiers are among the best trained and most respected in the world. After training, you just need to build up a few month's experience, then you can go abroad and work on cruise ships or in the US and get hefty tips (which were illegal in UK casinos). This sounded great, especially as one croupier I worked with in 'Froggy's Casino' on Moortown Corner in Leeds told me she'd dealt blackjack to the tit-and-bum obsessed rap group 2 Live Crew on a boat and had received hundreds of dollars in tips from them over a couple of hours. This sounded incredibly glamorous.

The reality of life as a croupier in a minor Leeds casino was somewhat less so. Shifts ran from 2-9pm, or 9pm-4am. You'd be expected to throw one double shift a week, where you'd start at 3pm and finish at 3am. If you worked a night shift, you'd get a cooked breakfast on one of your breaks, at the unnatural hour of around 2AM. I don't think I've ever experienced such a pure ontological crisis as I have while eating shitty, heat lamp warmed bacon and eggs on my own, staring through a window at the stars/the bins round the back of the casino, at 2.12AM on a Tuesday morning. And you really needed to do a double shift, as the money was pitiful. For a full-time job for which I had trained unpaid for six weeks, I was taking home around £115 a week. And it was a job where, on a double shift day, I was standing up for 12 hours, dealing cards or pushing roulette chips around, constantly working out sums in my head while observing the many rules and regulations of British casinos. Your work is scrutinised by a pit boss, who will pull you up on any mistakes, or intervene if you get an aggressive gambler. They'd also tell you to go for a break if you were on a losing streak, something which still baffles me.

The casino industry is built on a cold, hard mathematical fact, and that's that over time, the house will win. The manager once expressed this to me as a percentage – and even if it was only 3 or 5%, the house would win that over a period, even with the day-to-day fluctuations of people hitting a lucky streak. Even if you take into account illegal or frowned-upon activities like card-counting, which pit bosses were trained to recognise, the odds are always in favour of the house. These are games of chance, apparently, but not much is really left to chance in the way they're designed. Which, of course is the attraction for both the house and the punter. Luck, ultimately, doesn't exist, or is rendered unimportant by the way the games are configured. And yet if, for example, you're dealing roulette and some punter is betting the house maximum (which I think was a measly £50 at our place) on black, and you come up with black three or four times in a row, your pit boss would send you for a break, to try and break the punter's streak. There'd be sympathetic shrugs and comments about how it's not your night. I found this staggering. It wasn't my money. Win or lose I was taking home the same pittance, and who's to say that the croupier who relieved me isn't going to hit black for the next ten spins? If you build a game where the odds are always stacked to make you win, there's no room for superstition on the part of the owners. That should be left to the punters.

As strange as I found this stuff, that wasn't my real problem with the job. Nor was it the occasionally rude customers who'd scream at you if they lost, or call you an unlucky omen for them (even though I was employed by the casino with the sole purpose of removing money from the wallets of gamblers) or on one occasion throw a very heavy crystal ashtray at my head. I liked most of my colleagues, I liked the maths and I liked the brushes with minor celebs – British javelin star Mick Hill or the now irredeemably tarnished Jimmy Savile (who wouldn't gamble himself. He'd sit and have a coffee while one of his minions placed bets for him). No, my real problem was with the hours and their effect on the rest of my life.

If you worked an afternoon shift, you'd have your morning to yourself, at a time when all your friends are at work, and you'd finish at 9pm, a bit too late to go out by the time you'd got washed and changed. If you worked the evening shift, you were setting off for work just as your friends were getting ready to go out, and the casino mini-bus would drop you off at home around about 5am. I would go to bed at the same time my mum was getting up for work, the birds tweeting. After just over two months of this I was a shadow of my former self. I was sallow, tired and irritable and had no social life to speak of. But I was saving for a trip to New York with Dan, the trip of a lifetime to the Mecca of hip-hop, and I needed money.

My dad stepped in to help. There had been nearly a year between my dad leaving and me finally going to see him. He'd made no attempts to contact any of us, but we knew from friends of his who'd seen him around that he didn't live very far from us, and had opened a stall in Morley market, a few miles away. It took a while to get up the courage to approach him. After all, he'd made the decision to cut all of his family out of his life, and it was obvious he felt that we'd all sided with mum, even though there'd actually been no big central drama or event to take sides over. He'd just left.

What had changed in the interim is that I'd grown up – at least a little bit – and could approach my dad with the confidence to do things differently, on my own terms. I wasn't going there to ask him to come back, far from it. I'd just decided I wanted my dad in my life. I started seeing him regularly towards the end of the first year of 6th form, and after some planning and, against the objections of my teachers, I took three weeks out of school and had a fantastic holiday with him in Florida. This wasn't like the holidays of my childhood, where I sulked in the back of the car while being forced to go to places I had no interest in and hang out with people I didn't want to meet. No, it was symbolic of our new relationship.

We decided on it together, we planned it out on a map and we both chose places we wanted to go to, we hired a Pontiac convertible and drove, top down, with the stereo blasting out music we both liked. We did the Florida theme parks and had a blast. We drank with wonderful Buffalo Bills fans as their team got beaten only a mile away in the Super Bowl. We went out to eat and talked politics. He drove me to record shops and waited while I sifted through the racks.

His reunion with Susan, and the establishment of reasonably friendly terms with my mum, would come later, but I saw my dad regularly from then on, and when I was on holiday from school I helped him out on his market stall. While I was at the casino, he could see that I'd become a bit of a depressed wreck, and asked me how much money I needed to earn to get to New York. He offered me a job on the market – the stall had now become a shop – working normal hours for the same money I was earning at the casino. I almost bit his hand off. I wasn't going to get to deal cards to 2 Live Crew on a floating pleasure palace, but I wasn't going to go insane either.

Sixteen
Things Fall Apart

Sometime after the first demo, but before Countdown left the group (spoiler alert) - but I'm not entirely sure when because none of the surviving tapes have dates on them - we rehearsed a couple of new tracks as a trio. You can tell this was at a time when Countdown wanted a bigger role (and he definitely deserved one) as all three of us rap on both of them. We'd listened back to our first demo and pinpointed a few issues, not the least of which was that the long, undisturbed verses delivered by me were a bit endless and tedious. Even the songs that we liked seemed to drag a bit. The formula needed punching up a bit.

We were inspired by the manic energy of Long Island rap group Leaders of the New School, whose debut album *A Future Without a Past* had been released in 1991. Without trying to sound old school (in the way that Jurassic 5 or Ugly Duckling specifically attempted to), they captured some of the magic of the earliest club-based rap routines of the late 70's, the kind of multi-voiced stuff that the Cold Crush Brothers did, cutting over the top of each other, finishing each other's lines, chanting choruses in unison. They did this not in a retro way, but in a way that seemed new, helped in no small part by the Bomb Squad production, the same people responsible for Public Enemy's unique sound. Plus, also, hip-hop in the early 90's was generally getting more shouty and chanty, and relied less and less on one rapper just holding court with little else to distract you.

We basically tried to copy this approach – with limited success, it almost goes without saying – on "Grab the Mic and Drop Bombs". We each delivered a verse, but shared the mic throughout, coming in on each other's punchlines and generally creating a whole bunch of noise in the background, something that is now known as 'ad-libs' but which we just called the 'shouty bits'.[76]

It's not yet time to pass the mic
Cough, cough, that's my asthma... syke
Got breath left yet I flow def
The needle picks up fluff, like my bum cleft

It was all in this vein (please note that I didn't just say 'Cough, cough', I actually provided the relevant sound effects of a man struggling for breath. I was a method rapper), and it did what it was intended to do, which was to add some much needed pizazz and energy into our songs. That also extended to changing our sound somewhat. Dan, as the group's producer, had always been open to Martin and myself bringing records we wanted to sample to the table. I used to go to Leeds Library and borrow jazz and funk records I couldn't afford to buy, and listen to them not just for a musical education, but

[76] Ad-libs are now part and parcel of pretty much every rap song, and are usually provided by the artist themselves or by one of their mates/hangers-on. I've witnessed ad-libs being laid down in a recording studio in New York and it was somewhat disconcerting. The rapper, having finished laying down his actual verses, went back into the booth and then did his ad-libs over the backing track with the vocals now on top. He had headphones on and he could hear it, but I couldn't hear anything, apart from him going 'Yeah... ughhh... C'mon.... Yeah.....' to himself for four minutes. It just sounded like he was in there getting a blowjob from a ghost.

with an ear for bits we could use. We usually sampled jazz, but for "When the Sun Goes Down", I'd found a much more funky bit on an album by War. I arrived at Dan's with the sample, the song's concept – all three of us recounting some events that happen at night – and my verse ready to go.

...and then the lights come on, the city centre filled with a throng
Of people, the streets hum to their own song

I then paint a picture of Leeds city centre on a Saturday night that makes it seems like a panel from Bosch's *The Garden of Earthly Delights*, a vision of hell that had no basis in reality whatsoever. Someone gets stabbed and is left with a five inch scar, someone gets randomly punched by someone on a pub crawl (which had actually happened to me, but in Nottingham, so there's at least some verisimilitude) and another guy gets a bottle smashed in his face for talking to the wrong girl.

The city centre gets me peeved
So the only big night out I get now is Vic Reeves
Take heed, it's just not safe in town
Better watch your back, when the sun goes down

Dan's verse is not dissimilar, but it's more about being offered drugs (we were, and remain, quite square individuals and none of us ever took any drugs, except for the occasional puff of someone else's weed when hip-hop had a big 'blunt' [77] phase and we tried,

---

[77] Wikipedia: "A blunt is a cigar hollowed out and filled with marijuana." That doesn't describe the blunts Dan and I tried and failed to roll on about two occasions before giving up and deciding that kind of thing wasn't really for us anyway. Our attempts looked like they'd been made by a nervous Parkinson's

unsuccessfully, to roll a couple of those) in town and some bloke doing an E and then jumping off a building. Again, none of this was really based on reality or first-hand experience, but was seemingly invented by our own distaste for the music associated with ecstasy – house – and based on tabloid scare bullshit.

Martin's verse was more realistic, and was definitely tapping into headlines about a spike in car theft at the time with his rhymes about a TWOCker (Taking Without Owner's Consent) called Johnny:

So foot to the floor, police sirens roar
Close behind, two or three more
Chasing, chasing, more members to his dream
The echoes of the night as the tyres scream
The suburban street was like a movie scene
He was the movie star, like Charlie Sheen

So there you have it, your average night in Leeds when the sun goes

---

sufferer using Jeremy Beadle's fingers. No offence. Why did we want to smoke 'blunts' rather than just the spliffs many of our generation were perfectly happy with? Because they were a big thing in hip-hop. Named for the Phillies Blunt brand of very inexpensive cigar (although Dutch Masters, Swisher Sweets, White Owls and El-Productos also passed into every rap fan's lexicon), which could be bought for a couple of dollars at bodegas and corner shops throughout America, they started to be referenced in song after song in the early 90's, and bootleg Philly Blunt T-shirts became temporarily fashionable, even if ultimately they were just the hip-hop generation's version of an 'I Like the Pope, The Pope Smokes Dope' T-shirt. I had one, obviously.

A more lasting cultural reference to Phillies may also be found in Edward Hopper's famous and much spoofed painting *Nighthawks*, where the diner actually carries a Phillies advert, but for me it was all about the endless songs about blunts, preferably enjoyed while I was failing to roll one properly. Redman's "How to Roll a Blunt", Diamond D's "Stunts, Blunts and Hip-Hop" and Nice & Smooth's "Blunts" are just three classics, while KRS-One's "I Can't Wake Up" sees the rapper adopting the point of view of a blunt being passed from person to person. Which is as creative as hip-hop songs about blunts ever get.

down: Stabbings, bottlings, ecstasy deaths, car theft and fatal crashes. I'm surprised we weren't offered a job with the Leeds Tourist Board.

All these great leaps forward came to end when Dan went on his college exchange program. He got a placement interning at Kiss 108 radio station in Boston from January to April 1992, which was a pretty sweet gig. He worked on "Matty in the Morning" which, at the time of writing, has been going strong since 1981. His side line was hunting in the bins for unplayed hip-hop promos, of which he found plenty. With Dan so far away, there was no official Prehistoric Ages business, but I was at Martin's house all the time anyway.

Between the group's two demos – the *Led Zeppelin I* and *II* of the Leeds rap scene, obviously – Martin and I did a few bedroom sessions to try out new material. What brave direction would we be heading in? Well, it turned out I was still making the same mistakes as on the first demo – writing songs based on samples that took my ear. Influential Bronx rap crew Boogie Down Productions had released their second album in 1988, *By All Means Necessary*, complete with a cover where rapper KRS-One recreated a famous picture of Malcolm X at a window with a gun. It was an instant classic. Tucked away at the end was a spoken word piece where KRS attacked hypocrisy about violence. He made serious points about how violence in movies and in many aspects of real life went unchecked, but when hip-hop depicted acts of violence in lyrics, it was attacked by moral arbiters and even legislated against.

Of course, my teenage mind reduced these lines about giving children a lookalike gun at Christmas being regarded as non-violent, while a KRS-One album was, to a rant about how giving toy guns to kids breeds violence. Perhaps in my lefty-liberal do-gooding brain, this was the correct position to take. I still don't know if it is. I have no idea about gender stereotyping in toys. I haven't the foggiest about whether putting toy guns into the hands of children leads to them wanting real guns later. And even if it does, can they get them? After all, I was in Leeds, not the Bronx. You can't just buy a gun over the counter. And if I did believe these things, then how does that square with me thinking, as I did then, that film and TV and music and video game violence should be completely uncensored because there's no obvious or proven causal link between these things and real violence? Obviously, I hadn't thought it through, but I was 18, so that's allowed. I acted like I knew the answers, and that was fine as far as my lyrics were concerned. Hence "Under the Christmas Tree".

Under the tree, I see a gun
Just one, but that's enough to make you run
How can you have peace, when a gun's a release?
For a kid's tensions, he'll never cease

I really do disappear up my own fundament here. I'm totally on board with the causal link between toy guns and real violence and am determined to ram the point down the listener's throat. The 18-year-old unwed father of none proceeds to deliver a sermon on parenting:

On Boxing Day your kid is playing
With his plastic gun, he's spraying and slaying
It ain't real but it teaches his mind
What he could do with a real life nine
His friends on the floor pretend to be dead
A rush of excitement goes to his head
"What would it be like if I had a real gun
I'd be on top, I'd be the one"

If there was any doubt about this water tight argument – one that

I've really nailed with my incredibly lifelike depiction of the thought processes of the aforementioned child – then all doubters and naysayers are put into place by this couplet:

It's a fact that it happens like that
'Cos your kid plays cricket when you buy him a bat

There you go, another world problem solved. What's that you say? Not all people bought cricket bats by their well-meaning but ultimately wrong-headed parents end up playing cricket? Sorry, we've moved on now. Do try to keep up. However, listening to this track again, and cringing at every single, well-meant word I rapped, I still think, in my best Northern Yellow Pages advert voice, "I were right about that sample."

Martin and I also found the time to record a couple of C90 cassettes of me and him clowning around, that we'd then send to Dan in Boston. These were supposed to consist of us doing rough versions of new songs we'd created but in reality were just one and a half hours of us freestyling, guffing into the microphone, doing silly voices and impressions, cracking each other up and talking utter rubbish until the tape was full. I don't know if Dan ever listened to these idiotic tapes when he got them, but I sincerely hope he has subsequently destroyed them and they never see the light of day.

It had been a while since the debacle at the No Sell Out night in York, and we were also now ready to take the stage again. Unfortunately, we didn't have a live show and were pretty unlikely to be booked based on our recorded history so far. But an opportunity knocked in the form of a rap battle at Mr Craig's nightclub in Leeds. Mr Craig's, situated on New Briggate in the city centre, was opened by Peter Stringfellow in 1980 in a forlorn attempt to inject some 'London glamour' into Leeds and looked exactly as you might imagine a nightclub opened by Peter Stringfellow in 1980 in a forlorn attempt to inject some 'London glamour' into Leeds would look. It limped on in all its neon and chrome glory into the 90's, home to some pretty naff nights, and its one rap battle was perhaps only the second and last time I went inside. With Dan away, and Martin only rapping sporadically, I decided I was going to take the crown.

I didn't take the crown, but I didn't make a complete tit of myself either. There were actually some pretty decent rappers in attendance – including Leigh Kenny aka LSK who went on to work with Faithless and Nightmares on Wax. It wasn't a modern rap battle where you proceed through the rounds, vanquishing your opponent or being eliminated. No, it wasn't really a battle at all, more like a talent show where every rapper got to perform their bit and some judges decided if you won or not. I'd written some new lyrics and rehearsed them diligently. These are lost to posterity, and the only bits I can remember are a line about "I get down like Shep and John Noakes" and a routine where I involved Countdown in a hip-hop version of "Move Over Darling" (almost certainly because I'd just picked up an old Doris Day album at a charity shop in the search for samples. A fruitless one in this case) which wasn't as bad as it now sounds, but didn't exactly wow the crowd or the judges (i.e. the manager of Mr Craig's and the DJ, neither of whom liked or played hip-hop) either. I didn't deserve to win, and didn't.

We also filled the time by making some music that I'd railed against on our first demo – hip-house.[78] I'm not sure why I did a

[78] Among the many musical prejudices I've always had, and in many cases still do (I still can't stand The Smiths, The Stone Roses, The Happy Mondays, Shirley Bassey or Lulu, for various reasons, and now in my 40's I've got a feeling they have calcified into permanent dislikes), my hatred of hip-house was perhaps the most

complete 180 from abhorring this musical sub-genre in every other verse from our first demo, to spending a few evenings making some. Perhaps my mind was broadening and my tastes were becoming more Catholic or, more likely, it was just boredom. Either way, "Different Kind of Music" and "Music Has the Power", the two hip-house 'excursions' I can find in my box of cassettes (in the P.A. Archives, available now to any museum that wants to house this stunning collection), aren't really masterpieces of their kind. The hip-hop beat that underpins the former is actually quite good, and the cliché house music noises we overlay it with aren't too bad either. They just don't go together. The same goes for "Music Has the Power", but I actually rap on that one, and my attempt at one of those short, jaunty hip-house verses that rappers once did isn't my finest hour either.

Music has the power, a vocal shower
Plug in the source 'cos now we're
Coming again on the hardcore techno tip
Take a sip, we all come equipped

---

irrational. I liked house music. I liked hip-hop music. Couldn't the two together work? Well, they did, for most people. It wasn't really the music I didn't like, it was just people messing with hip-hop, which I was incredibly possessive and territorial about. I also rapped at great length on various songs about hating 'rave', and was joined in my hatred of that scene by the rest of the P.A. Posse and some of our extended rapping family. Thinking about it, it was a self-important reaction to a music that was all about fun, dancing and hedonism when I wanted music to be full of dull and dismal life lessons and lectures.

Reflecting now, with a marginally more open mind, hip-house threw up its share of classics, and the ones that cleaved closest to the classic House Sound of Chicago template (your Marshall Jeffersons and the like) were the best. A bit of tried-and-tested house piano and a producer-cum-rapper like Tyree Cooper could throw up a top song. And the brilliant 1989 pirate radio staple "The Chief" by Toni Scott – which I advise you to check out if you're not already familiar with it – does not sound in a million years like it was made by a Dutchman.

'Cos music fills me up with force
So we can dance and unite of course
So come on y'all take my hand I'll lead the way
Music has the power, okay?

A vocal shower of shit, more like. Hip-house rappers tended to be full of life and vim, adopting a tone that fit the happy-go-lucky-let's-all-have-a-big-bag-of-drugs-and-dance-like-tits material. I sounded like I'd spent three days digging a 12 foot deep grave for a giant and was still at the bottom. These songs are also six and seven minutes long respectively, which renders them interminable. Still, we were filling a void (in ourselves, not a void felt by any consumers of music, clearly). And Martin was no longer content to just play the scratch and cut DJ either, which is fair enough as he was full of ideas. He didn't ask us to collaborate on *One Man Band*, his 1992 solo project, but I gave him a couple of song titles for it anyway, from my vast archive of unwritten but niftily-titled tracks.

P.A. Posse 1.0 split up almost by accident, like we'd glanced away for a moment and when we looked back it was over, but we didn't really know why. Martin moving away from me and Dan as slowly but as surely as a glacier carves out its valley (hmm, glaciers... Good subject for a poem). There was no big fall out, no big row.[79] No clash

---

[79] I didn't trust my memory on this – perhaps I'd forgotten a blazing row over the future lyrical direction of the group or about if we should use a trombone sample or not on an interlude. So I asked Martin what he remembered: "When Dan was away in Boston, I had the sampler for a bit and worked on my solo LP. Apart from that I'm not sure what happened next. I remember Prehistoric Ages changing to Progressive Agenda, which was far too intelligent for little old me. None of us fell out, just took different directions."

Dan's take is pretty much identical: "I think Countdown was doing his own stuff like the *One Man Band* demo which I always thought was dope, especially "I Wreck The Mic". So we'd already decided we were doing our own thing then. I remember finding it quite hard to collaborate on production as he was an all-of egos. It helped that there was absolutely no money or contract issues to come between us, as no one had offered us either. Martin just kind of started a solo career as something to do while Prehistoric Ages was on hold and we all just accepted that an era had come quietly to an end.

Relations between us all were good, so good in fact that DJ Countdown appears on our next project, contributing scratches (which Dan was never very good at and I'd never even tried) and a verse on the posse cut to end all posse cuts.[80] Dan and I perhaps had more of a

---

rounder too. He could rap and produce and so could I (in the loosest sense – but there's no doubt that we could). But I remember when we were both actually working on a beat one of us would try and take over, not aggressively but we were both very hands on and had our own techniques, so I guess it was a bit frustrating. Maybe when he did his first proper solo demo that was the trigger for him and the rest was psychological. You can quote me on this but I frequently wonder if I hadn't sold my sampler and if I'd really pursued music where it would have taken me, as I was really into the creative aspect and production. No regrets but it was definitely a great period of our lives being carefree and making music. Worse groups made it – like Stereo MC's – but not being in London at that time hindered us."

[80] The posse cut is one of those things that, like 'The Golden Age' that we covered earlier, I'm very pernickety about. So, just to make my feelings abundantly clear: A posse cut is a record that, according to Wikipedia, contains four or more rappers. This is wrong. As far as I'm concerned, if you're a solo rapper and you invite at least two people onto your song, that's a posse cut. If you're a group of three rappers and you invite one more person onto your song, that's not a posse cut. For me, the posse cut has to involve guest appearances by a minimum of two rappers who aren't in the group. The early songs by Grandmaster Flash and the Furious Five and Afrika Bambaataa and the Soulsonic Force might have a big group of rappers on them, but they're all members of the group, they're not drawn from the group's extended posse. They are not posse cuts. A solo artist or group who invite two other rappers to perform with them are most definitely making a posse cut, as are a bunch of disparate rappers who band together on a one-off basis to make a track. So, the cuts and albums by the hip-hop super group The Gravediggaz are not posse cuts or albums, as they formed a cohesive group to make a couple of albums. There are posse cuts on there though, as they invite two or three guest rappers onto a couple of songs. By contrast, Marley Marl's *The Symphony* is a posse cut, because the four rappers assembled there aren't part of the same group even if, confusingly, they are all part of the 'Juice Crew'. Look, it's

bond with each other than we did with Martin, who had different interests to us away from hip-hop, and other friends who he probably was closer to. He had more confidence with girls, and he'd hang around town chatting to them out of the window of the legendary P.A. Craft. Dan and I were maybe a bit more reticent/useless.

It was strange to think that Countdown had left the group that he and Dan had started before I was even on the scene, so we didn't feel it was right to continue using Prehistoric Ages as a name. But as what little repute we did have resided entirely in the 'P.A. Posse' tag, we decided to keep that. But what would the P and the A stand for now? Dan and I arrived at our momentous name change – I shit you not – when he stayed over at my house one night and we shared a bed like Morecambe and Wise on TV, lying there in our pyjamas with a list of words written under 'P' and another list under 'A'. What would capture our sense of positivity and mission to educate the enslaved masses and bring new light to bear through the medium of hip-hop? How do we convey our commitment to real social and mental change by making music without catchy choruses? We'd need a list! And thus Progressive Agenda was born. Don't snigger, we could well have been called 'Positive Action'.

Dan returned from Boston in April of 1992, having made plenty of friends both there and in the Big Apple who had offered us places to stay if we made it over there in the summer. Perhaps I should have been putting the money earmarked for this trip aside for university, especially as the three years spent there would turn out to be the most penurious ones of my life, but my heart was set on a trip to New York. The. Home. Of. Hip. Hop.

---

perfectly simple! Wikipedia also makes the unforgivable error of calling NWA's "Parental Discretion Iz Advised" from their *Straight Outta Compton* album a posse cut, as it features all of NWA and single guest The DOC. I will be writing them a stiff email.

Seventeen
Big Apple Rappin'

We started our holiday in Boston, staying with college friends of Dan's, Sherri and Sharon. They were lovely, showed us the sights, gave us our own room and saved us a shitload of money. We'd hang around Harvard Square, buying records and comics and basically feeling like this was the best place in the world. And we hadn't even got to New York yet. Our habits were pretty much the same as they were in Leeds, where we'd buy records and then go to Dan's house to play them immediately. But doing the exact same thing in a basement in Boston gave it an extra frisson – we hadn't had to wait for those records to be imported to Leeds, and they were less than half the price. But still, being in Boston felt like the warm up act for the main event.

We got the Greyhound coach from Boston to New York, an eventful journey that took about twice as long as it should have as the coach broke down en route. The whole journey had got off to a bad start as Dan and I couldn't sit together, and while he was down at the front next to some snoozing Grandma, I was on the very back seat next to some borderline insane guy, who would hoot and holler at unexpected Tourettesy intervals, occasionally shout and swear at the driver all the way from the back, and then just started rolling massive spliffs for him and his girlfriend, which they smoked without regard to laws or courtesy. All the other passengers were shooting him shifty 'Is this guy going to go bananas with a gun or a knife?' type looks for the entire journey. And so was I, from one foot away.

Just as we got to New York, the bus ground to a halt and the driver informed us, somewhat racistly, that we were going to be there for a while, but we couldn't get off the bus as this was a really bad neighbourhood and we'd likely get robbed or worse (it was Harlem). We were there so long, waiting for a replacement bus, that a local pizza company took pity on us and delivered a bunch of free pizzas. I'd taken the opportunity to move down the front of the bus to stand in the aisle and talk to Dan, largely because my back seat neighbour had reacted badly to this unforeseen delay and was issuing actual physical threats to the driver, albeit still from the full length of the bus. He then shot down to the front when the pizzas arrived and, bless him, went to great pains and efforts through the scrum of people reaching for a slice, to reserve some for me, saying, "I got you, my man, here's some pizza for my backseat man." We were firm friends from then on and, while I declined his offer of a spliff once we were back under way, we exchanged phone numbers. Although I think his had about three digits too few to actually be a real one and mine was entirely fabricated.

My first taste of New York was even more awesome (and even more intimidating) than I ever dreamed it would be. I walked out of the bus station into a New York heatwave, ill-prepared for how oppressive Manhattan could be in summer. The sheer scale of everything was stunning, I felt my weedy asthmatic chest being crushed both by the air and the spectacle. I'd been off the bus for less than ten minutes when some random homeless New York guy was up in my face, coating it with saliva, tugging at my bag and leaving a lasting impression that absolutely everyone in New York (and on the buses to New York) was mad and shouty.

We weren't staying in Manhattan itself, but with Jen, a friend of Dan's out in Long Island. Coming from a maisonette in Beeston, I was in constant awe of the size of the houses and was chuffed to be given my own en suite in what I saw as a mansion with manicured grounds, but by middle class Long Island standards was probably the equivalent of a three up, two down. We'd go to Jones Beach and chill with Jen and her girlfriends. Dan and I got so severely sunburnt on the first day there that we couldn't even put our sneakers on, and had to smear our swollen feet with aloe vera. As painful as it was, it had the happy side-effect of getting us out of a Toad the Wet Sprocket concert the girls were determined to drag us along to. Dan had a little thing going on with Jen, and as her parents were away he was desperate to take full advantage of that. She invited a friend over, Rachel, who was charmed by my accent but obviously not that charmed by me as I didn't get so much as a snog.

We really only had one full day to explore Manhattan which, as any fule kno, is completely impossible. We had with us a hand-written page of addresses of record shops, record labels and even the location of the famed hip-hop magazine *The Source*.[81] Our aim

[81] *The Source* is a legendary magazine that started out as a newsletter, became the leading monthly hip-hop magazine in the world and then pissed away all its good will with a succession of editorial scandals involving publishers, editors, writers and excessive fawning coverage of groups that the editor was a member of and the publisher had a financial interest in. However, in the late 80's and early 90's under the leadership of Jonathan Shecter it was brilliant, combining cutting edge reporting about rappers and hip-hop culture with some hard-hitting political journalism about topics like police brutality. Early issues were extremely difficult to come by in the UK, and Dan and I would stock up on them whenever we travelled to London, in the few places cutting-edge enough to stock them. Such was the magazine's stock that a '5 mic' review (5 out of 5, basically) could cement your album as a classic. Very few were accorded, although the fact that they gave one to the exceedingly forgettable Lil' Kim album *The Naked Truth* in 2005 amid rumours that the publisher of *The Source*, David Mays, was dating Lil' Kim's manager, is a barometer of how low the publication had fallen.

was to visit as many of them as possible, to try and blag some records and promo freebies. I'm not sure what we were going to do at *The Source*... raid the back issues department, perhaps? We didn't really grasp the distances in play, or the effects of the heat. Nor that when we – a very small world, indeed – bumped into a bunch of Leeds hip-hop friends (including Paul aka Wiz from the aforementioned Breaking The Illusion rap group and Crash Records) they wouldn't really want to trek to all these places on a wild goose chase in 100 stifling degrees.

So the day petered out with us walking exhausting distances to places that were either usually closed or in giant skyscrapers that wouldn't let us in, or were just post boxes. The only thing either of us had to show for our labours was that we each bought a T-shirt from Spike Lee's 40 Acres and a Mule concession in Macy's, peered out from the top of the Empire State Building like the truly thrilled tourists we were and, importantly, copped a bunch of vinyl from Tower Records (R.I.P.) and Music Factory (also R.I.P.). The latter being perhaps the most legendary hip-hop record shop ever.[82]

---

[82] The original Music Factory was based in Times Square, although there was also a branch in Jamaica, Queens, where a young LL Cool J used to buy his records. When that one closed it became Music Dynasty for a while. Both were great places, but we didn't venture out to Queens, so our joy was in going to the Times Square branch and buying classic records with the 'Music Factory' stickers on the sleeve. Because of its midtown location and proximity to all the major NY radio stations, it was a hub for DJ's, MC's, producers and artists in the 80's. Radio kingpins Red Alert, Mr Magic and Chuck Chillout would get their vinyl there. If a record was on the wall in Music Factory, it was going to sell well.

It was owned by a guy called Mannie but Stanley Platzer, aka Fat Stan, ran it, and he was a musical guru. You could hum a few bars of anything to him and he knew it. And not just hip-hop. His all-encompassing musical knowledge was a thing of wonder, and Music Factory was just as famous for stocking the *Ultimate Breaks and Beats* range of records, the original compilations of the records from which the earliest hip-hop DJ's culled the breaks that invented the genre. As mentioned earlier, Times Square is much safer for tourists now compared to the 70's and 80's. It's full of chains, theatres, a giant Hershey's store and tourist trap

We didn't get to meet any rappers or see any shows, but we did get a sense of the hustle and scale of the city that gave birth to the music that had brought us together and then driven us to its shores. It's not hindsight – even as we sweated our way up Broadway I had the feeling that I was somehow experiencing or being patched into the soul of the city. I was wide open to New York, a place that had given me not just music, but structure, purpose and meaning.

These days you can book yourself onto one of several competing 'hip-hop tours' of New York. Often they're hosted by retired rappers, largely those who got their start in the late 70's and early 80's and were yesterday's men by the time the real money rolled in to the genre. The music industry has no place for them, they didn't have the kind of record deals that guarantee them a comfortable dotage so – and twas ever thus – they have to get out and hustle for a living. These bus tours are fun, and it feels good to contribute to a legend's retirement fund, shake their hand, get their autograph, hear them reminisce in the flesh about the time they battled so-and-so at such-and-such long defunct club.

The anecdotes were well-worn long before these tours started. Repetition has given them a polish, and the rapt audience swallows them wholesale even if, in reality, there's another rapper out there who was on the other end of the same battle and remembers it differently. Hip-hop history is like all history, it's largely written by the winners, and if the Cold Crush Brothers defeated the Fantastic Romantic Five, then tour host Grandmaster Caz is going to tell you about the key part he had to play in that victory.[83]

---

restaurants. I preferred it when it was full of sleaze, street walkers and shops like Music Factory.

[83] Of the many early rap battles, the one between the Cold Crush Brothers and the Fantastic Romantic Five at Harlem World, New York on July 4, 1981 is one of the most legendary. It's pretty easy to hear it these days, and it has even

There's some revisionism in there too, although not of a particularly sinister kind. People who look back on hip-hop's early years often do so with rose-tinted spectacles, seeing it as a time of good-hearted battles, positivity and coming together in brotherhood. It was all love, peace and hair grease in the collective imagination. In reality it wasn't like that. It was brilliant and thrilling, it goes without saying, but there was still bitter rivalry, gangs, guns and fights. The subject matter wasn't all edifying either – another popular myth held as fact by the majority of ageing hip-hop fans, or those that have abandoned it altogether.

They scoff at today's music and denounce it as consisting exclusively of violence, guns, sex and consumerism, full of shallow and overpaid artists. Well, scratch the lyrical content of even the very earliest rap battles and you'll get the same stuff, with the exception of being overpaid. Battle raps were brag raps, and those brags included stuff about how much gold you had, what car you drove and how hard you were. Guns, sex and sexism came as standard. And why wouldn't it? The motivations of the people making hip-hop in 1980 aren't that much different from those of artists nearly 40 years

---

been released on vinyl, while there are also many unofficial CD and MP3 compilations of early rap concerts, with understandably patchy sound quality. It's not the most significant battle, however. For starters, neither of the groups put in their best ever performances and, while it's great, it doesn't have the relevance, say, of the time in December that same year at the same venue when Kool Moe Dee of the Treacherous Three dissed Busy Bee in a way that signalled the coming of the new era of MC's. Yup, by 1981 people were already being lined up for retirement. What is special about the battle is that it catches the interplay of multiple MC's that was so thrilling and typical of the time, and that it inspired the next generation of rappers. Run DMC, who were very much the next level of hip-hop and moved it away from the original template in numerous daring ways, drew on it for their brilliant 1983 recording of "Here We Go (Live at The Funhouse)". Funnily enough, the Fantastic Five were judged to have won the battle on the night (and the prize of $1000), but once the bootleg tapes of the event circulated round the streets, most people thought the Cold Crush edged it. Me too.

later. It's evolved sonically, gone in many of the fascinating new directions I've already written about, but it's still about the beat and the rhyme. And if you really hold to the belief that hip-hop subject matter has changed, you're cherry-picking your examples. Conscious rap? Yep, we have some of that now, and we had some in 2000 and 1990 and 1980. But it has always been a small corner of the larger picture, no matter how high profile Public Enemy or KRS-One were. If anyone tells you that the New York rap scene in 1979 traded merely in life-affirming rhymes from a bunch of philanthropically minded saints, they're imagining a New York that never existed. Hip-hop was never 'pure' from the start. It was always much more interesting than that. It was a mongrel born of a clash of other genres and mongrels, of course, live longer.

So while these tours are fun and I commend them wholeheartedly (if not unreservedly), they don't tell the complete story. And nor can you get it by just stomping to these famous places yourself, standing alone while you try to summon the ghosts of the past. You need to do both. Later in life, I'd have the once-in-a-lifetime opportunity to accompany Dan as we gathered together some of the original participants from the climactic concert from the landmark hip-hop movie *Wild Style* at the derelict outdoor amphitheatre where it took place.[84] For us, it was the perfect day. We

---

[84] *Wild Style* is a 1983 movie by Charlie Ahearn that mixes documentary and drama. It's largely seen by hip-hop fans as the more authentic big brother to *Beat Street*, although to be honest the acting isn't all that much better (and in some cases notably worse), even if it is by non-professionals and people directly involved in the scene. What's so brilliant about it is that it's a very authentic portrait of the hip-hop world in 1981 and 1982, when it's largely set and filmed. The scripted parts might seem somewhat amateurish, but they vividly capture the then close interplay between the graffiti scene and rap music. Best of all are the various pieces of live performance: Grandmaster Flash deftly scratching on two turntables, Double Trouble rapping on their stoop, the teenage Rock Steady Crew

met a handful of living legends of the music we adored, and we reunited them for the first time at the place where they'd stamped their names on history.

They hadn't been back since. An eyesore that most people just walked or drove past as they went about their daily lives was for them the repository of so many dreams, and for us the home to a near-mythical gathering. They chuckled and joshed each other as they reminisced. Our photographer and friend Mike Lewis captured them posing and at ease. It was beautiful. But just as beautiful was to stand there after they'd left, among the crumbling, graffiti'd, empty wreck, an oasis of memories in a city that moves on restlessly. You need the people there, and you need it without – legends don't become legends without the passing of time.

You can experience New York as a tourist destination, you can experience it as a storied city or as a symbol of the new world, you can experience it as somewhere to go eating or shopping, or you can experience it as the home of the most glorious music to ever emerge from a speaker. I think we did all of these simultaneously on that first visit. What we weren't stupid or delusional enough to do was to try to shop our little demo to any of these labels. We already knew we weren't quite ready (yet) to break New York.

---

breakdancing, Busy Bee working the crowd, The Cold Crush Brothers and the Fantastic Five facing off on the basketball court.

The soundtrack itself is a classic, while both it and the film itself have provided hundreds of samples for artists. The climactic concert at the amphitheatre, recorded in May 1982, is a thing of beauty, with future hall-of-fame breakdancer Crazy Legs going wild on stage, before legends like Rammellzee and Grandmixer D.St do their thing. I still get excited about it now and I first saw it nearly 30 years ago. In an era before smartphones and even before portable video cameras, where such scant original footage of hip-hop's birth exists, this is as close as it gets.

Eighteen
Cold Chillin' in the Studio

Headnods and Broomsticks took shape over most of 1992 and was finally finished in 1993.[85] It started with a surge of activity in the summer after we got back from New York, but then it only moved forward when I came home for holiday from university. I'd got into pretty much all of the colleges I'd applied to, after my A-level grades turned out to be markedly better than I or my teachers expected – I'd absolutely tanked my mock exams. But my choice was simple, because I wanted to go back to Nottingham.

I'd lost touch with all my friends there in a mere four years, but it was still a city I loved, so I took a place on a Humanities degree at Nottingham Trent University, and lived in halls on Clifton Campus. Even though I was in one of the final years of students fortunate enough to get a grant, I was still almost instantly skint. What money I should have saved from my year working had been spent on a flight to New York and the stacks of vinyl I'd brought back with me. This meant I couldn't really contribute towards the studio time we'd

[85] *Headnods* instead of the *Bedknobs* of the 1971 Disney film's title, because hip-hop fans usually responded to music they liked by nodding their head in time, as I've mentioned before. Often this was the only response a DJ or a performer would get, if the crowd were a bit too cool for school. Serried ranks of people in baggy jeans all nodding their heads. I couldn't think of something clever and punning to replace *Broomsticks* with then, and I still can't now.

booked at Christmas to work on the demo. Dan, who was working by then, bore the brunt.

Still, I'd put the hours in on the songs, and was confident we'd got the material to make a vinyl EP not only a possibility, but a resounding success. We went into the studio already rehearsed and ready to go. I can only assume the sound engineer thought we were a bunch of tools. Songs we thought we knew backwards just didn't sound right once they were subject to professional equipment. The flaws – my weedy voice, our (mostly my) inability to keep time, our ultimately limited and amateur technical knowledge of how to actually record songs – were ruthlessly exposed.

Songs required take after take, verses were added, expunged, rewritten in the vocal booth. What we thought would take three days stretched on beyond a week, the final polish postponed for another time. I'm sure this is fine if you're an artist with an indulgent record label or deep pockets, but we were burning through Dan's little bit of spare money very quickly. But still, it took shape, although with all the arsing around and me having to go back to university constantly, and working in the office for my sister Tracy's joinery firm to make ends meet, we did occasionally feel like we were stonemasons working on a cathedral that would only be completed 30 years after we'd died.

After an intro track we launch the EP (I'm going to call it an EP rather than a demo from here on, because that was what it was intended to be) with "A Simple Life".[86] Of all the tracks we ever

---

[86] When I listen to an old soul or jazz or pop or rock or metal album, what they usually do, with very few exceptions, is just kick straight in with the music. You press play, you get a song. At some point in hip-hop's evolution, someone decided you needed not just songs, punctuated by skits (see earlier footnote) but also an Intro and sometimes an Outro. These can make sense if the song is a concept album, as it can introduce you to the story the artist is trying to tell. But

recorded, this one holds a special place in my heart. Okay, much of it is Prehistoric Ages by numbers, transplanted straight into Progressive Agenda material. I'm almost certain we're rinsing poor old Jimmy Smith again for the main sample. There are the usual well-chosen hip-hop scratches and samples (Dan's record collection was starting to take on an awesome aspect, and there was gold to be plundered from it) and the usual nods to shared cultural icons of our childhood – Worzel Gummidge in this case. But the track is also the most clear-cut love song to hip-hop I've ever written, and goes some way towards capturing, in just a few lines, a lot of what I'm trying to express with this book.

Well, sat thinking what I oughta write
Back in my days with my Mongoose on the quarterpipe
We had the backspins going on, the tape

---

the majority of hip-hop albums that have Intros and Outros aren't concept albums. They just start with an Intro anyway because, well, why not?

Intros don't follow a hard-and-fast pattern. Some of them are almost songs, with a bit of music and rapping. Sometimes it'll just be a loop of music, thrown away – producers such as Pete Rock, Large Professor and The Beatnuts were buggers for studding their albums with 10 or 20 second loops that sounded incredible and then disappeared almost immediately, leaving you wanting more (or sending producers scurrying to find out what sample they'd used). Other Intros are most definitely skits, and will involve attempts at comedy, or sexual sound effects, while others are just the rapper talking over music, welcoming you to the album. The Outro is often the same, but usually with a few shout-outs from the rapper to the people that made it all happen etc., even though these same people are all thanked at great length on the sleeve notes.

The vast majority of Intros and Outros, like the vast majority of skits, are pointless, tedious and well worth deleting if you're listening to an album on your portable digital media player of choice. My theory is that once someone did an Intro, everyone else realised they could, and no studio engineer or A & R man was ever brave enough to tell a crew of stoned rappers, many of whom would be carrying guns, that maybe they shouldn't because, at the end of the day, who wants to hear this self-indulgent shit? So we're stuck with the Intro and the Outro, even though no good has come of it.

Is Knight of the Turntables, and it was great
With the Pumas and Nike cagoules
Clocking as cool as we viewed the Rock City duels
Fools followed the trend for a month or two
Then left for a new fad to pursue

So far, so nostalgic. At this stage I'd been into hip-hop for around 8-9 years, which felt like a pretty long stint. It was only the beginning. Other rappers have done this kind of sepia-tinted self-mythologizing, and often better, but that's just the scene-setting before the crux of the track:

As rap evolved it solved the problems for a kid
Who didn't know about race or how the other half lived
I was a pre-teen racist, I faced this
I changed this, now it's the basis...
People judged on the demos, that was the formative
Years for ears, hip-hop to storm the kids
Hear myself two years ago I sound so contrived
But now I just flow and I stride
And my life is simple, I'm enjoying it
It hasn't been long, since I was a boy and shit
The expletives flowed, I talked about ho's
The smell of bullshit didn't penetrate my nose
Who's heard of gangstas in Leeds?
Now only when I'm down or clown, do I wear a vexed frown

It's entirely natural to disown your past material, to be embarrassed by it as I clearly was (and am) and I'm already doing that with these lyrics. And I am more relaxed on this track, a bit breezier, more at ease. But the most important thing is that I think this was the first time I'd ever really reflected on what rap music meant to me, the way it had changed my life and the new horizons it had opened up to me. I wouldn't have read Alex Haley's *Autobiography of Malcolm X*, without KRS-One recreating his pose and sampling his words, or Eldridge Cleaver's *Soul on Ice* if Ice-T hadn't referenced it in music and interviews.

The years before had been about me experiencing and soaking up hip-hop, discovering old and new music, being swept along with it. Now I was at an age where I could reflect on how much my life had changed and how much of this was down to my favourite music. And also how I'd found my place within it – as I say explicitly, we know we can't be gangsta rappers, so what kind of rappers can we be? Well, we can be slightly funny, slightly earnest, slightly silly and slightly honest ones. Dan contributes four lines to the song, coming in twice with a couplet in the middle of my second verse. And because it fits the theme (and also, let's be honest, because hardly anyone heard our first demo and so couldn't complain about us cannibalising ourselves), one of those couplets is an old favourite:

No need to be a rap star
Just collect respect and say 'cheers, ta'

I think it works even better here. There's no manifesto or one-sheet with this project, full of justifications and pronouncements. I think "A Simple Life" works pretty well as a manifesto all on its own. Of course, I can't really disagree with any reader who is of the opinion that musicians should make music and not manifestos. In 1994, the rapper (and now actor) Common released a fantastic track from his

Resurrection album called "I Used to Love H.E.R."[87] It's a well-executed conceit, using the ebbs and flows of life with a woman as a metaphor for his increasingly troubled relationship with hip-hop. "A Simple Life" is in many ways a much more blatant, less metaphorical song that could alternatively be called "I Really, Really Love H.E.R."

"As the Diction Flows" was going to be a rare track where Dan raps first, with us perhaps being more democratic now that we were down to just two members. I've still got a typed lyric sheet for use in the studio where his verse is first. I then reasserted myself and wrote another verse to open the track, with Dan's one verse being sandwiched by mine. As the title and the lyrics make clear, we were obviously trying to be show-offs and clever, using big words willy nilly, despite me being a callow undergraduate and Dan doing a HND. I don't know why, but I still remember Dan's verses better than my own. Perhaps they're actually more memorable or, as I prefer to think, I have to remember them because Dan didn't exactly have a great track record in that department...

"Now the diction's flowing, the grass is greener
No need for lawn mowin', or slow mowin'
Check the skill cross code so move back from the curb, herb
Bics are disposable but still drops verbs ya nerd
So we make observations and speak our mind

[87] Common, who was quite the conscious rapper back then, clearly thought hip-hop had become too shallow and commercial by 1994 and had fallen out of love with it. In the way of things, he later went on to make songs with many of the people he was decrying, and his 1997 track "Retrospect For Life" is so nakedly anti-abortion and pro-life that I've never quite liked him since. Just to drill home, if I haven't done so enough already, hip-hop's love of the clunky acronym: The 'H.E.R. In "I Used to Love H.E.R." stands for 'Hip-Hop in its Essence is Real'. Ugh.

Wake up those who are blind like mankind
So Scam informs and I too drop vocab
Lovely concoctions we produce in our lab
Then we grab the mic to drop a nice sentence
Feel tension, if ya don't get a mention
Step to a club, freak to dubs, drink a beverage on draught
Intellect, respect the fact that we're not daft
Sport boots that aren't flimsy, watch tellys...
...consult dictionaries
Mental recession from crews who lack duration
Fake gangsters step off you cause vexation

And then I come in:

As I execute the elocution, you say golly gosh
He's got more flavours than a traffic light lollipop
It just flows from my tongue like a greenie
Friends like Whodini, rocking flat caps, taking cat naps
Making fat tracks for the rap spacs and the droolers
The cub scouts and ging-gang-goolers
Like blood through my veins to my brain
It's a cancerous pain like Roy Castle or Marti Caine
Refrain, cease, seckle and ponder
Ask, Wee Willie Winkie, where will he wander
The choicest cuts like meat dripping with blood
Footwear is always worn unlike Zola Budd
Peace to the homeless and Mr Wendal
Living the good life (like Pete Rock?) no like Felicity Kendal

And so on in this vein. None of this really makes much sense, it's largely non sequitur after non sequitur, put there because they rhyme.

But it's abundantly clear by now that we're not all that good at political engagement, and the one track on this EP that attempts a bit of that – the really quite rubbish "Outside the System, Looking In" – is the last nail in the coffin and we'd never attempt that type of thing again. "As the Diction Flows" is really just a freestyle track of boasts, brags, punchlines and flights of lyrical fancy. I commend it to you wholeheartedly.

While much of the hip-hop I loved then, and still love now, is lyrically interesting and stands up to some scrutiny, a lot of it wasn't. Many, many of my favourite tracks are full of similar nonsense to those verses I've just included above. I give you the entire recorded career of Nice & Smooth. And my seriousness about hip-hop faded with time, as it does for most, but not all, fans. Because, if I'm honest, it was never hip-hop's lyrical content that hooked me on that day that Richard Kirk played me that fateful cassette of *Electro 2*. It was the sounds. I came to love the lyrics, and have always enjoyed the way they've fluctuated between the high-brow and the gutter, but ultimately I can pretty much listen to any old rubbish being spouted as long as the music is good.

I also like to reflect on how my relationship to the lyrics has changed. I can still listen to a Public Enemy record from 1987 and feel the swell of power in those words, and remember how they impacted on me, but rap lyrics about sex that I thought were ribald and hilarious in 1989 now make me cringe. In fact, I now pretty much fast forward any track that has explicit descriptions of sex. It might be something in my own psyche, or might be that I'm correct in thinking that rappers in their mid-twenties don't really need to be telling us on what piece of furniture they wipe their dicks after ejaculating. Although the 15-year-old me would have been all ears.

"Outside the System..." is not, by any measure, in the same ballpark of awfulness as "The Steppages of History". If it was, I would not be prepared to discuss it further. I would delete it from history and hide under a pillow until it had definitely gone away. In some ways, it's a corrective to that track. Whereas "Steppages" was all 'sorry for these awful things perpetrated by our forefathers and the whole white patriarchal society we are unwitting pawns of', this is a little more fighty. It simultaneously stands up for hip-hop against external figures (usually US Republicans and the odd uninformed British MP) trying to use it as a scapegoat for society's problems, while telling hip-hop to put its house in order by not portraying all white people as 'devils' (which was a bit of a thing in Afrocentric hip-hop at the time[88]) when some of us are long-suffering white rap

---

[88] Afrocentric hip-hop, often called 5% hip-hop by some people on account of the Afrocentic 5 Percent Nation whose frankly weird views are often espoused by songs in this sub-genre, is one of my favourite things ever. It arrived in the late 80's and, a few diehards swimming against the tide aside, had largely disappeared by about 1993. It included a lot of people who, like me, were inspired by Public Enemy and wanted to make more socially and politically conscious music. It also included a lot of religious cranks. Afrocentrism in hip-hop largely came down to rappers deciding to tackle issues affecting the black community, challenging the white hegemony and in some cases affecting a modernised style of traditional African wear. The gold that rappers loved to wear was replaced by beads and African symbols. There were varying degrees of Afrocentric hip-hop. Some artists, such as X-Clan, went the whole hog, dressing like lost tribal kings and dealing with some pretty heavy theology in their records. Others just did a bit of pro-black flag-waving and referenced a book or two they'd read.

And there were some right chancers as well. Philadelphia's Schoolly D, one of my favourite rappers ever and one known for sex and bragging raps with titles like "Mr Big Dick" and "Fat Gold Chain", saw which way the wind was blowing and recorded an album called *Am I Black Enough For You?* in 1989. It had eight different tracks that contained the world 'Black' in the title. Despite all of this, it has barely any Afrocentric or 'uplifting' lyrical content at all and largely contains the same pussy, weed and gold-obsessed raps that Schoolly specialised in. It is obviously brilliant. Other rappers did similar amounts of bandwagon jumping. One second they were making albums full of diatribes about the devil and pork all wrapped in pictures of pyramids then, once the winds of change had blown hip-hop in a different direction, were back on the party or gun-toting raps the next year. Others, of course, looked upon it with disdain and decided to keep ploughing

fans who love this music and would do anything for it. And, just for good measure – because once you've started sorting the world out in a three minute rap track, why stop there? – there's a bit where we tell black female rappers to stop selling themselves short by playing the same game as male rappers and by calling themselves bitch, which Dan captures quite succinctly:

I don't buy Boss, I'd rather buy Monie Love
Peace to Ladybug, it's more meaningful to my earlug.

Boss being a gangsta rapper, Monie Love and Ladybug being more friendly, positive, De La Soulish type females. Dan and I trade lines on this song, constantly cutting in on each other which, taken with the wide-ranging lyrical approach, results in a bit of a mess. The one good thing about it is that it shows some of the same development as "A Simple Life", with us taking an aerial view of what our rightful place in hip-hop should be, understanding this ever-growing culture in the light of our own backgrounds and experiences. That might sound a little like the kind of exercise a therapist might ask you to undertake, or a creative writing seminar, but it's just something we did without thinking too hard about it. No music talks about itself as much as hip-hop does, and we were just joining in.

---

their own particular furrow and maintained their openness to eating bacon sandwiches.

One of the more troubling aspects of Afrocentric hip-hop is that it replaced the constant sexist denigration of women in rap lyrics with an equally queasy veneration of true black women as 'queens' but only if they acted like them. They were still considered beneath contempt if they ate swine or laid with a white man. What with this, the streak of homophobia running through it, and the pitifully stupid stuff about an ancient black scientist called Yacub creating the white race in a laboratory thousands of years ago, there is much to deride in Afrocentric hip-hop, but I still enjoy playing X-Clan's "Fire and Earth" or Two Kings in a Cipher's "Kemit-Cal Reaction" a few times a year.

PROGRESSIVE AGENDA

OUTSIDE THE SYSTEM LOOKING IN

Nineteen
Yo! Bum Rush the Show

Writing and recording our EP was taking up a lot more time than we expected, and with us both having other commitments, leisure time was in short supply. But one thing we always made time for was the rare visits to Leeds or a nearby city from our rap heroes. Martin used to drive us, even after the group had split up, but occasionally we couldn't all make it and we'd venture out on our own. I was used to standing by myself in a hip-hop venue from an early age.

When I was still 15, Public Enemy were playing Leeds University, and I was desperate to see them. At this stage, I'd only been to those early jams and, earlier in 1988, I'd gone back to Nottingham, back to Rock City, to see the Cold Chillin' Tour with Falco, before we lost touch for ever. That was a legendary tour and a legendary night. I got to see Marley Marl, Biz Markie, Big Daddy Kane, Kool G Rap and Roxanne Shante – all future hip-hop hall-of-famers and at the time all making stunning landmark records produced by Marley's 'House of Hits'. Excitingly, the acts didn't just perform their own singles, but combined together as well. Biz beatboxed for Roxanne as they performed their "Def Fresh Crew" collaboration live. Biz's singer TJ Swan even turned up, wearing a silk string vest that I immediately coveted even though it would have looked obscene and ridiculous on my gangly teenage frame. I'd got the bug for live hip-hop done right, and I heard Public Enemy did it right.

I didn't know anyone who was attending – I'd only met Dan the once at this stage – so I was going by myself. I was no longer intimidated at gigs, although the mood of the times led to a lot of people – right wing newspaper columnists and misinformed parents – being up in arms about these 'black radicals' stirring up trouble. Annoyingly, the show was on the exact same night as the 16th birthday party of my best friend Paul. I was going to get a taxi from the gig straight to the party, but I'd be playing catch-up on the drinking front. It wasn't like I was going to miss many girls though. When we were 15, Paul and I didn't really attract many girls into our social circle. It would just be nerds, every one of them a virgin. But there'd be booze, so I still wanted to be there.

The show was incredible. Public Enemy were – and still are – one of the best live acts in music history. Despite the fact that the music was born out of live performance, and was one that existed purely in that arena until the first rap was laid down in a studio and released on vinyl, hip-hop never had a great reputation for dazzling audiences live. It still doesn't. Certain collectors and aficionados still swap tapes and flyers of the legendary shows that predated hip-hop as we know it. Some of the acts on these bills – the Cold Crush Brothers, for example – went on to have actual recording careers, but there are many who never made it out of the live arena. They only got to rap over the DJ's breaks, they never got to rap over actual brand new production.

Some old hip-hop heads think about its first days as a golden age for performing, but the truth is a little more nuanced. Some of the routines that have survived are brilliantly entertaining, and some of the lyrics and chants so inspirational they're still referenced in modern rap years later. But the truth is that in those very early shows, the rapper is merely an adjunct. The DJ is the draw, and the rapper an added bonus. The DJ is at the top of the bill, gets the people dancing, the rapper adds a little something extra, injecting some flavour and personality into the show. The fact this balance started to tip in the other direction perhaps explains a lot about hip-hop's live woes. As the importance of the DJ declined, as producers emerged and breaks were forgotten about, the rapper took centre stage. Only DJ's with extravagant skills in cutting and scratching kept top billing – Will Smith might have eclipsed Jeff Townes in the thespian world, but The Fresh Prince always came second to DJ Jazzy Jeff in their early shows.

Why is this problematic for hip-hop as a live entity? Well, the same attribute that makes hip-hop so rich and communicative and great for home listening – the abundance of lyrics per song – can drag it down at a show. It's such a different art form to singing, so different to melody in the traditional sense, that it's a brand new experience. I'm not saying it was as earth-shattering as when the talkies came in and silent cinema died, because hip-hop and other genres could co-exist, but in a similar manner hip-hop audiences got to experience their music in a fresh, unique way. You weren't focussing on the melody or the riff or the chorus so much as a fan of classical or rock or soul or pop would. You're focussing heavily on the 48 lines that the rapper has to get through.

I don't want to oversimplify. I know there are rap artists who have great songs with negligible lyrics. No-one is really listening to the verses of Onyx's "Slam", they're just waiting to throw themselves about to the chorus, but that's an experience more akin to that of a rock or metal gig, and not how the vast majority of hip-hop is experienced live. No, the thick rump of live hip-hop, especially in the days when it was an emerging art form rather than the behemoth that it is now, was about a man on the stage who had a microphone and a hell of a lot to say to you.

If that man can say those things in a way that's interesting and engaging? You've got a live show. If you've got a man who can't – you've got a lot of people at an event that sounds like bad spoken-word poetry set to music played through a shitty sound system. I've been at countless hip-hop nights like this. A bunch of people emerge on stage, run through their verses while bumping into each other and leave to a notable absence of calls for more. They've clearly never sat down to think about how they might translate their music into a live performance. I feel their pain. How do you entertain an audience when you don't have a budget and all your music consists of you delivering 48 lines of boasting / impassioned but naïve politics / highly intricate insider drug-trade information / deeply degrading sexual detail (delete as applicable)? What if you're a brilliant rapper but you can't do choruses and your producer's music sounds great on vinyl or through headphones but muddy live? These are all real-world hip-hop issues that artists have failed to combat. It's not surprising that the hip-hop band emerged.

This isn't as big a thing as it could or perhaps should be. The Roots[89] are perhaps the most famous, but in my humble opinion,

[89] The Roots' early recordings seemed a bit worthy. They were called things like "Organix" and "Proceed" and that, coupled with the live band thing, seemed a bit too much like hard work. Hair shirt hip-hop. How wrong could you be? They're not just a cracking live band – although some fans have correctly complained that there are too many solos these days – they've now released over ten very different, interesting and progressive hip-hop albums. They've achieved more fame as the backing band for *The Tonight Show* on American TV but for me are also notable as one of the few bands who have a drummer (the walking musical encyclopaedia known as Questlove) as their front/spokesman. Especially surprising considering their rapper, Black Thought, is one of the more erudite, intelligent and highly regarded out there.

Stetsasonic[90] definitely got there first. They even called themselves 'The hip-hop Band'. It seems an elegant solution – you still get to do rap and all the lyrics, but you've got the more propulsive live sound of a band behind you, perhaps with a real drummer, guitars and bass, keyboards, the lot. The Beastie Boys had a similar thing going on, although it was quite an organic progression as they started out as a punk band. But, of course, there are always going to be problems when you broaden your appeal. You'll lose the more purist hip-hop fans, the ones who want you to be one man with a drum machine and a DJ.

If 30 years of hip-hop fandom have taught me anything, it's that there are plenty of people happier in a sullen crowd of five watching a dreadful performance than they ever would be among 5000 at a stellar, for-the-ages concert. They want to be among the few, not the many, and more power to those miserable bastards. I've been one myself. These are people who can't admit that Run DMC's "Walk This Way" is a brilliant pop record. For them it's the record with which the Hollis, Queens legends jumped the shark. These are the people who, at very grimy, sweaty and hostile underground club nights, went absolutely mental to Kris Kross' "Jump" and House of Pain's "Jump Around", when they were released on import vinyl and they didn't know who the artists were, and stopped jumping around to either of them the precise second they entered the charts, turned

[90] Stetsasonic, who I mentioned earlier for their sampling-championing classic "Talkin' All That Jazz", released three albums on Tommy Boy Records and were one of the most original and interesting groups of the 80's. While their contemporaries were generally going down the 'one MC and one DJ' route, Stetsasonic had seven members, incorporated live instruments into their recordings and live shows and were as adept at bragging rhymes as they were at political or romantic raps. One member, Prince Paul, would go on to produce De La Soul's debut *Three Feet High & Rising*, form horrorcore group The Gravediggaz with Wu-Tang Clan member The Rza and generally have a pretty atypical career.

into crossover classics and they became aware that they were made, respectively, by a couple of kids and a bunch of tattooed white Irish New Yorkers. I was in the same Leeds club, with the same clientele, when these records emptied the bars and, a week later, emptied the dancefloor. Rap fans have often been too school for cool, so cross over at your peril. These people might like your records, but they will not like your hip-hop band.

It's a sad state of affairs that many of the great rappers are dreadful live performers. If you could bottle the gravitas, power and charisma that Rakim bought to his recorded material, you'd die rich. But live, his stately monotone was stultifying, turning anthems into dirges. It didn't help that in Eric B he had one of the worst DJ's alive – there was no falling back on turntable trickery if Rakim's stuff wasn't cutting it. EPMD's 'slow-flow' style was a breath of fresh air on brilliant songs like "You're a Customer" and "Strictly Business" from 1987 onwards – on stage they were akin to a pair of asthmatic lunks slowly sucking the last traces of oxygen out of the room (and I know one when I see one). I saw them recently, as part of the burgeoning retro circuit, and while it was nice to see them getting a pay day and lovely to see a full room in London some 20 years after they last released a decent record, only nostalgia coupled with wilful blindness could convince you they'd improved any as performers. Those finely crafted lyrics and punchy stanzas flow like milk through a pair of headphones, but they curdle over a PA.

Yet many major rap acts think they can come over to the UK, perform their one hit single, shuffle about the stage with a bunch of their no-name mates, and charge £30 for the privilege. Such acts often get short shrift – reactions have ranged from booing to bottling to stage invasions. If a hip-hop artist or group treats a UK audience with disdain, things can get ugly very quickly. By contrast, those who take the time to engage with their audience – De La Soul, for example – or put some thought into their live performance – Kanye West, who might rub a lot of people up the wrong way but rarely phones it in – are cherished by their crowds. Jurassic 5's recorded output was decent but disappointing compared to their live shows, which were a direct throwback to an almost mythical era of late 70's hip-hop show, and Ugly Duckling are likeable but limited on record, but always great fun in the right sized room.

Whether a big stadium charging £8 a pint or a sweaty venue with blocked toilets and adventurous fire-control policies, some things never change with live hip-hop. You'll be asked by the artists to make some noise. They'll be insistent on that point. They'd prefer said noise to be of the 'motherfucking' variety. And then all bets are off. You might be asked to scream the DJ's name (not so much these days), you might be split into two and pitted against the other side of the room for who can make the most of the aforementioned motherfucking noise. These tricks are overused, hoary and simple, but they work. They'll get even the most recalcitrant audience stoked if they do it just right (again, I cite De La Soul as peerless executors of this approach) and then, when they drop in the first notes of that last big single they released, you'll go crazy apeshit bananas.

What the groups with finesse have learned is that if you just plough through your catalogue, no matter how brilliant and studded with gems and certified club bangers, you're just adding 48 lines to 48 lines to 48 lines, until eventually you're subjecting the audience to hundreds of couplets with no respite. No, break them up, tease it out, and it's much more palatable. And you can chop the last verse off, if you don't mind. People have stopped dancing by halfway through anyway... They're like a wind-up toy that runs out after one and a half minutes, and they're saving their energy for the next big single you play. Keep it succinct, keep it lively, keep it popping and get the energy up.

It has taken hip-hop nearly 40 years to learn that it's best as a live event if you can distract the audience from thinking about what it actually is they're witnessing – which, just to reiterate, is a man (or very occasionally a woman) doing 48 lines of lyrics per song at you. That stuff might fire the synapses at home in your bedroom when alone, or if eagerly analysing the latest release with a like-minded friend, but it's no-one's idea of a fun night out when you've already got to contend with lukewarm Red Stripe, a toilet flooded with heroic amounts of piss and a definite news-making inferno if even a stray ember should alight on the alcohol-soaked floor.

It's easy to be cynical about live hip-hop. I've gone from being the boy down at the front desperately trying to reach the hands of his heroes to the man at the back nursing a pint I've just paid far too much for. But some things are true down the ages, and one such thing is that Public Enemy kick arse live. Put Public Enemy in the right kind of room with the right kind of sound and their sonic soup goes down a treat, given a huge helping hand by a stage show that included not just the authority of Chuck D and the clowning of Flavor Flav, but also the pseudo-paramilitary movements of the S1W's – the Security of the First World. If you got into the front row of a Public Enemy concert – which I did a few subsequent times, if not on this occasion – then the crush and the thrill as they launched into "Bring The Noise" or "Fight The Power" was the closest hip-hop ever got to a mosh pit.

I came out of that 1988 concert buzzing, soaked in sweat, and the proud owner of a brand new official Public Enemy baseball cap that I'd bought on the way out. I wouldn't dream of wearing a hat now – I just haven't got the head or face to carry one off – but for years I wasn't without one. At university it was a preposterous and pretentious baggy flat cap – one that riled my one-time housemate and future radio 'personality' Christian O' Connell so much that he ripped it from my head and tossed it into a heaving crowd of students in Nottingham's Rock City club one night (at a student night, their legendary hip-hop jams long a thing of the past), never to be seen again. In my mid-teens, it was a selection of baseball caps – and yes, they were occasionally worn backwards.[91] A white boy in a baseball cap is a common sight now – it really wasn't at that time, not in Leeds.

I stood waiting for a taxi to take me to Paul's party, the sweat drying on me, the adrenaline starting to die away, and promptly got mugged. This wasn't like the 'taxings' I'd had at jams in Nottingham, which always felt like a friendly contractual arrangement, where it was mutually agreed in advance that I'd begrudgingly give up a small amount of money in return for not being punched in the face. No, this involved pushing, it involved a couple of punches and, most distressing of all, it involved the four black men who did it calling me 'white boy' disdainfully and stealing my Public Enemy cap.

I didn't know their motivations, so I'm not going to try and draw out some pompous larger 'truth' about white people perhaps being interlopers at a black music event we weren't really welcome at. I don't think there's anything to that – any hip-hop gig in the UK for an act of that level, outside of London, will pretty much be dominated by white people. But at the time I wasn't just shocked by my mugging, I was hurt. In my naïve teenage brain I was politically rooting for the rights of black people worldwide. Hell, I was spending my money at a Public Enemy concert – it doesn't get more

[91] Although, among the many terrible hats I wore over the years, none were as hilarious as Dan's Osh Kosh B-Gosh hat, which I think he'd bought in America. It's what a man with a train set in his loft would wear if he was pretending to be the station agent, while his wife secretly carried out a string of affairs and his children looked at him with barely disguised scorn. I'm not judging. It was just a hat.

pro-black than that. I almost wanted to shout, "I'm on your side!" at them – like that would have helped. I dwelled on it for months, when what I see now is what they probably saw: A skinny kid (this was a long time ago, granted) on his own with a pretty great hat who looked like an easy touch.

My overly dramatic reading of the situation aside, what I should have done is taken it as a simple lesson – don't go to hip-hop concerts on your own. Whenever I did, something bad happened. I once joined a coach trip from Leeds to Birmingham to go and see NWA, Eazy E and Above the Law play. It was so undersubscribed it turned into a mini-bus trip (which is absolutely baffling – NWA! Dr. Dre! And yet only seven people from Leeds wanted to go), a mini-bus that promptly broke down en route. I didn't know anyone else on the trip and no-one talked to me the entire way. We missed all the opening acts and most of Above The Law.[92] The only thing that rescued the evening was that Eazy-E threw a sweat-drenched Holiday Inn towel into the crowd and I caught it, saving it for years before my mum washed it one day and eradicated the all-important DNA traces.

On another occasion, LA rapper Ice-T brought his Rhyme Syndicate crew to The Leadmill in Sheffield with a line-up that included Lord Finesse, one of my favourite MC's and producers of all time.[93] I've no idea why Dan and Martin didn't join me – they

---

[92] Whose 1990 debut album *Livin' Like Hustlers* is a masterpiece of early Dr. Dre production and who would go on to make other stonkingly good records like *Uncle Sam's Curse*. I also liked the fact that one of the group members was called Cold 187um, which I didn't even know how to say.

[93] It's pretty baffling now to contemplate just how big and matter-of-fact Ice-T has become. As a rapper he was often the absolute epitome of the kind of thing that parents warned us about and the media thought was 'bad for the kids'. He appeared in early movies about hip-hop, recorded some of the most respected West Coast albums of the 80's, and then went on to become properly huge, helped in no small part by various controversies you can read about on the internet. He

loved Ice-T, they loved Finesse – but I assume it was something to do with their girlfriends. Or maybe they had a premonition that I would worm my way to the front row only to have an asthma attack halfway through Ice-T's set and would have to worm my way to the back to spend the rest of the evening puffing on my inhaler while a legendary gig took place yards away from me. Never. Go. Alone.

Anyway, shaken by my experience, angered by the theft of a hat I'd paid £15 for only 30 minutes earlier (and my hair now looked a right state), and stinking of sweat and fear, I got a taxi to Paul's 16th. There were no girls there, obviously. I drank half a bottle of Lamb's Navy Rum, threw up everywhere and fell asleep in a chair. Oh what a night.

---

then moved into acting and has carved out a decent niche there as well. But he's not too big for hip-hop. I saw him again at the screening of a documentary called *The Art Of Rap* that he narrated in 2012 and his live show was still brilliant.

Twenty
Serve Tea, Then Murder

I wasn't exactly living the hip-hop life at university in Nottingham. I was permanently broke, so much so that I even ended up checking ID's on the door at my campus' student union bar, for the princely sum of £10 per night. The grant would come in, pay for my rent, leave a bit for food, and nights out had to be strictly rationed. Tricky in what was definitely a party house. And my record collection wasn't getting any bigger either. It has an entire room in my house at the moment, 31 years of obsession bowing the floorboards, but I managed to take my complete record collection to university in 1992 – all two boxes of it. I was enjoying revisiting Arcade Records, acting like I was taking some trip down memory lane to the haunts of my youth when, in fact, it had only been five years since I'd last been in there. It was strictly window shopping though.

Happily I wasn't in a houseful of hip-hop haters. Living cheek by jowl with nine teenage strangers has its unique stresses, but as only myself and a lad called Oliver Scull were big vinyl buyers (and my buying was on hiatus), there were very few fights about music. Ollie, I'm happy to say, has become a close and lifelong friend, and he even played up to my hip-hop fandom by dubbing himself 'O-Real' as we bonded over our mutual love of artists like NWA and Cypress Hill. In wearisome student fashion, we'd all take turns breaking into each other's rooms when the inhabitant was at lectures. The room would then be trashed and defaced, clothes emptied from drawers, scatological German pornography hidden under pillows, that kind of thing. When it was my turn, they really hit me where it hurt – they de-alphabeticised my two boxes of records. The mental scars were deep.

At the end of each term it was back to Leeds, back to working in the office for Tracy, and back to using the money I earned there to help book more studio time for *Headnods*... Maybe it's because it was something we truly believed, or maybe we were just trying to explain to ourselves the reason why we had turned down the only offer of a record deal anyone had been foolish enough to dangle in front us, but we decided to make a record about only producing our own material. "Production Artist" sees Dan explaining why he crafts all our stuff, which seems a bit silly now. Who else was going to be daft enough to waste their time and beats on us and why do we think that's something worth patting ourselves on the back for?

Yeah you can do what you want when you do your own stuff
Not tied down to play blind man's bluff
Nuff respect to myself 'cos I dig in my own crates
And sometimes off the shelf
Good health, drop bombs like a plane
You know my name, money's not the aim
'Cos I've got about 53p in my purse
No need for a producer to reimburse
Cash settlement, a nice round sum
An outside beat maker? I'd rather ask my mum
But she doesn't like rap so it looks like I'm on my own
To make beats like those kids on Meanwood streets

Call up Marley Marl or Jermaine Dupri?
[We can do that Greenpeace] Yep, that's me
But I don't want credit 'cos it's a joint venture
And I'll love hip-hop until I need dentures

At least we're realistic. When it came to producers we could have afforded to pay, legends like Marl and Dupri were a little out of our range. Maybe we should have asked Dan's mum after all. The eagle-eyed scrutiniser of lyrics will have noticed the usual contradictions: 'Nuff respect to myself' versus 'I don't want credit', but what Dan makes clear is that we're in this together, whether for good or ill. We thought we had our own unique, original and particular sound, and we were just waiting for the world to catch up with it. Although, had that happened, I'm sure Dan wouldn't have turned down a fat cheque to produce for somebody else. My verses top and tail his, but I think he says it best especially as, a few pithy points aside, I get distracted.

So take a running jump with your big name producer
I'll be myself even if it makes me a loser
Not really bothered about chart hits
So the productions by the artist, Production: Artist.

I like this song – and I think Dan's production work, with a lovely jazz piano and a beat break down at the end drives our point home – but as much as anything else I loved recording it. It's one thing to look back and poke fun at our naïve lyrics, but I'd be lying if I didn't confess to having a wonderful time in the studio. When you're someone as nervous as me – someone who has to have two bottles of wine and eight poos before delivering a best man speech – then making your way to a vocal booth with a sheet of lyrics you've spent weeks honing, is both frightening and exhilarating in roughly equal measure. You can't wait for people to hear your work for the first time, and you don't want to fuck it up.

There were moments where I couldn't deliver a line the way Dan thought it would work best and he'd get exasperated as I failed again and again. And there were moments when I did a line in a new way to all the other takes, cutting out a word or lengthening another line so it felt and sounded just right, and I could see Dan nodding his head in appreciation. This is what I lived for – writing lyrics and laying them down. Even though just the two of us were making this track, we had our crew in the studio with us, and in the last seconds of "Production: Artist" you can hear them all in the background – SADE singing baritone, Horny Baker joining me in a daft chant about Northern motorways, Countdown doing some vocal scratching. We recorded a silly outro with them, a couple of quick skits we never used.[94] It sounds, on the tape, like fun, which

[94] I could have bundled a footnote about skits in with the earlier one about Intros and Outros but, truly, it deserves its own. Although I wish it didn't. Whereas the Intro and Outro top and tail an album, the skits are dotted throughout, and depending on the self-indulgence of the artist, can soon mount up, especially when they're not little 10 second interludes, but two and three minute things. It's hard to pinpoint the first ever skit, but the first ever skit-heavy album was De La Soul's *Three Feet High and Rising* (1989), largely due to the influence of producer Prince Paul, a man whose entire career was punctuated heavily with skits. The skits take the form of a gameshow and, because they're not obnoxious, they're some of the few skits listeners don't automatically skip past. Ironically their follow-up album, 1991's sour (but also brilliant) *De La Soul is Dead* is full of skits that are largely annoying as the group try to distance themselves from the image they portrayed on their debut. But these skits are still charm itself compared to most, which break down into three main types: Skits that are about sex, and usually have the artist fucking several orgasmic women through a crescendo of aahs and oohs. Skits that are about someone getting shot in a hail of fake-sounding gunshot. Skits where the rapper and his mates think they're funny.

Okay, there are other types, but those three categories account for maybe ninety percent of recorded skits. Occasionally a skit will complement the track it's attached to, but just as often it'll ruin it, or take you out of the world the music has

it was. I'd been serious about hip-hop all my life but now I was doing what I wanted to do: Making the rap of the future with my friends.

"Time to Start Peeping" is just your standard brag-and-boast track, with Dan and I trading allegedly witty punchlines in our usual vein. By peeping, we don't mean it in the everyday sense, but in the hip-hop sense of the time, which is to check something out. There were lots of records out about that time called things like "Peep the Skillz", "Peep Game" and such, and we were just joining in. We literally did go around in everyday life saying things like 'peep my new sneakers', although in truth this lasted all of about five minutes.

Keep your eyes peeled for the real deal feel
Selling hip-hop, not selling apples like Pete Beale
Not an Eastender, I tend to
Bend your earths to the North and serve it up like a vendor
So if it's time to peep, peep from your shutter

---

created. That's another problem with them – they're too literal. A song about how a rapper's 'bitches' are after his money? Okay, whatever... Followed by a skit in which some 'bitches' are after his money? We get the point, mate. Some people are fond of skits, and this is why a quick search on the internet will give you access to lots of different lists of people's favourites. Others, like me, routinely delete them from the track listing before listening digitally, or get ready to skip the vinyl or CD along. I seriously don't want to ever hear another rapper having fake sex on a record, I don't want to hear another broadcast from DJ Salt E. Nuts on station WBALLS or hear some non-thespian mangling some dialogue from *Scarface.*

Grudgingly, I will accept a couple of skits. Black Sheep's "U Mean I'm Not" from their 1991 album *A Wolf In Sheep's Clothing* is a note perfect mockery of the type of hardcore gangsta rap that Black Sheep specialised in the polar opposite of. De La Soul's aforementioned gameshow skits are fine, and the numerous ones dotted through the Wu-Tang Clan albums – both collectively and on their solo projects – were a good window into their world when they first came out and revolutionised their corner of hip-hop. But, 20 years later, do I want to sit through a fiftieth listen to that bit where they sew someone's anus closed and force feed them? No, I do not.

'Cos the rhymes so smooth you can't believe it's not butter
Or Anchor, it melts on my toast and I thank ya
For being here this evening, it's time to start peeping

Nothing ground breaking, but in terms of a brag track perfectly functional. I'd also like to go on record and say that I was the first rapper in the world to use the 'can't believe it's not butter' line. I've heard it many times since, used by both UK and US rappers, but my usage predates them all by years. Small victories.

As much fun as recording the preceding tracks was, it all paled in comparison to recording our posse cut masterpiece, "Drinking Tea with the Lads". I've got a faded photo from the studio that day. Me, Dan, Countdown, Horny Baker, Boyd, SADE, Part 2. We're in our hip-hop gear, mugs of tea in hand. I still have discernible facial bone structure. It captures what was not only the most fun I'd ever had in my brief recording career, but also the most artistically rewarding. The posse cut had been my idea. Not a greatly original concept I'll grant you, but the lyrical theme, getting all of Progressive Agenda, DJ Countdown, SADE and New Flesh 4 Old to rap about having a cuppa, and for the musical backdrop to change for each rapper – that was my idea.

Why tea? I suppose it was just a continuation of our attempts to be real and Northern. We weren't smoking blunts and sipping Hennessy XO in the studio – we were taking it in turns to put the kettle on and make a brew. I took a vocal sample from a group called Taking Your Business, one of them saying "A Sexy hip-hopper" and decided that we'd start our respective verses with our names and then that sample would drop in, to give the song some structure and unity. I even picked out some of the music, working closely with Dan to find stuff that would marry with the beat. That bit that Horny Baker raps over? A track called "Landscape" by The Mohawks on the B-side of their heavily sampled "The Champ". Again, I wasn't pushing any boundaries, but if the 11-year-old me could have seen the 20-year-old me rapping in a proper recording studio with a posse of friends, all working towards an idea I'd sketched out on one of my notepads? It would have blown his stupid, crap sneaker-wearing mind.

Okay, so perhaps the world isn't crying out for rap tracks that celebrate beverages that also clock in at over eight and a half minutes, but I can still listen to this track with love, over 20 years later. Dan (a sexy hip-hopper) sets the tone with talk of Ken Dodd, chocolate digestives, Jeremy Beadle and Paul Raymond magazines and then SADE (a sexy hip-hopper) comes in:

I've got the metal kettle that shakes and makes a racket
Plus the nice price Rich Tea, 23p a packet
My lips start to pout, then I scream and shout
And I strain through my brain and the flavour floods out

His verse grows more deft and complex as it goes on, a fine debut from the newcomer. Then the DJ turned one man band Countdown (a sexy hip-hopper) delivers his verse:

Drinking tea with the lads, what's the taste is it Tetley?
Oh my gosh it's PG
Granules, more tricks up my sleeve than Paul Daniels
I pull them out like a gun in H. Samuels...

You get the picture. Tea. Lots of it. I'm not Scam on this track, I'm Sweaty Convict (a sexy hip-hopper). I know. I'm not proud. My verse starts with talk about my old chopper (the bike, that is), takes in Avon cosmetics, Ryan Giggs, Chewbacca, Joey Deacon, Russell Hobbs, scones and a barely disguised diss of Braintax. New Flesh 4 Old (sexy hip-hoppers all) bring up the rear, Part 2 (coffee, two sugars, Bakewell tarts, Kajagoogoo) and Horny Baker (Gazza, the gold run on *Blockbusters*, Regal cigarettes) deliver two excellent, very different verses. And then Boyd... does what Boyd does. An entirely improvised and meandering spoken word bit that is either anti-climactic or entirely fitting, depending on where you stand. And then it's a wrap, eight minutes and 38 seconds, the peak of my small ambitions, a song about drinking tea. The best thing I ever did.

BOSTON

Twenty-One
White Lines

Like the Robin Hood of the hip-hop world that I never was, I fell foul of the Sheriff of Nottingham. I'm not joking. I didn't think that was even a thing in the real world, but it turned out it was, and that he was also campus warden at my university. And like the fictional sheriff is so often depicted when squaring up to the Merry Men, he was a humourless arsehole. And, not to heap all the blame on his shoulders, I was a drunk arsehole. One night of drinking with a small bunch of fellow Manchester United fans at the student union bar, celebrating the Red Devils' first league title in our lifetimes, and I was under threat of being sent down. Perhaps I deserved it. It's not often you get a free pass for calling a figure of authority a 'cunt', and I wasn't getting one. The Sheriff recommended that I was kicked out of the whole place. At a special hearing I expressed my mortification, my profound regrets, made guarantees about my future behaviour. He sneered and emphasised how he wouldn't settle for anything less than the end of my time at Nottingham Trent.

I was the first person in my family ever to go to university. I was about to become the first to ever be forcibly ejected from one as well. Luckily, my tutor intervened and negotiated the Sheriff down, citing my reasonable academic performance and my genuine remorse. However, I still had to move off campus, despite the fact that I'd paid up until the end of the year. I got a letter stipulating that I was allowed on campus for lectures, but must stick to the main paths, and certainly never deviate to the accommodation blocks. As pretty much every friend I had at college lived in those blocks, this was harsh. If understandable. I did 'cunt off' the Sheriff of Nottingham, after all. I wasn't going to not see my mates, however, so every couple of days I'd sneak back into J Block, and my 'friends' would constantly pretend they were about to phone the campus warden to come and collect me.

With no money and only a couple of months left of the academic year, I was forced to squat in the house of a friend of a friend. They kindly gave me a roof and a room, and also a head start on my former campus-mates in the fascinating world of student houses. The halls of residence, with their cleaners and insulation and electrics that were up to code were like the Palace of Versailles compared to what was out there. The house we lived in in the second year was the absolute pits, like the set from *The Young Ones.* I woke up every morning to be greeted by fresh slugs sliming their way across the carpet, and the landlord had taken a novel approach to electricity where it wasn't so much carried through cables as freely available in the atmosphere. There was a whole corner of my room that hummed like a Tesla coil.

I'd been the last to arrive for that academic year, and the others had picked the best rooms before I turned up. Ollie's was a sun-trap on the top floor, mine a slug-trap on the bottom, the prime candidate for the almost constant burglaries in Nottingham's Meadows area. Although all any burglar would have found would have been some slugs fizzing in piles of salt and whatever scheisse-filled German porn mag Ollie or Tom had placed under my pillow. It didn't help that my neighbour was a homunculus who decided to hire a sun bed to sleep in like it was a normal bed, so that every morning I was greeted by a scorched Hobbit.

Graduation was still some way away, and I didn't have a clue what I wanted to do if I managed to avoid any further disciplinary action and make it there. The dream, however unrealistic, had always been a career in hip-hop, but as I only saw Dan in holidays, that was merely edging forward. Would it still be there in 1995?

The *Headnods and Broomsticks EP* was in the bag, but we never pressed it up. We never even sent it out to any record labels so that they could ask us to work with the Stereo MC's and we could say no again. Why not? To this day, I don't really know. Is it the great lost British rap record? Of course not, but nor would it have been the worst thing ever committed to vinyl.[95] After spending all the time and money in the studio, dragging our collaborators in to record their bits, polishing and tweaking the finished product, playing around with the sequence of tracks for maximum impact, we just mothballed it.

With Dan working and me studying, maybe we just didn't have the time and money to commit to putting it out. To find a pressing plant, listen to the test pressings, design labels and stickers, go shop

---

[95] Every person you ask will have a different opinion on what the worst hip-hop record ever is. Often it'll be by an artist they hate, or a bit of pop-rap they resent, or a piece of pisstakery like the Morris Minor and the Majors stuff. But for me, it's usually stuff by artists I like. In Outkast's case, love. Yet somehow, in 1998, they did their best to ruin their otherwise brilliant *Aquemini* album with the track "Mamacita", which is easily, by some margin, their worst record. There are hundreds, if not thousands, of tracks I routinely skip when listening to albums I like. Hell, I even turn off *It Takes a Nation of Millions* by Public Enemy – to drill the point home, the best album recorded in musical history – before "She Watch Channel Zero" comes on. But I don't hate these records, they're just disappointing. The only hip-hop record I think I really hate, and my nomination for the worst ever, is the completely charmless "Ain't No Nigga" by Jay-Z featuring Foxy Brown. A sample used better by everyone else who ever sampled it and two horrible vocal performances. It's terrible.

to shop asking them to stock it, promoting it in a pre-Internet era. We'd never thought that far ahead, to be honest. Conceiving, writing and recording the EP was the fun bit, we weren't prepared for the slog of actually making it into a physical product and then marketing it. And perhaps, deep down, we knew it wasn't quite good enough. Did it have the effortless charm and soul of Breaking The Illusion? Not really. Were we as good at rapping as Braintax? No, we probably weren't. We didn't believe in it enough to put it out there for the public to judge. After all the time and effort we'd invested, we weren't mentally strong enough to send it to *Hip-Hop Connection* where the review might be scathing. Deep down, did we know that the music buying world wouldn't be interested in two white rappers from Leeds, obsessed with tea and minor TV personalities?

My documented lack of talent aside – a talent that was limited, as we've already established, to a few half-decent punchlines and an ear for an apposite vocal sample to drop into a track, the rest was enthusiasm – there's also the white rapper thing. I didn't fail because I was a white rapper, far from it, but it's worth exploring the white rapper issue. It's a tricky one to contend with, encompassing as it does issues of race, racism and, once we dig into it, concepts of 'soul' with all of the baggage that brings along. And that's before we get into history, capitalism, education and whether or not 'reverse racism' exists. I don't think we'll get this covered in a 200 word footnote.

You could start by saying, 'But Andrew, why do you want to go down this path? There isn't really a white rapper issue (as you insist on calling it) is there? After all, I've got lots of music from The Beastie Boys and Eminem in my collection. They sold millions of records. If there's an issue it's entirely in your mind. Is it because you never got a record deal? Go on, you can tell me.'

It's not. And it's really, really difficult to examine what being a white rapper is/was (even one at an exceedingly low level) without treading on a few issues. Even when I was being mugged at hip-hop gigs (for pocket change and baseball caps), I never felt excluded from the scene. After all, in the UK, white people embraced hip-hop in huge numbers, and at the gigs I attended there were often as many white people as black people, sometimes more. I'd argue that the main hip-hop collectors in the UK (and Europe) are white people (there isn't the time or space here to go into why that is, and I should add that there are notable exceptions) but obviously the main hip-hop artists aren't.

I don't think I've ever had anyone tell me I couldn't rap because I was white (it was usually because, well, I couldn't really rap) or that anyone into hip-hop has ever said I shouldn't be into it because I was white. The only people who've ever told me that I shouldn't be into hip-hop were reprehensible and entirely ignorable white people at school who told me it was 'nigger music'. So to say that I have first-hand experience of white exclusion from hip-hop would be nonsense. But as I say, it's not that simple.

The fundamental question is, can white people make hip-hop music that is as good as that made by black people? If not, why? And if they can, why are there so few notable white rap artists? I find it helpful to bear something else in mind – I see lots of black footballers at an amateur and professional level, but I don't see many black football managers. Are they not as good as white managers, or is it a matter of opportunity? If you think it's the former, I'm not sure how you've got this far into a book about hip-hop music.

So, let's say there's a camp who, if pushed, would say that white people can't make hip-hop that is as good as that made by black people because white people lack 'soul'. They might say that white people don't have an innate sense of rhythm and can't ride the beat on time. The people saying this might be of either colour, by the way.

Let's say there's another camp who might opine that white people can't make hip-hop because they lack the shared racial experience that has been uniquely expressed and channelled by hip-hop music over the last 30-odd years. That it's a music made by black people to express a black point of view. White people have their own avenues of expression and should stick to those. Again, this view could be expressed by either white or black people. I've heard it from both.

Another camp points to Eminem, The Beastie Boys, Macklemore, Iggy Azalea and says, well, it's clear that white people can make hip-hop and very successful they are too. Another camp points to Eminem, The Beastie Boys, Macklemore, Iggy Azalea and says, well, it's clear that white people suck at hip-hop and can only make music that appeals to other white people, students, liberals and the stupid.

At this point you might groan and say, well, it's essentially something that can't be resolved. Some people like white rappers, some don't. But there've been some successes, so why are you even banging on about it at this length? Well, it's because there is a white rapper issue. It didn't affect me – my talent flew too low to trouble the radar – but it has affected many. And it often goes unsaid, but then so much does. Yet there has always been an opinion about white rappers that has some things in common with old-fashioned opinions about British rappers. When rappers from these shores were making great records in the 80's (I'm referring to Hijack, Demon Boyz, Hardnoise, Silver Bullet and a few others), many critics and fans didn't have any time for them. They had time for lesser songs, or songs that fit better into what they were expecting hip-hop to sound like. Basically, you had to be 400% better than a US artist had to be to even get noticed.

I feel the same is true about white rappers. There used to be an assumption among large swathes of hip-hop fans (of all races and colours) that your run-of-the-mill white rapper wasn't as good as your run-of-the-mill black rapper for deep-seated reasons alluded to in the last few paragraphs. White rappers had to bring something else to the party. The white New York rap duo 3rd Bass were signed to Def Jam and released a brace of critically acclaimed albums, but both times I saw them live they received a very cool response. Both times they out-performed the black artists they were supporting, both times they got cold-shouldered. They also found themselves embroiled in a diss war with the radically Afrocentric hip-hop group X-Clan. The Beastie Boys got a similar reaction to their early material, but managed to side-step it by pitching their later material to a largely college crowd, heavily white. Lots of black people love The Beastie Boys, of course, but they could only forge out a long career by moving slightly closer to rock and appealing to a much wider demographic.

Hopefully I made it abundantly clear at the start of this section that the 'white rapper issue' is a thorny and complicated one, with no clear answer or narrative. Some things you feel and, no matter how hard you try, struggle to explain. Many of the notions of 'soul' that white rappers have fallen foul of come from black music fans. And many of them come from the kind of white music fan who celebrates cerebrality in music over emotion. There are many different sides and angles to it. I've heard enough great white rappers and enough great black rockers to know that most of the boundaries put up between genres with spurious justifications are absolutely bullshit. And one of the many areas where hip-hop in the present day has improved on hip-hop in 1990 is that it's more racially open. But we still live in a world where the people behind the brilliant magazine *Ego Trip* made a TV talent show in 2007 called *The White Rapper Show*, hosted by one third of 3rd Bass. It ran for one series.

Given the huge numbers of white people into hip-hop, given the crowds who've tried their hands at being rappers and DJ's, the general lack of success at a mid-level is the most noticeable to me. Eminem was a phenomenon, up there with some of the biggest sellers of all time. But he's an exception, and I'm looking for artists who combine moderate critical acclaim with moderate sales as the true test of the health of a genre. It lives or dies on its footsoldiers, not its heroes. And when you dig into the artists who sold a few thousand records and whose careers are remembered fondly for flickering briefly, there aren't many white guys in there.[96]

So, again. Did they lack talent? Were they the victims of conscious racism? Unconscious racism? Did they not believe in themselves? Was it at the record label level? Did the laudable pro-black push in some hip-hop make people think you shouldn't sign white rappers?

I don't want you to think I'm mewling. Again, any white rapper issues didn't directly affect me, as my talent or lack thereof had already taken care of Scam's career path. I'm just exploring the issue – were white rappers marginalised because black hip-hop fans were racist, consciously or subconsciously? I don't think so, but I can't rule it out. Were white rappers marginalised because white hip-hop fans were racist and only wanted to hear black people rap? A bit. Can black music fans be accused of racism anyway, when much of racism

---

[96] This isn't the *Ego Trip Book of Rap Lists* but here are 10 tracks by white rappers I definitely love: RA the Rugged Man – "Stanley Kubrick", Yelawolf – "Pop the Trunk", Eminem – "Just the Two of Us", Paul Wall – "They Don't Know", Bubba Sparxxx – "Deliverance", Non Phixion – "Black Helicopters", Cage – "Radiohead", Goldtop – "Introduction", 3rd Bass – "Steppin' to the AM", Beastie Boys – "Hold It Now Hit It".

is about economic power?[97] I honestly don't know. Did my being a white British male from Northern England give me a certain frame of cultural reference and set of shared experiences that I thought could be better expressed than it was being in hip-hop? At last, a question I can answer. Yes. Definitely. And I failed.

---

97 While we're on this, Ice Cube was definitely being a racist dick when he recorded "Black Korea" in 1991 and rapped about Korean store owners with their "Chop-Suey asses". Honestly, Ice, you've recorded a couple of albums about how your race is mistreated, marginalised and stereotyped and you're going to then go and make a track about how Korean people are all shopkeepers, complete with racial slurs?

Twenty-Two
Movin' on

Or had we failed? Was there one last chance for that rap career? By now we didn't even dream of fame or riches, just of minor recognition for our continued efforts in the Leeds rap scene. Could we at least get a 12" out there, something to show the grandchildren on Moon Base 5?

Dan and I recorded one last track as Progressive Agenda and, as I was persisting in being called Sweaty Convict (and when I wasn't, actually being called it by some people in our small circle of rappers and DJ's, which is a bit strange come to think of it: "Alright, Dave?" "Yeah, not too shabby, Sweaty Convict."), we called it "Sweaty Convict's Theme". We didn't even really finish it. It only exists in three increasingly amateurish takes that collapse into giggles every time. We'd probably had a bit to drink.

"Sweaty Convict's Theme" sums up our careers in many ways. It has an organ sample, it has a vocal sample (from De La Soul's brilliant and strange "Afro Connections at a Hi 5 (In The Eyes of a Hoodlum)", it has a *Hong Kong Phooey* sample and it has a porn film sample. The lyrics are puerile and chock full of contemporary references. As ever, you can work out when we recorded something without resorting to carbon dating. In fact, let's not underplay the puerility – this is perhaps our silliest and most childish, tactless and tasteless song. And it has some extremely strong competition.

It's a black thing, a white thing, hell, it's just a Panda
You'll get chopped by machetes in Rwanda
What lurks in Gabrielle's eye socket?
My tape's so fat you couldn't fit it in your pocket

We're not only sharing mic duties, we're sharing verses, lines and words, cutting in on each other, finishing each other's rhymes. It's a true collaboration.

Don't fuck, or you'll get took, to the butcher shop
For some chop chop suey
Hong Kong Phooey I'm the number one super Jewy
Something goes wrong, I strike out like Myra Hindley
But I don't kill kids 'cause my limbs are too spindly
You were comatose, what did you miss
I put nails through Christ's wrists just because I was pissed
And you hissed, booed, the Sweaty Convict was lewd, crude
You died on stage like Tommy Cooper in full view
Kids run your garments, run your garms kid
Kids get your garms ran by the garm runner Scam
Or gran run your purse, run your purse gran
Or get your purse ran by the purse runner Dan
I drop this in your mind it lingers
I also drop the mic 'cause I have Beadle fingers

Poor old Jeremy Beadle, we never could leave him alone. These lyrics only scrape the surface of how silly this song is. There are other lyrics I can't bring myself to share, there are ad-libs and impressions, corpsing galore and us joining in with the porn star moans on the backing track. Fun to record? Obviously. Fun to listen to? Obviously not. We'd never before recorded a track that we didn't play to anybody, and we'd recorded some complete rubbish.

This was our post-Prehistoric Ages light-hearted agenda taken to the extreme, with absolutely no thought going into the lyrics except, if we're being honest, the urge to make each other laugh. And while we never dreamed of sharing this song or sending it to anyone – we weren't daft or deluded enough to imagine anyone would ever want to sign us to a three album deal on the back of such juvenile frippery – it didn't quite die or disappear.

Shortly after we'd made this, and with no concrete plans to make any other music, Part 2 from New Flesh 4 Old asked Dan to record some music with him for a new project. It may have been jingles and idents for some radio show but, if that was the case, the radio show remained jingleless. I tagged along as Dan and two thirds of the new look New Flesh 4 Old (Part 2 and Bang out of Order were present. Toastie Taylor couldn't make it. Horny Baker and Boyd had moved on) went into a recording studio in York.

I don't know what derailed the jingle-making. But before long we were taking the bare bones of "Sweaty Convict's Theme" and recycling and repurposing them for a new track. While Dan did the work, I again will take sole credit for the concept. I'm not sure how I arrived at it, but at some point I found myself saying, out loud: "We should make a track where Dan, the producer, is Scaramanga from the *James Bond* movies, and each of us rappers is one of his three nipples." Hence "The Three Nipples of Scaramanga". And I wonder why I never made it as a mainstream rapper...

We all wrote our lyrics there in the studio, refashioned the music, recorded it and mixed it. By the end of play, there were no jingles to be heard, but we had a track. Dan appears only at the end, introducing his three nipples in a doom-laden, portentous voice. Am I proud of this one, despite the hastily assembled and once again silly lyrics? Hell yes.

I'll take no shorts even if my legs were stumps
My rhymes flow like my girl on the 28th of the month
I'm aiming strobe lights at epileptics
Your mind has one track, mine has two, call me Scalextrix
Eating rappers is my favourite dish
I burn MC's like Laurence Fishburne burns fish
Dispose of them, like my crew dispose of Rizlas
Got more girls phone numbers on my list than Schindler

These are, pretty much, the last rap lyrics I'll ever write. It's clear that 12 years of fandom and love of hip-hop culture had only taken me as far as a bunch of punchlines stuck unevenly together, displaying at best a partial understanding of menstruation and a complete misreading of how Oskar Schindler did his heroic thing. I still love this song, however. All three rappers are hugely different in style and approach. I'm the most traditional in terms of flow, the silliest in content. Part 2 is still Part 2, leaping breathlessly between concepts, many of which aren't immediately apparent but come out after repeat listening, while Bang Out of Order fits into that New Flesh niche of interesting, unusual MC's with a style all of his own.

It seemed a waste just to pocket the discs of the recording and do nothing with them. I asked everyone's permission, came up with the collective name of 'Bloody Beat Haemophiliacs' (I couldn't even begin to reason why) and sent the tape off to *Hip-Hop Connection.* At that time, they had a monthly column called 'Demo Blaster' or, more prosaically, 'Readers' Demos', where Northern hip-hop figure Dave 'The Ruf' (who was label owner, recording artist, DJ and record dealer all in one) reviewed demos sent in with the assistance of a different UK rapper each month. I made sure ours was anonymous, and we didn't mention our real names on the track. In fact, we nipples were identified on the track as The Bearded Nurse, Squinty Nadzack the Children's Friend and Percy Topless the Big Bugger.

We were all little known enough to slip under the radar, although New Flesh would soon have a record deal and would go on to release some acclaimed music (with a line-up always in flux, the only constant being Part 2). It's clear that Dave 'The Ruf' and his guest reviewer didn't have the foggiest who any of us were. I've kept the cutting, obviously. I probably wouldn't have done if they'd been totally scathing. But as this is the only review I ever got in my life, and it was a for a throwaway track recorded in one day and sent in under a false name, I'll take it. His guest reviewer that month was a guy called Loire from a British group, Hearts of Darkness, who released a couple of records on The Ruf's label. I send out my heartfelt thanks to him for not slagging us off.[98]

---

[98] The review in full, just in case my future biographer can't find it in the teetering tower of shit upon which I have bestowed the lofty name 'Archives'.
INFO: Very little known about this strange bunch of freaks. This track was produced by Scaramanga for Rude Bastard Productions. Fuck all else is known.
PRESENTATION: Brief letter with no telephone number or address and a line stating "Don't call us, we'll call you" – Mafia style – but we're not scared 'cause our dads are well hard.
MUSIC: Simple rhythm track bounces along with a mad slowed down 'house' synth played as a four-note hook. Nice little drum rolls and occasional scratches, but really the music is just a backing for the madness of all the different emcees to show their wild and crazy lyrics, and in that context the track works.
OPINIONS:
L: "This reminds me of First in Command."
R: "Nah, the quirkiness of this is more like the Parlour Talk tape. The emcees are fucking crazy bastards, they've got good flows and original madcap ideas and phrases. Sometimes crews seem to try and 'find' character voices for their rappers which can backfire if they are too gimmicky and sound wack, but all these guys are safe except for one who's borderline."
L: "Heavily influenced by that Doctor Octagon weird vibe. Nice to hear a good

York, all things considered, was very good to me. The nervous calamity of the 'No Sell Out' concert is now a fond memory. Recording "Three Nipples..." got me my only press. And I even had one more chance to shine. London rapper Blade performed at St. Sampson's in York.[99] Once a derelict church, it had now been turned into a charity and a centre for old men.

It was all young men this night, and the place was packed to see one of the few UK acts of that time with a passionate enough following to fill out a small venue. Were we, as local hip-hop luminaries, invited up to share the stage or to open for him? Don't be silly. No-one knew us, beyond passing record shop acquaintances you'd nod to. No, our chance came at the end of Blade's set, where he left the mic on and invited anyone who wanted to, to get up and freestyle. Countdown and I seized the chance.

We climbed up with a handful of others, stood there nodding our heads as we waited for our turn, then did about a minute each. I probably did my "Three Nipples..." lyrics while Martin did something from his solo project. Applause, cheers, bo bo bo's... there

---

drum break instead of all the bollocks drum programming I keep hearing nowadays."

R: "Musically for me though it needs more variety. I like the breaks that build and work with an emcee's flow rather than just rhyming on a backbeat."

L: "Yeah, it's a bit shallow and is missing something. However, they're not copying anyone and are doing their own thing, they've got potential."

R: "Definitely, but I've got to hear more than one track of the madness. I want more info and more tracks!"

Sorry to let you down Dave, but that was it for the Bloody Beat Haemophiliacs. "The emcees are fucking crazy bastards." I'll take that.

[99] Blade, who I had the pleasure to meet a couple of times in later life, was an Iranian of Armenian descent and who, despite only moving to London when he was seven, was better at rapping in English than I ever was. His late 80's debut "Lyrical Maniac" set the template for his career – hectic, passionate music that wore its heart on its sleeve. He'd go on to have a top 30 hit with "Ya Don't See the Signs", a collaboration with the late Mark B, so fair play to him.

were none of these. People weren't sticking around to hear local rappers share a microphone, they'd been here for Blade. The only people left were the ones who wanted a go, to grab their moment to shine. York was very good to me, but it never got carried away. The last rapper puts down the microphone. Lights out, party's over.

Twenty-Three
Long Live Hip-Hop

Hip-hop is dead, according to many people. It's an album title, a mantra, an endlessly repeated cliché on the internet. It's a neat little capsule phrase that is easy to use, to share, to meme. The only problem is that it's bullshit.

What people who say that really mean is not that hip-hop is dead to them, but that they're dead to hip-hop. This wonderful music waits for no fan. How different does electro sound to disco rap, disco rap to sample-heavy golden age music, jazz rap to trap music? It never stops or slows, but people do. When someone tells me hip-hop is dead, I don't argue. They're already lost to it, the argument has run its course in their mind. They'll have their memories, their own form of nostalgia, perhaps their own old tapes and lyric sheets which they'll cling to like their first teddy bear, tucked away in the attic. Something to show the future of what they once were. And if they want to retreat to that world, that's fine – it's what most music fans do. It's what mums and dads do. You should feel perfectly comfortable becoming like them, and screwing your face up at the sound of your children's music tastes. It's only natural. But that's not enough for me.

I enjoy looking back. Hell, this entire book is an exercise in doing so. But I'm also enjoying the here and now of hip-hop. You only like the hip-hop you grew up on? That's cool, nothing wrong with that. You only appreciate the stuff you and your mates breakdanced to, or the Wu-Tang Clan era? That's entirely your right. But the minute you take that path, you disqualify yourself from any argument about hip-hop in all its colossal entirety. You opt out. Hip-hop is as alive right now as it ever has been. You could even call it a Golden Age if, sorry to hark back, that name wasn't already taken. And that's because this is the nature of hip-hop's DNA. It's not fixed, like mine. Hip-hop is something that multiplies and mutates, leaving hybrids all over the place. Yes, it was born in The Bronx, but now it's of no fixed abode, and one of the joys in life is discovering it everywhere, often in the most unlikely corners.

I don't want what I grew up on to be frozen forever as some exemplar of what hip-hop is or should be, as something that only me and my mates could enjoy. It's not just 'real hip-hop' if it's got a rapper, a DJ, scratching, a beatboxer and some blokes body-popping in the video.[100] As much fun as that was, it was only a tiny period of

---

[100] I can't believe I got this far into the book without mentioning Human Beatbox. For the totally uninformed, it's the act of making percussion with your mouth, like that bloke out of the *Police Academy* films I mentioned earlier. While there are still many brilliant beatboxers around today, who rack up YouTube hits by the million (or, like my mate Kela, end up doing a Rowntree's Fruit Pastilles advert and dating Patsy Kensit for a while), in hip-hop terms it's definitely an early to mid-80's phenomenon. Hip-hop invented and popularised it (although you could throw Bobby McFerrin into the mix), and it was a staple feature of many songs. Many people's first exposure to it may have been when Doug E. Fresh's "The Show" hit the charts in 1985, but it had already been around for a couple of years. An incomplete list of beatboxers who made life more pleasurable by covering us with lots of their spit as they imitated drums and basslines must include Greg Nice (The Incredible Sound Machine), Rahzel, Doug E. Fresh (The World's Greatest Entertainer), Ready Rock C (The Human Linndrum), Biz Markie (The Inhuman Orchestra), Buffy of the Fat Boys (The Human Beatbox – he definitely needed a better nickname), D-Nice (The Human TR808), Run of Run DMC, DMX (Just-Ice's sidekick, not the rapper), Jock Box of The Skinny Boys, Wise of Stetsasonic (The Devastating Beat Creator), Beatmaster T and Sipho (RIP) from The London Posse. Rahzel managed to bring it back to records in the

time. If you equate it to a person's life, it's like saying I was only the 'Real Andrew' when I watched *Jamie and the Magic Torch*, ate Farley's Rusks and didn't have pubes.

The hip-hop is dead argument goes hand in hand with people saying that hip-hop now has nothing to say. It's interesting to wonder if, with its current lyrical preoccupations, it would convert and educate me now. It made me appreciate issues of race, but why didn't it make me sexist and homophobic at the same time, as many of the artists I listened to were both of those things? Or does hip-hop, regardless of the actual lyrical content, simply work to let white people understand black experience, which can be as racist, sexist and homophobic as white culture is (but in entirely different ways)? On a basic level, at the very least, it does that.

I've heard lots of people say that they gave up watching the fantastic HBO series *The Wire* pretty quickly, as they couldn't fathom what was being said or what any of it meant. Or they had to constantly pause and rewind it. I've never heard any hip-hop fans say that, because all the argot and slang and drug terminology that makes *The Wire* so authentic-seeming is all part and parcel of hip-hop. A lifetime spent listening to rap is the perfect primer for watching *The Wire* (you're also able to recognise the numerous rappers who have roles in it).

I'm clearly not one to say that hip-hop isn't all it used to be and, while sympathising with the 'real hip-hop' brigade, I also find them tiresome in the extreme. People who embraced hip-hop because it was different no longer like it because it currently sounds different

---

late 90's, after becoming the beatbox for The Roots (along with another guy called Scratch, who specialised in, erm, vocal scratching), but it didn't really capture the joys of 80's classics like "My Beatbox Reggae Style", "Three Minutes of Beatbox", "Breath Control", "The Original Human Beat Box", "Def Fresh Crew" or "Make the Music With Your Mouth".

to how they first experienced it. They have the same attitudes to music that, for me, hip-hop was tearing up in the first place. But it is undoubtedly a different thing to the people who are living with it now. When I got into hip-hop it was shockingly new and original, only a few years old, finding its feet, still taking baby steps. Someone discovering hip-hop today is getting into something that has nigh on 40 years of history and has not only found its feet but has its feet under the table. I'm not saying they won't be as thrilled by it as I was, and that they won't have their lives changed irreversibly, just that they're doing it under different conditions.

It will make it easier that they can look back on that history of chart success, on rappers becoming household names, on the fashion that hip-hop pioneered becoming mainstream. They'll have role models from their cities, their towns, their neighbourhoods. We have British rappers now who do get respect worldwide, who sell records abroad. It will also make it easier that they no longer have to worry about breakdancing because, to be honest, that was always a hard sell.

So if I was discovering hip-hop now, a completely different beast from the 1984 model with only some shared DNA, maybe it would impact on me in a different way. I'd have to dig a bit deeper to find the political content (there's plenty of it about, if you look, but largely not from artists who I actually want to listen to or who are in any way cutting edge musically). But it's not like I went looking for the politics in the first place. I was converted by *Electro Two*, a compilation that may well have contained Grandmaster Flash & Melle Mel's anti-coke classic "White Lines (Don't Don't Do it)" but also consisted of almost wordless instrumentals from The B-Boys and Hashim that grabbed me in the guts. It was just a happy coincidence that hip-hop became political shortly after that, and it was artists who were musically brilliant – Public Enemy, Stetsasonic,

KRS One – who led the way. It wasn't the lyrics, it was the noise that pulled me in, and I'd still get sucked in by the noise hip-hop makes now.

Twenty-Four
When the Pen Hits the Paper

In the end, neither Prehistoric Ages nor Progressive Agenda troubled the charts. They aren't names that stimulate the memories of the UK hip-hop fraternity. Mention Hardnoise or Hijack to anyone who grew up with hip-hop when I did and they'll wax nostalgic, reach for their 12"s, quote some lyrics at you. They wouldn't even know who we were. You'd have to ask a very small, very selective sample of people in Leeds to garner even the faintest glimmer of recognition, and even then they'd probably know Prehistoric Ages, but not Progressive Agenda. And there are no flyers to dig out, no posters of concerts past. No scarce pieces of vinyl that were only available in strictly limited quantities to the cognoscenti. Our rap careers, ultimately, flopped.

After graduating in 1995, and starting work (my very first proper job was actually as a P.A. – not Progressive Agenda, sadly, but a Personal Assistant to the Principal of a Leeds Further Education College) all roads pointed to London. Dan and Barrie had already moved down, and as I'd split up with Sarah after graduation, there was little keeping me in Leeds except for family and friends like Robin and Lucy. And the latter would soon be in London themselves.

I'd decided to be a journalist and had had a few freelance pieces published while I lived with my mum. I was making ends meet working as a supervisor in a depressing local video shop (sadly, the *Electric Blue* series was no more[101]) when I got an in at a publishers, left Leeds behind and moved south to share a house in Golders Green, North London, with Dan and Barrie. Yet despite our proximity, despite the evenings and weekends we spent in each other's company, we never recorded – or even talked about recording – any music together. It was if we'd left childish things behind, and the topic never came up. Hip-hop was still a huge part of our lives, and we were in the best place in Britain to experience it. Concerts, club nights, record shops – they all put Leeds to shame. If we'd wanted to relaunch the P.A. Posse, this was the place to do it. But we didn't even think about it. We worked, went out, made new friends, got new girlfriends, got on with life.

When did the lyrics dry up? When I was at university, probably. Life got in the way of the endless jottings, and my college textbooks and notebooks aren't defaced in the same way my school ones were. Somewhere along the line, before we'd even recorded our last music together, before I summoned the effort to write "Sweaty Convict's Theme" and "Three Nipples", the dream had already died. The hopes and energy that we once had for making it in hip-hop we now redirected into our careers and relationships. We found fulfilment elsewhere.

It can hurt to reflect on things that you'll never get to do. The climber who is now too old and weak to try an ascent of Everest again, after failure before. The would-be writer with nothing but rejection slips. The rapper who didn't ever get to rap, to hold the crowd in his hand. But I don't really see myself that way. I see my

---

[101] In fact, there was no pornography in the Dewsbury Road branch of Choices Video at all. What there was instead was a female colleague who showed me pictures of her dead baby on my first night in the job, and later sexually harassed me. Great times.

failed hip-hop career as a success in other ways. I got to play at being in a band, I got to meet friends whose funerals I'll attend, or will attend mine. I went into a studio, laughed, drank and made music that I'll never forget. Those decaying cassettes and those yellowing lyric sheets embarrass me, yes, but not as much as they give me joy to pore over now and then. At my wedding party, Dan and another close friend Nat shared DJ duties for a while and, in between the guaranteed dance floor fillers and air-guitar classics, they cued up one of our demo tracks as a surprise and played it. Everyone was non-plussed, apart from me and the two DJ's themselves. It was the biggest audience a P.A. Posse track had ever had, and no-one knew what it was. We've all put that part of our life away – Dan's wife Susie had never even heard "Drinking Tea with the Lads" until, more than 20 years after we made it, I forced it upon her one day – but we're all acutely aware of what it did for us, what it made us.

And it's not only what our anti-climactic hip-hop careers turned us into, because this book isn't solely about that. It's about what hip-hop itself with all its flaws, its positives and negatives, its restless shape-shifting, did for us. We were changed in ways that the casual music fan can't imagine. As different as the genres are, musically, ethically, everything-cally, our hip-hop generation had a lot in common with punks, with mods, with Smiths fans, even with ravers. Music wasn't something background, something you tuned in and out of. It spoke to you, it gave you life and it expressed that life in ways you yourself couldn't always articulate. *Electro Two* isn't just an old compilation I'm fond of. It's my heartbeat. I can't imagine my world and my life without it.

I did, eventually, find my niche in hip-hop: Writing about it. I'd grown up reading *Hip-Hop Connection* in my teens, and in my 20's I became a journalist for it. First I was contributing the occasional LP review, a piece about a concert, small stuff. Over time, I wrote more and more until I was Contributing Editor, doing thousands of words a month, speaking to rappers on the phone and in person, writing features and columns. I got to play pool with The Beatnuts, ask Salt 'n' Pepa where they bought their lingerie and interview Lauryn Hill while she was in the shower. I got to walk out on an interview with a rude and monosyllabic Method Man, have Prodigy from Mobb Deep fall asleep on me, ask J Dilla over dinner, a couple of years before his death, what his name would be if he was a porn star. I spoke to Jay-Z, EPMD, Jazzy Jeff, Schoolly D, De La Soul and Eminem. Rappers I loved, rappers I despised, rappers I was indifferent about but I thought I could still write something illuminating and truthful about. I got to write hatchet pieces that elicited hate mail, I got to write hatchet pieces that had people calling me 'hip-hop's greatest writer' (I prefer to quote that one). I got death threats over pieces I wrote, I got death threats over pieces that I didn't actually write. I also got to write pieces that expressed nothing more than my undying love for this music.

The fun was in not doing this alone because, something the eleven year old hip-hop fan in me would never have believed, I had lifelong friends who felt the same way as me. I launched *Fat Lace*, an independent magazine with Dan, Barrie, Robin and Mike. DJ Yoda came on board. We had contributors from around the world and we poked fun at rappers in a way no-one else would. I was still in a posse and, with *Fat Lace* and *Hip-Hop Connection*, we had finally carved out our place in hip-hop: As chroniclers of its wonder and absurdity. People who adored it but were aware of its foibles and failings. In a way, our approach to rap journalism was like our approach with Prehistoric Ages and Progressive Agenda: we wanted to leave something of ourselves in it, using the humour we had ultimately failed to channel in our music. Irony, satire and sarcasm may have been our tools, but love for the music and its characters was always our guiding principle.

Dan, Robin and Yoda got to inspire and move crowds in a way I never would, as DJ's, performers and radio hosts. Dan also got to release a record, contributing an instrumental track to a 1996 compilation called *Organised Sound.* He called it, fittingly, "Progressive Agenda". Me? I don't regret a thing. I got to live my dream. I tried to rap, I failed. It never shook my adoration for or faith in hip-hop. For over 30 years it has been a central part of my life, and I've been lucky to have every second of it. I used to rap along in my bedroom to Public Enemy and the powerful, political lyrics of Chuck D. Twenty years later I was in a hotel room in London, interviewing him as he had his hair cut at 3AM after a concert, for a chapter in my *Book of Hip-Hop Cover Art.* A year after that, at a record launch party in London, I walked into a room in a hotel and Chuck D, still and forever my hero, called to me by my name. Young Scam, writing rhyming couplets in a chemistry exercise book at school, would never have believed such a thing could happen. The wonder of it.

Epilogue
Unfinished Business

Summer, 2003. The Oh! Bar in Camden, North London, an evening called The Lyric Pad. It's a fortnightly rap battle where some of London's best known MC's cut their teeth, and where hopefuls line up to take a shot at them. Somehow, I'm on stage, holding a microphone for the first time in nearly ten years. Ten years where I've never even thought about rapping again, ten years without writing a lyric, thinking up a fictitious group name or buying records for samples. Ten years of retirement from the somewhat sedate ride (less rollercoaster, more spinning teacups) that was the P.A. Posse. And yet here I am, my bowels in turmoil, eight pints of Guinness inside me, about to do it all over again.

The difference this time is that I'm getting paid. I'm writing an article for *Muzik* magazine in the wake of the release of the Eminem film *8 Mile*, which centres on rap battles. It's a knockout competition, and we're going to see if I can proceed through the rounds to the final, even though I'm up against people who do this every fortnight, who do this for a living. I've written all new lyrics just for the occasion, lots of barbed disses and insults to skewer my opponents. In truth, I've found it a lot harder to remember them than I used to. Once upon a time they sank straight in. I must have rehearsed this lot 30 times and they're still not sticking. Perhaps it's because this time they're not for the studio, for a demo, for the P.A. Posse. They're for one night only.

I have never, in 20 years of life in hip-hop, been in a proper rap battle. I've never had someone facing me on stage in front of the paying public (with some friends and well-wishers dotted throughout) who wants to humiliate and defeat me. When I face my opponent in round one, he goes first and is standing so close to me, his words a blur, that I'm getting spittle on my face. It's like being bollocked by a Sergeant Major. It's my turn to riposte, and nerves get the better of me. I'm rushing to try to get to the punchlines which aren't coming out clearly enough, my freshly written lyrics wasted, stumbling over the bits that are supposed to be the best ones. "You're almost as bad as me," my opponent taunts, and the crowd laugh with him. At me. He goes again, and even though he's not really very good at all, he's still winning, as I'm about 10 years too old for this shit, and this hungry tyke is taking me to the cleaners because I've frozen. It turns out that the eight pints of Guinness I saw off to calm myself was nowhere near enough.

A chink of light: He loses his way, his flow falters and breaks. I step in. It's my last chance. It's all or nothing, and now I'm in his face. I'm signalling to the crowd, rallying them to my cause, getting them to round on an MC when he's down. And the lyrics? Ones that I didn't rehearse that day. Ones that I hadn't said in a dozen years but spring fully formed from my lips as if brand new. They're vintage P.A. Posse lyrics. And because I know them so well, they roll straight off my tongue and into the mic. I know where the punchlines are, where to stop for emphasis. And my old jokes, my old naff stuff full of Joey Deacon and Laurence Fishburne and dear old Jeremy Beadle, it's enough for this opponent. I get cheers, I get laughs and I get the victory. I'm back.

Round two. And after this the quarter finals, the semi-finals, then the final itself beckons. I can't, can I? I'm up against a nice kid called Archer whose opening salvo is decent enough, but shouldn't trouble me if I can recreate the vibe from round one. I've calmed down inside. I only wanted to avoid the shame of falling at the first hurdle, so now I find I'm able to remember more of my new lyrics. And they're doing the job. In fact, my first eight lines go down a storm, the crowd on my side again, the thrill rushing through my body, my veins popping. And then... nothing. They're gone again. I had my foot on his throat, and now I can't summon a single word to finish him. My brain chugs through the gears, trying to dredge up some more P.A. Posse classics... but I can't. I've lost.

I leave the stage, and say goodbye to the microphone once again. Because, ultimately, the P.A. Posse stuff was never good enough in the first place. It never really cut it and neither did I. All I was good at was doing exactly what I did later that night – I went home and turned that battle into words, into an article. I found my place in hip-hop by talking about the greatest thing the US ever gave us, their finest export, and how it's experienced in the UK. Something like this book.

The people in this book, including myself – we weren't the only ones. Not by a long shot. Thousands and thousands of people shared the UK adventure of hip-hop in the 80's, 90's and beyond. We shared in the triumphs and tragedies, the rich times and the lean, the shunning and the acceptance, the rise and rise and rise. Every hip-hop fan who lived in a provincial town and had to get the bus, train or a lift from mum to a record shop, their pocket money at the ready. Every hip-hop fan who coveted sneakers, bodywarmers or Dapper Dan outfits worn by their idols, and had to make do with what their parents bought them.

Every hip-hop fan who practised headspins in their kitchen, frightening those same parents. Every hip-hop fan who went to the one concert or jam their town ever hosted and stood there nodding in time. Every hip-hop fan who scratched his head at a lyrical reference he wouldn't understand for another decade, or who always got the lyrics wrong, or still does. Every hip-hop fan who listened to John Peel or Tim Westwood or Mike Allen, blank tape at the ready. Every hip-hop fan who wrote in to *Hip-Hop Connection*, traded cassettes in the post or the playground or bodypopped at the school disco. Every hip-hop fan who hoisted a portable cassette player, whether pumping or pathetic, onto their shoulder and walked around town. Every hip-hop fan who picked up a mic to rap, or a turntable to scratch or a sampler to produce, all with a dream. And every hip-hop fan who put those things down to get on with the business of life. Down, yes, but not away, still tucked safely in a corner of the heart. Where hip-hop is alive, and always will be.

Chapter Credits:

Prologue: The Show (Doug E. Fresh & The Get Fresh Crew, Reality Records, 1985)

One: Children's Story (Slick Rick, Def Jam Recordings, 1989)

Two: Step In The Arena (Gang Starr, Chrysalis, 1990)

Three: Back To The Old School (Just-Ice, Fresh Records, 1986)

Four: I Can't Live Without My Radio (LL Cool J, Def Jam Recordings, 1985)

Five: Travelling At The Speed Of Thought (Ultra Magnetic MC's, Next Plateau Records, 1987)

Six: This Is Something For The Radio (Biz Markie, Cold Chillin', 1988)

Seven: My Vinyl Weighs A Ton (Peanut Butter Wolf, Stones Throw, 1998)

Eight: Rebel Without A Pause (Public Enemy, Def Jam Recordings, 1987)

Nine: Hip-Hop Hooray (Naughty By Nature, Tommy Boy, 1993)

Ten: Me And My Posse (Divine Sounds, Reality Records, 1986)

Eleven: Just A Friend (Biz Markie, Cold Chillin', 1989)

Twelve: It's A Demo (Kool G Rap & DJ Polo, Cold Chillin', 1986)

Thirteen: Please Listen To My Demo (EPMD, Fresh Records, 1989)

Fourteen: Enta Da Stage (Black Moon, Wreck Records, 1993)

Fifteen: Girls I Got Em Locked (Super Love Cee & Casanova Rud, Elektra/DNA, 1988)

Sixteen: Things Fall Apart (The Roots, MCA Records, 1999)

Seventeen: Big Apple Rappin' (Spyder-D, Newtroit Records, 1980)

Eighteen: Cold Chillin' In The Studio (The Original Jazzy Jay, UNI/Strong City, 1989)

Nineteen: Yo! Bum Rush The Show (Public Enemy, Def Jam Recordings, 1987)

Twenty: Serve Tea, Then Murder (Hardnoise, Music of Life, 1991)

Twenty-One: White Lines (Grandmaster & Melle Mel, Sugar Hill Records, 1983)

Twenty-Two: Movin' On (Master Ace, Cold Chillin', 1990)

Twenty-Three: Long Live Hip-Hop (Taking Your Business, Bad Boy Records, 1987)

Twenty-Four: When The Pen Hits The Paper (Freak L, Urban Rock Records, 1989)

Epilogue: Unfinished Business (EPMD, Fresh Records, 1989)

Photo Credits:

Cover: Mr Bojangles flyer c/o NG83: When We Were B-Boys
Title: PA Posse demo shoot: DJ Greenpeace, SCAM, DJ Countdown
Prologue: DJ Greenpeace & SCAM
P.20: SCAM & DJ Greenpeace in the P.A. Lab
P.28: Postcard courtesy of Susan Brown
P.34: Mr Bojangles Jam, Nottingham, mid 1980s
P.60a: DJ Greenpeace & SCAM: Twin Peaks
P.60b: Foresight, SCAM, DJ Greenpeace: Triple Stage Wackness
P.88: Draft "A Simple Life" lyrics, 1993
P.97: DJ Greenpeace & DJ Countdown: Hip-Hop Buskers
P. 107: John Smeaton 6th Form Talent Show, 1991. SCAM, MC Paul Chatterton
P.122: PA demo cassette inlay, 1991
P.129: PA demo booklet cover
P.138: East/West Records rejection letter
P.164: DJ Countdown, SCAM: Pretty boys surviving up north
P.183: Draft artwork for *Outside the System, Looking in* demo
P.203: "Drinking Tea With the Lads" recording session. Left to right (back): S.A.D.E., DJ Countdown, SCAM, Horny Baker, DJ Greenpeace. Left to right (front): Part 2, MC 4-9
P.224: "Drinking Tea" session. SCAM, DJ Greenpeace, S.A.D.E.
P.233: DJ Greenpeace, SCAM: Progressive Agenda

Huge thanks to DJ Countdown the One Man Band aka Martin Allan for the loan of many of these photos.

Acknowledgements: Countdown, Horny Baker aka Ash Kollakowski, Rob Pursey, Brett Dickinson and all those who responded to questions and filled in for my terrible memory. Susan Brown, Tam Emery, Justin Quirk and Dan & Susie Goldberg for your proofing and editing help and kind and useful feedback. All errors in the final version are mine alone.

About the author

Andrew Emery is a journalist who has written about hip-hop music for over 20 years, most notably for *Hip-Hop Connection*, *The Guardian*, *The Face* and *Arena*. He co-founded the satirical hip-hop magazine *Fat Lace* and is the author of *The Book of Hip-Hop Cover Art*. He lives in Yorkshire with his beloved wife and dog. He is currently writing *Adventures with Rappers*, *Promo Only: Vintage Hip-Hop Memorabilia* and *The Biographical Dictionary of Hip-Hop*. He blogs about hip-hop at wiggazwithattitude.com – sign up for all the latest book news, exclusives and free previews of forthcoming work.

Reviews are the lifeblood of independent authors. If you've enjoyed the book, I'd appreciate your honest opinion over at Amazon, Goodreads or wherever you picked it up. Many thanks.

Made in the USA
San Bernardino, CA
19 December 2017